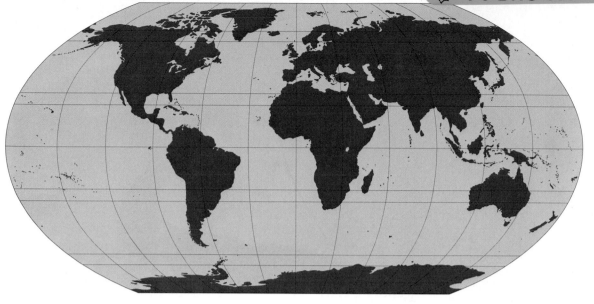

Geography is the science of space and place on Earth's surface. Its subject matter is the physical and human phenomena that make up the world's environments and places. Geographers describe the changing patterns of places in words, maps, and geo-graphics, explain how these patterns come to be, and unravel their meaning. Geography's continuing quest is to understand the physical and cultural features of places and their natural settings on the surface of Earth.

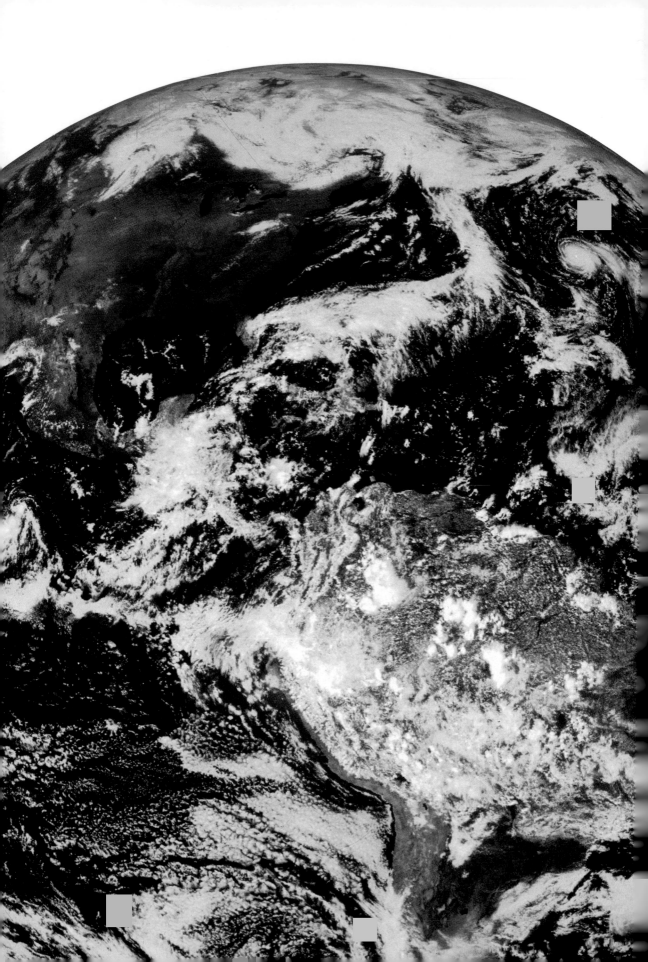

What Every Young American Should Know and Be Able to Do in Geography

GEOGRAPHY FOR LIFE

····································

NATIONAL GEOGRAPHY STANDARDS 1994

GEOGRAPHY EDUCATION STANDARDS PROJECT

Developed on behalf of the

American Geographical Society
Association of American Geographers
National Council for Geographic Education
National Geographic Society

1994

. . . .

By the year 2000, all students will leave grades 4, 8, and 12 having demonstrated competency over challenging subject matter including. . . geography, and every school in America will ensure that all students learn to use their minds well, so they may be prepared for responsible citizenship, further learning, and productive employment in our Nation's modern economy.

Goals 2000:
Educate America Act,
Section 102

. . . .

This publication has been prepared by the Geography Education Standards Project with grants from the U.S. Department of Education, the National Endowment for the Humanities, and the National Geographic Society.

The grants have been administered by the National Council for Geographic Education.

Grantees undertaking such projects are encouraged to express freely their professional judgment. This publication, therefore, does not necessarily represent positions or policies of the federal government, and no official endorsement should be inferred.

THE GEOGRAPHY EDUCATION
STANDARDS PROJECT

ANTHONY R. DE SOUZA, Executive Director
National Geographic Society

RUTH I. SHIREY, Project Administrator
National Council for Geographic Education

NORMAN C. BETTIS, Project Co-chair
Illinois State University

CHRISTOPHER L. SALTER, Project Co-chair
University of Missouri

ROGER M. DOWNS, Writing Coordinator
The Pennsylvania State University

AUTHORS

SARAH WITHAM BEDNARZ
Texas A&M University

NORMAN C. BETTIS
Illinois State University

RICHARD G. BOEHM
Southwest Texas State University

ANTHONY R. DE SOUZA
National Geographic Society

ROGER M. DOWNS
The Pennsylvania State University

JAMES F. MARRAN
New Trier High School

ROBERT W. MORRILL
Virginia Polytechnic Institute and State University

CHRISTOPHER L. SALTER
University of Missouri

COMMITTEE CHAIRS

SAUL B. COHEN, Advisers
Hunter College–CUNY

SUSAN W. HARDWICK, Content Development
California State University–Chico

A. DAVID HILL, International
University of Colorado–Boulder

LYDIA LEWIS, Writing
National Geographic Society

MICHAEL J. LIBBEE, Environmental Education
Central Michigan University

RAMSAY SELDEN, Oversight
Council of Chief State School Officers

THOMAS J. WILBANKS, Content Advisory
Oak Ridge National Laboratory

(cover) Diego Ribero's 1529 world map "Carta Planisferio." BIBLIOTECA APOSTOLICA VATICANA
(right) Riverton, Wyoming. DAVID P. JOHNSON

Our galaxy—the Milky Way—is a spiral, a common
type. Several hundred billion spinning stars revolve
around its center. Midway out, stars—including our
Sun—move at about 500,000 miles per hour, taking
250 million years to make a single circuit.

TABLE OF CONTENTS

. . . .

Preface

···

The inclusion of geography as a core subject in Goals 2000: Educate America Act (Public Law 103-227) is the culmination of a decade of reform in geography education. There is now a widespread acceptance among the people of the United States that being literate in geography is essential if students are to leave school equipped to earn a decent living, enjoy the richness of life, and participate responsibly in local, national, and international affairs. In response to this desire for a geographically literate society, educators and parents, as well as members of business, professional, and civic organizations, have built a national consensus regarding the study of geography and produced *Geography for Life: National Geography Standards 1994*.

These geography standards identify what American students should learn—a set of voluntary benchmarks that every school and school district may use as guidelines for developing their own curricula. The standards for grades K–4, 5–8, and 9–12 specify the essential subject matter, skills, and perspectives that all students should have in order to attain high levels of competency. The standards provide every parent, teacher, curriculum developer, and business and policy leader with a set of challenging expectations for all students.

The purpose of standards for geography is to bring all students up to internationally competitive levels to meet the demands of a new age and a different world. For the United States to maintain leadership and prosper in the twenty-first century, the education system must be tailored to the needs of productive and responsible citizenship in the global economy.

Geography for Life: National Geography Standards 1994 is a vital contribution to the achievement of the goals enunciated in the Educate America Act that "all students learn to use their minds well, so they may be prepared for responsible citizenship, further learning, and productive employment in our Nation's modern economy . . . ."

We urge you to read the National Geography Standards, share them with friends and colleagues, and reflect on the urgent need for a geographically literate society. Consider what must be done to implement the standards so that all students, regardless of background or aspirations for the future, can grow to be productive and enlightened citizens in a democracy and in today's global society.

THE GEOGRAPHY EDUCATION STANDARDS PROJECT

···

CHAPTER 1

The Geographic View of Our World

Geography *is* for life in every sense of that expression: lifelong, life-sustaining, and life-enhancing. Geography is a field of study that enables us to find answers to questions about the world around us—about where things are and how and why they got there. We can ask questions about things that seem very familiar and are often taken for granted.

For example, most people know the map of states in the United States. But not all of us know why some state boundaries, especially in the West, consist of straight lines, whereas others, especially in the East, appear to wander here and there.

The answer is based on an understanding of geography. State boundaries in the West were often created before settlement. They were drawn by people who were far away and who lacked specific information about the geography of the area. These state boundaries were imposed on the land, often following lines of latitude and longitude. Most boundaries in the East were drawn after settlement, by people who knew the land from long personal experience. Therefore these boundaries often reflect the grain of the land—rivers, ridges, lakes.

Let's continue to look at maps and to ask some even more challenging geographic questions. We'll begin with the world as a whole, shift to the United States, and then focus on a single state, Pennsylvania.

"A Map of the British and French Dominions in North America,"
third edition, by John Mitchell, London, 1755. This map was drafted for
the Lords Commissioners for Trade and Plantations. Its hand coloring
emphasizes the extent of colonial charters at a time when France vied for
the Ohio Valley. JOSEPH H. BAILEY

1. Light is evidence of large numbers of people and cities; dark means the absence of people and cities. You can see great clusters of cities—from Boston through New York, Philadelphia, and Baltimore, to Washington. This is the original megalopolis, the nation's economic and political powerhouse.

THE WORLD AT NIGHT

WHAT DOES LIGHT INDICATE IN THESE THREE EXAMPLES?

IDENTIFICATION CHART

G = natural gas burn-off
F = agricultural fires

NORTH AMERICA

1 G (Prudhoe Bay)
2 Fairbanks
3 Anchorage + G
4 Edmonton
5 Winnipeg
6 Calgary
7 Medicine Hat
8 Vancouver
9 Seattle
10 Portland
11 Interstate Highway 5
12 San Francisco–Oakland
13 Los Angeles
14 Honolulu
15 San Diego
16 Phoenix
17 Tucson
18 El Paso
19 Chihuahua
20 Dallas–Ft. Worth
21 Torreon
22 Guadalajara
23 Monterrey
24 Mexico City
25 Puebla
26 G (Tabasco)
27 Tampa
28 San Antonio
29 Houston
30 New Orleans
31 Miami
32 Jacksonville
33 Atlanta
34 Kansas City
35 St. Louis
36 Norfolk
37 Washington, D.C.–Baltimore
38 Phildelphia–Newark–New York City–Long Island
39 Boston–Providence
40 Montréal
41 Quebec
42 Aurora borealis
43 Pittsburgh
44 Buffalo
45 Toronto
46 Cleveland
47 Detroit
48 Chicago–Milwaukee
49 Minneapolis–St. Paul
50 Denver
51 Salt Lake City

CENTRAL & SOUTH AMERICA

52 San José
53 Panamá
54 Bogotá + G
55 Quito + G
56 Lima
57 Santiago
58 Rosario
59 Buenos Aires
60 Montevideo
61 Pôrto Alegre
62 São Paulo
63 Rio de Janeiro
64 Brasilia
65 Salvador
66 Recife
67 Manuas
68 Caracas + G
69 Puerto Rico
70 Kingston
71 Havana

AFRICA

72 Casablanca
73 G (Algeria)
74 F (sub-Saharan savanna)
75 G (Nigeria)
76 G (Gabon)
77 Kinshasa
78 F (Southeast Africa)
79 Capetown
80 Durban
81 Johannesburg
82 F (Matagasy [Madagascar])
83 Nairobi
84 Khartoum
85 G (Libya)
86 Aswan
87 Nile River
88 Cairo + Nile River delta

2. Here, light is evidence of energy or power, not people and cities. What you see are flares from the burn-off of oil and natural gas fields in the Persian Gulf region. Imagine what this would have looked like during the Gulf War in 1991.

3. This triangular-shaped area is in the Sea of Japan. Here there are no oil and gas fields, no cities, and very few people. There is a valuable resource being exploited, however. It is the Japanese squid-fishing fleet, lit up at night for round-the-clock harvesting.

EUROPE

121	Milan
122	Munich
123	Rome
124	Prague
125	Vienna
126	Budapest
127	Athens
128	Bucharest
129	Odessa

ASIA

130	Istanbul
131	Israel
132	Ankara
133	Damascus
134	Baghdad
135	G (Saudi Arabia & Persian Gulf States)
136	Teheran
137	Karachi
138	Lahore
139	Ahmadabad
140	Bombay
141	Delhi
142	Himalaya Mountains
143	Bangalore
144	Colombo
145	Madras
146	Hyderabad
147	Allahabad
148	Patna
149	Calcutta + Ganges River delta
150	Dacca
151	F (SE Asian highlands)
152	Teheran
153	Rangoon
154	Singapore
155	Bangkok
156	Ho Chi-Minh City (Saigon)
157	Manila
158	Lanzhou (Lanchow)
159	Hong Kong
160	Taiwan
161	Jing-Bao/Bao-Lan Railroads + Yellow River
162	Nanjing (Nanking)
163	Shanghai + Yangtze River delta
164	T'ai-yüan
165	Beijing (Peking)–Tianjin (Tientsin)
166	Pusan
167	Seoul
168	Osaka-Kobe-Kyoto
169	Tokyo–Yokohama
170	Japanese squid fleet
171	P'yongyang
172	Shen-yang
173	Sapporo
174	Vladivostok
175	Trans-Siberian Railroad
176	Irkutsk
177	Novosibirsk
178	G (Surgut, Biberia)
179	Omsk
180	Tashkent + G
181	Sverdiovsk
182	Chelyabinsk

AUSTRALASIA

183	Jakarta
184	Northwest Cape
185	Perth
186	Adelaide
187	Hobart
188	Christchurch
189	Wellington
190	Auckland
191	Melbourne
192	Sydney
193	Brisbane
194	G (Sulawesi, Indonesia)

CREDITS: United States Air Force / DMSP Archive, National Snow & Ice Data Center, NOAA, University of Colorado / Text & image © 1995 W.T. Sullivan, III, University of Washington, Seattle
Poster design & image processing by Kerry Meyer / Power © 1995 Hansen Planetarium, Salt Lake City, Utah, U.S.A.

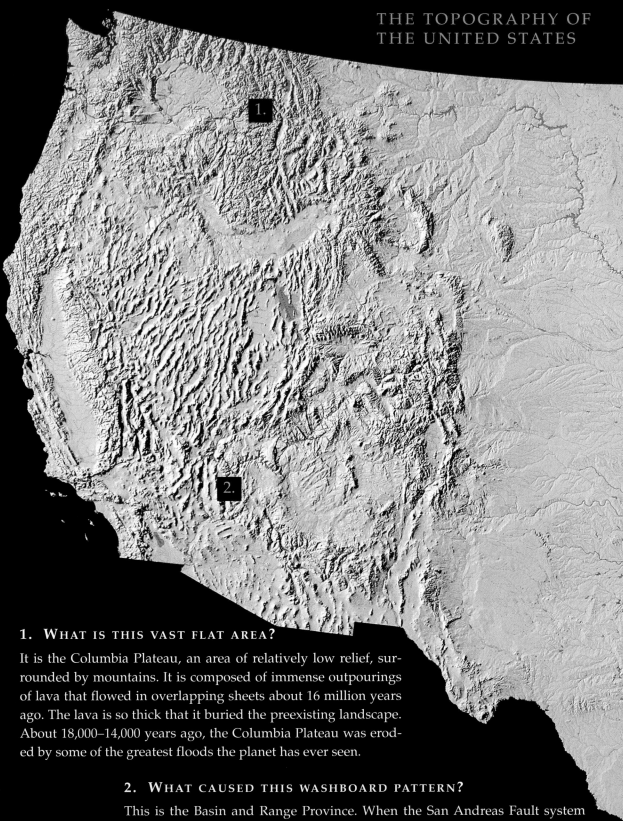

1. WHAT IS THIS VAST FLAT AREA?

It is the Columbia Plateau, an area of relatively low relief, surrounded by mountains. It is composed of immense outpourings
of lava that flowed in overlapping sheets about 16 million years
ago. The lava is so thick that it buried the preexisting landscape.
About 18,000–14,000 years ago, the Columbia Plateau was erod-
ed by some of the greatest floods the planet has ever seen.

2. WHAT CAUSED THIS WASHBOARD PATTERN?

This is the Basin and Range Province. When the San Andreas Fault system
developed about 20 million years ago the province was stretched and started
to break into blocks, separated by faults. Some of these fault-bounded blocks
dropped down; others rose up; still others were tilted. Erosion of the uplifted
blocks has half-buried surrounding lowlands in sediment.

4. WHY IS THIS SHORELINE SO UNEVEN, SO COMPLICATED?

Before the last ice age (the Pleistocene epoch), the Susquehanna River flowed through the center of what is now the Chesapeake Bay. The river and its tributaries formed a dendritic pattern, like the veins of a leaf. After the ice age, sea levels rose, drowning the lower parts of the valleys of the Susquehanna and its tributaries and creating today's shoreline.

3.

4.

WHY ARE THE MAJOR RIVERS OF THE MIDWEST— THE MISSISSIPPI, OHIO, AND MISSOURI— SYMMETRICALLY ARRANGED?

e Missouri and Ohio Rivers were formed as spillways that approxi- ately paralleled the southernmost extent of the North American ice eet. The Mississippi served as a gutter running to the Gulf of exico, following the downwarp in the middle of the continent. The ssissippi has since filled that downwarp with its alluvial sediments

THE OFFICIAL STATE ROAD MAP OF PENNSYLVANIA

1. WHY IS THERE SO MUCH FOREST IN THIS PART OF PENNSYLVANIA?

This is a plateau of sandstone with poor soils and few mineral resources. After lumber companies exhausted the timber supplies, the land had little value and reverted to public ownership. Subsequently, the land was reforested, and it has been maintained as forest land by state and federal governments.

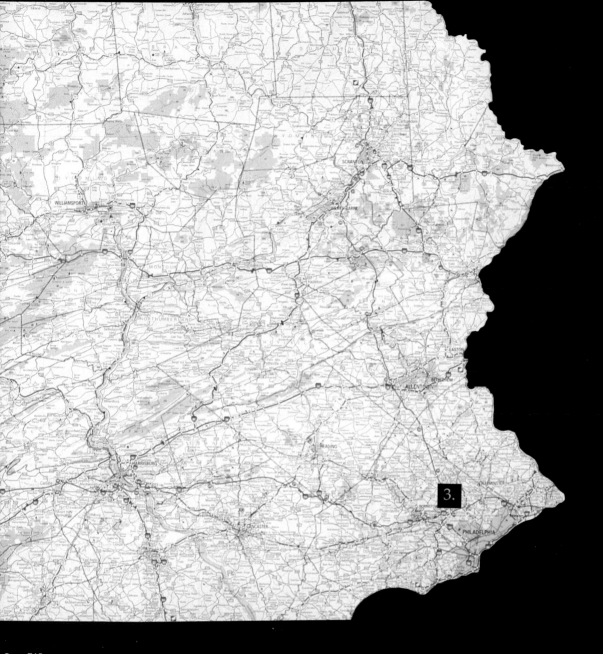

2. WHY IS THE PENNSYLVANIA TURNPIKE HERE?

It was constructed as a New Deal project that connected the east (Philadelphia) with the west (Pittsburgh) and followed the abandoned right-of-way of the South Penn Railroad Company. Opened in 1940 as the nation's first multi-lane superhighway, the turnpike demonstrated that Americans were willing to pay for a high-speed, limited-access, long-distance toll road; it was the precursor of the interstate highway system.

3. WHY IS PHILADELPHIA LOCATED HERE?

It is at the junction of the Delaware and Schuylkill Rivers. As a drowned arm of the Atlantic, the Delaware provides access to the sea. In colonial times, the Schuylkill provided access to the interior, especially to the rich agricultural area of southeastern Pennsylvania's piedmont.

BASE MAP REPRINTED COURTESY OF THE COMMONWEALTH OF PENNSYLVANIA, DEPARTMENT OF TRANSPORTATION. ORIGINAL MAP BASE COPYRIGHTED BY THE COMMONWEALTH OF PENNSYLVANIA, ©1994

WHAT IS GEOGRAPHY?

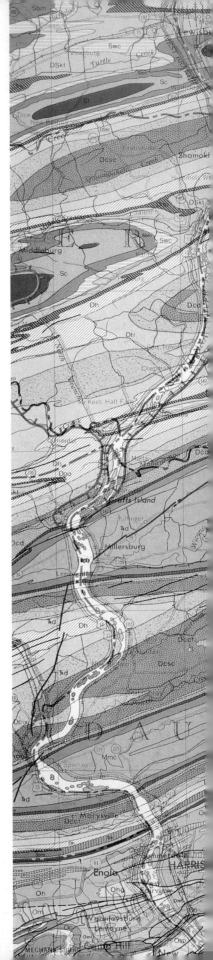

The preceding questions and answers exemplify the approach taken by geographers when looking at Earth: Where is something? Why is it there? How did it get there? How does it interact with other things?

Geography is not a collection of arcane information. Rather, it is the study of spatial aspects of human existence. People everywhere need to know about the nature of their world and their place in it. Geography has much more to do with asking questions and solving problems than it does with rote memorization of isolated facts.

So what exactly is geography? It is an integrative discipline that brings together the physical and human dimensions of the world in the study of people, places, and environments. Its subject matter is Earth's surface and the processes that shape it, the relationships between people and environments, and the connections between people and places.

The world facing students graduating in the year 2000 will be more crowded, the physical environment more threatened, and the global economy more competitive and interconnected. Understanding that world, that environment, and that economy will require high levels of competency in geography, because geography means a sensitivity to location, to scale, to movement, to patterns, to resources and conflicts, to maps and geo-graphics.

A stretch of Pennsylvania's Susquehanna River flows through swaths of four types of images—a geologic map identifying rock types, a regional map combining cultural and natural features, a Landsat image, and a topographic map.

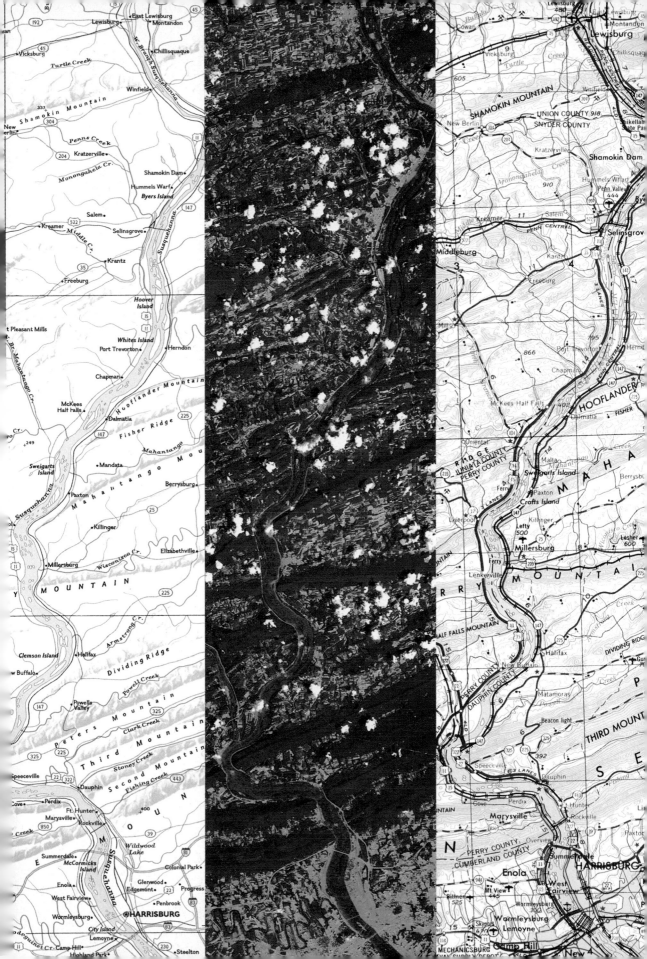

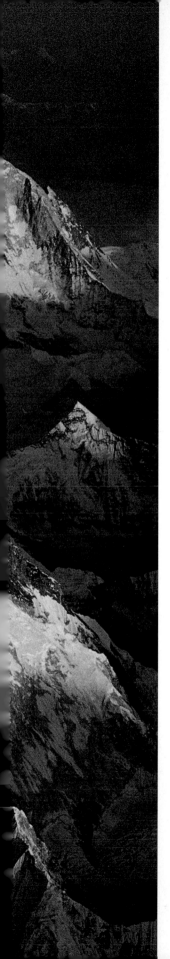

WHY GEOGRAPHY?

. . . .

A ll individuals need to have an understanding of geography, which means that they need to have an understanding of the spatial contexts of people, places, and environments on Earth. An isolated geographic fact does not constitute geographic understanding. For example, to know that Mount Everest is the highest peak in the world is not understanding geography until that isolated fact is put into a variety of spatial contexts. Geographic understanding requires that we know not only the location of Mount Everest but why it is the highest peak in the world. We must understand the physical processes that were responsible for its creation and evolution. We must understand why its location in the Himalaya has impacts on the Indian subcontinent in terms of access to water and downstream flooding, political security and territorial conflict, and transportation passes and barriers. To a geographer, Mount Everest is in the ecological nerve center of the Indian subcontinent. To a geographer, Mount Everest can only be understood in terms of its interlinked physical and human spatial contexts. We need this understanding of geography for reasons that range from the most profound to the most utilitarian:

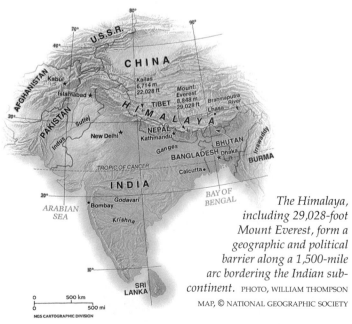

The Himalaya, including 29,028-foot Mount Everest, form a geographic and political barrier along a 1,500-mile arc bordering the Indian subcontinent. PHOTO, WILLIAM THOMPSON MAP, © NATIONAL GEOGRAPHIC SOCIETY

21

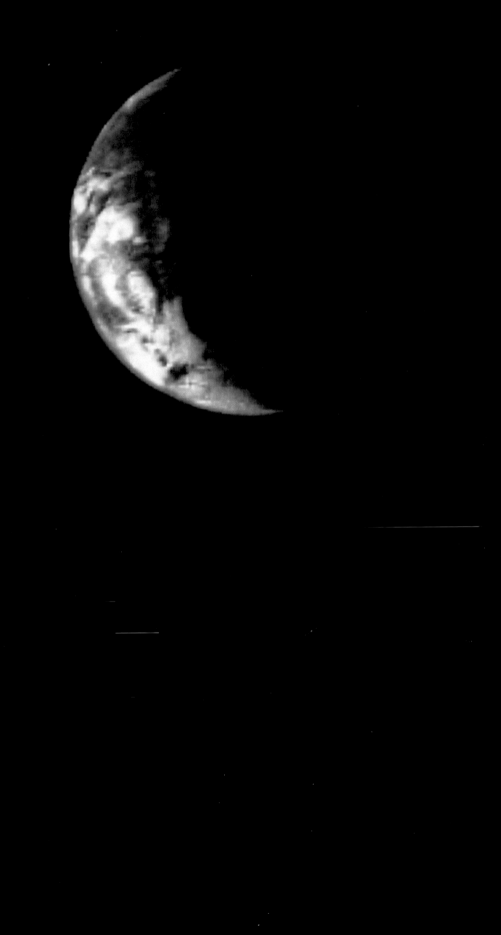

THE EXISTENTIAL REASON

In 1977, the U. S. spacecraft Voyager 1 set out on its epic journey to the outer solar system and beyond. When it had passed the most distant planet, its camera was turned back to photograph the solar system. Purely by chance, the camera recorded a pale blue dot in the vastness of space. Every human who has ever lived has lived on that blue dot—Earth. Humans want to understand the intrinsic nature of their home. Geography enables them to understand where they are, literally and figuratively.

THE ETHICAL REASON

Earth will continue to whirl through space for untold millennia, but it is not certain that it will exist in a condition in which humans can thrive or even live. Earth is the only home that humans know or are likely to know. Life is fragile; humans are fragile. Geography provides knowledge of Earth's physical and human systems and of the interdependency of living things and physical environments. That knowledge, in turn, provides a basis for humans to cooperate in the best interests of our planet.

(opposite) The Earth photographed September 18, 1977 from Voyager 1 at 7.25 million miles away.
(above) A man walking in the Sahel near Sinkat, Sudan. NASA; JAMES NACHTWEY

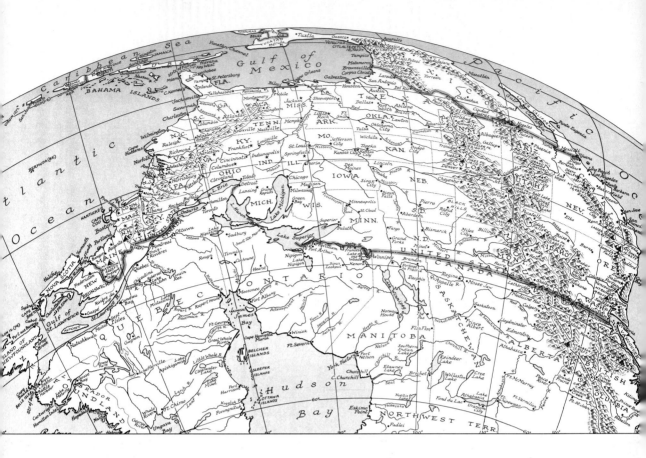

THE INTELLECTUAL REASON

. . . .

Geography captures the imagination. It stimulates curiosity about the world and the world's diverse inhabitants and places, as well as about local, regional, and global issues. By understanding our place in the world, humans can overcome parochialism and ethnocentrism. Geography focuses attention on exciting and interesting things, on fascinating people and places, on things worth knowing because they are absorbing and because knowing about them lets humans make better-informed and, therefore, wiser decisions.

THE PRACTICAL REASON

. . . .

Geography has utilitarian value in the modern world. As the interconnectedness of the world accelerates, the practical need for geographic knowledge becomes more critical. Imagine a doctor who treats diseases without understanding the environment in which the diseases thrive and spread, or a manufacturer who is ignorant of world markets and resources, or a postal worker who cannot distinguish Guinea from Guyana. With a strong grasp of geography, people are better equipped to solve issues at not only the local level but also the global level.

(above) A map of North America from the perspective of the Arctic Circle in northern Canada. (right) Geographic information systems (GIS) allow a cartographer to combine Landsat images by computer. Here, a mosaic map of North America is created at the Environmental Research Institute of Michigan using NOAA satellite images. © WORLD EAGLE; ANDREW SACKS

G eography education is the key to geographic competency. To achieve geographic understanding on a national scale requires a concerted effort by the educational system to ensure that all students receive a basic education in geography.

Geography standards are the key to geography education. The National Geography Standards represent a consensus on what constitutes a world-class education in geography for all American students.

In developing the standards, the Geography Education Standards Project used curriculum materials collected from many countries as well as materials familiar to most teachers in the United States, such as state and local curriculum frameworks and the 1984 *Guidelines for Geographic Education: Elementary and Secondary Schools*. Particular care was taken to use the framework and exercise specifications prepared for the *Geography Assessment Framework for the 1994 National Assessment of Educational Progress* (NAEP). Thus, these standards evolved from the geography community's thinking about what constitutes appropriate and challenging content (see Appendix A: Genesis of the National Geography Standards).

Two imperatives drive the National Geography Standards. First, geographic understanding must be set into a process of lifelong learning. There is an inseparable and seamless connection between formal educational contexts—preschool, K–12, college—and adult life. Second, geographic understanding must be set into life contexts: school, family, society, and occupation.

The standards are intended for life: lifelong in terms of commitment and life-enhancing in terms of purpose. Geography is empowering in practical contexts. Geography is enriching by helping humans understand their personal experiences.

The National Geography Standards aim to create a geographically informed person: someone who understands

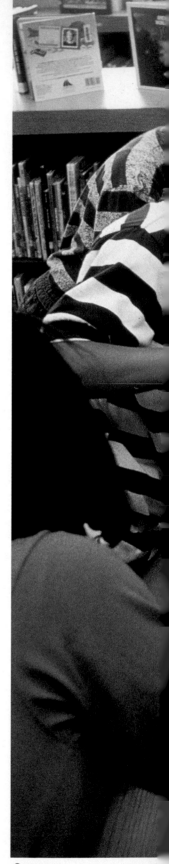

© UNIPHOTO

THE SAHEL, 1986, NIGER. STEVE McCURRY

NATIONAL GEOGRAPHY STANDARDS : 1994

that geography is the study of people, places, and environments from a spatial perspective, someone who appreciates the interdependent worlds in which we all live. The study of geography has practical value through the application of a spatial view to life situations.

THE GEOGRAPHICALLY INFORMED PERSON

T he power and beauty of geography allow us to see, understand, and appreciate the web of relationships between people, places, and environments.

At the everyday level, for example, a geographically informed person can appreciate the locational dynamics of street vendors and pedestrian traffic or fast-food outlets and automobile traffic; the routing strategies of school buses in urban areas and of backpackers in wilderness areas; the land-use strategies of farmers and of real estate developers.

At a more extended spatial scale, that same person can appreciate the dynamic links between severe storms and property damage or between summer thunderstorms and flash floods; the use of irrigation systems to compensate for lack of precipitation or the connections between temperature inversions and urban air pollution episodes; the seasonal movement of migrant laborers in search of work and of vacationers in search of sunshine and warmth.

At a global level, the geographically informed person can appreciate the connections between cyclical drought and human starvation in the Sahel or between the Chernobyl nuclear disaster and the long-term consequences to human health and economic activities throughout eastern and northwestern Europe; the restructuring of human migration and trade patterns as the European Union becomes increasingly integrated or as the Pacific rim nations develop a commonality of economic and political interests; and the uncertainties associated with the possible effects of global warming on human society or the destruction of tropical rain forests on global climate.

CHAPTER 2

The Components of Geography Education

ORGANIZATION OF GEOGRAPHY

Geography is composed of three interrelated and inseparable components: subject matter, skills, and perspectives. Subject matter is a distillation of essential knowledge and is the foundation for the geography standards. Subject matter is the basis on which geographic skills are brought to bear. These skills are: (1) asking geographic questions, (2) acquiring geographic information, (3) organizing geographic information, (4) analyzing geographic information, and (5) answering geographic questions. Knowledge and skills must be considered from two perspectives: spatial and ecological.

Mastering any single component of geography is *not* equivalent to mastering geography. All three—subject matter, skills, and perspectives—are necessary to being geographically informed. None can stand alone.

There is a related chain of knowledge that the geographically informed person must appreciate and command. Knowing population growth rates is not sufficient unless that knowledge can be related to an understanding of the resource base—the distribution of arable land, climate patterns—and to the transportation system that moves food supplies to consumers, and so on. Likewise, knowing where to find information on the distribution of population is not sufficient unless you know how to evaluate the reliability of that information, can relate it to maps of arable land and transportation routes, and can then speculate on the impact of changing population policies, migration patterns, or new crops on the patterns of people and rates of food production. This process returns you to the subject of population growth rates, completing a chain of knowledge involving people, places, and environments.

A Datoga child in Tanzania plays at being a homeowner and cattle manager. Large pebbles are cattle, small pebbles are calves; leaves represent gates to the different enclosures. MONIQUE BORGERHOFF MULDER

SPACE AND PLACE

. . . .

Understanding the relationships between people, places, and environments depends upon an understanding of space. Space is the environmental stage upon which the drama of geography is played out, and places are particular points on the environmental stage where the action occurs. In this respect, there is a parallel with the approach of history. History is concerned with understanding the temporal dimension of human experience (time and chronology). Geography is concerned with understanding the spatial dimension of human experience (space and place).

Space in the world is identified in terms of location, distance, direction, pattern, shape, and arrangement. Place is identified in terms of the relationships between physical environmental characteristics, such as climate, topography, and vegetation, and, such human characteristics as economic activity, settlement, and land use. Together, these characteristics make each particular place meaningful and special to people. Place, in fact, is space endowed with physical and human meaning. It is the fascination with and exploration of space and place that give geography its way of understanding the world.

THE SUBJECT MATTER

The roots of the word "geography" are found in two Greek words: *geo*, meaning Earth, and *graphia*, meaning description or depiction. The purpose of geography, therefore, is to describe or depict Earth. But there is no single way of doing that. Rather, Earth can be looked at in various ways.

As a physical object, it is an oblate spheroid with an equatorial circumference of approximately 24,902 miles; its surface is covered by water and land in a ratio of approximately 2.3:1; and that surface ranges from 29,028 feet above sea level to 35,840 feet below sea level (the top of Mount Everest to the bottom of the Mariana Trench).

As a physical environment, Earth is characterized by large-scale processes, such as the atmospheric jet streams that snake across its surface, and large-scale landforms, such as the Ring of Fire surrounding the Pacific Basin.

As a place in which humans can live, it offers such diverse habitats as the permafrost of Siberia, the tropical rain forest of the Congo River basin, and the Atacama Desert of Chile.

As a place in which humans *do* live, it displays intricate patterns of environmental modification (e.g., the polderlands of the Netherlands, or the terraced hills of the Philippines), as well as varied patterns of land use (e.g., the densely populated area of Hong Kong, the sparsely peopled central desert of Australia, and the automobile-based sprawl of southern California).

Geographers look at Earth in all of these ways—as a physical object, as a physical environment, and as a human place. Geographers also look at the world as a whole, to understand the connections between places, and to recognize that the local affects the global and vice versa. But in order to study Earth as the home of people, geographers must develop a framework that cuts into the connections between places.

Our framework consists of two levels. At the first level, the subject matter of geography is divided into six essential elements. By essential we mean that each piece is central and necessary; we must look at the world in this way. By element we mean that each piece is a building block for the whole. At the second level, each essential element contains a number of geography standards, and each geography standard contains a set of related ideas and approaches to the subject matter of geography.

A student awaits her commuter train in Shinjuku, Japan, an edge city of Tokyo. Nearly 3 million people per day use this station, the country's largest. DAVID ALAN HARVEY

THE SIX ESSENTIAL ELEMENTS

. . . .

The first element, The World in Spatial Terms, captures the essence of the geographic eye: the structuring of geographic information, the ordering of knowledge into mental maps, and the spatial analysis of that information. Given this essential grounding in the geographic way of approaching the world, the second element, Places and Regions, applies that geographic eye to the world: places and regions are the basic units of geography, and those units are seen differently by different people. The third and fourth elements, Physical Systems and Human Systems, cover the specific content of geography. Physical Systems looks at physical processes (climate, landforms, etc.) and then organizes these processes into functional units, ecosystems. Human Systems begins with population and then considers human activities, from culture to economics, settlement, and conflict and cooperation. The fifth element, Environment and Society, reintegrates the content of geography by emphasizing the interaction between physical and human systems and identifying the central role of resources in environment–society links. The sixth element, The Uses of Geography, shows how geography, taken as a whole, enables us to understand the past, interpret the present, and plan for the future.

Physical and human phenomena are spatially distributed over Earth's surface. The outcome of *Geography for Life* is a geographically informed person (1) who sees meaning in the arrangement of things in space; (2) who sees relations between people, places, and environments; (3) who uses geographic skills; and (4) who applies spatial and ecological perspectives to life situations.

The World in Spatial Terms

Geography studies the relationships between people, places, and environments by mapping information about them into a spatial context.

The geographically informed person knows and understands:

1. How to use maps and other geographic representations, tools, and technologies to acquire, process, and report information from a spatial perspective

2. How to use mental maps to organize information about people, places, and environments in a spatial context

3. How to analyze the spatial organization of people, places, and environments on Earth's surface

Places and Regions

The identities and lives of individuals and peoples are rooted in particular places and in those human constructs called regions.

The geographically informed person knows and understands:

4. The physical and human characteristics of places

5. That people create regions to interpret Earth's complexity

6. How culture and experience influence people's perceptions of places and regions

Physical Systems

Physical processes shape Earth's surface and interact with plant and animal life to create, sustain, and modify ecosystems.

The geographically informed person knows and understands:

7. The physical processes that shape the patterns of Earth's surface

8. The characteristics and spatial distribution of ecosystems on Earth's surface

Human Systems

People are central to geography in that human activities help shape Earth's surface, human settlements and structures are part of Earth's surface, and humans compete for control of Earth's surface.

The geographically informed person knows and understands:

9. The characteristics, distribution, and migration of human populations on Earth's surface
10. The characteristics, distribution, and complexity of Earth's cultural mosaics
11. The patterns and networks of economic interdependence on Earth's surface
12. The processes, patterns, and functions of human settlement
13. How the forces of cooperation and conflict among people influence the division and control of Earth's surface

Environment and Society

The physical environment is modified by human activities, largely as a consequence of the ways in which human societies value and use Earth's natural resources, and human activities are also influenced by Earth's physical features and processes.

The geographically informed person knows and understands:

14. How human actions modify the physical environment
15. How physical systems affect human systems
16. The changes that occur in the meaning, use, distribution, and importance of resources

The Uses of Geography

Knowledge of geography enables people to develop an understanding of the relationships between people, places, and environments over time—that is, of Earth as it was, is, and might be.

The geographically informed person knows and understands:

17. How to apply geography to interpret the past
18. How to apply geography to interpret the present and plan for the future

USING THE
EIGHTEEN STANDARDS
. . . .

While all of the National Geography Standards are applicable and relevant to all states and school districts, different emphases are possible and desirable. A state such as Alaska might emphasize the three Environment and Society standards, interpreting them prospectively by focusing on resources and the potential impacts of human activities on Alaska's physical environment. A state such as Pennsylvania might take the same three standards, interpreting them retrospectively by focusing on thé environmental consequences of resource extraction and exhaustion in Pennsylvania. Similarly, an urban school in Detroit might implement National Geography Standard 10—The characteristics, distribution, and complexity of Earth's cultural mosaics—by emphasizing intraurban migration, neighborhood formation, and ethnic diversity; whereas a rural school in Montana might emphasize National Geography Standard 12—The processes, patterns, and functions of human settlement—and concentrate on the economic and social problems of low density, dispersed settlements.

Illustrative examples can be tailored to local contexts. In discussing migration in National Geography Standard 9, a school district in California might examine migration from Southeast Asia, a school district in Florida might devote attention to migration from the Caribbean, and a school district in Texas might consider migration from Mexico and Central America. Similarly, a New England school district might discuss migration of French Canadians in the nineteenth century whereas a school district in Louisiana might look at the migration of Acadians in the early eighteenth century. School districts in Chicago and Baltimore might look at the flows of African Americans from Mississippi and Alabama in the early and middle twentieth century; whereas schools in Cincinnati and Cleveland might choose migration from Appalachia during the same period. In all cases, despite differences in specific place and time, the basic geographic concepts would be identical: push and pull factors, migration streams, migration fields, distances, the role of intervening opportunities.

Immigrants in the Registry Room at Ellis Island, New York, 1909. Of each, inspectors asked a barrage of questions—Where are you going? Have you ever been in prison? Do you have any money? NEW YORK PUBLIC LIBRARY

Reading the Text of These Standards

Each standard is identified by a number—in this case National Geography Standard 4—and grade level—in this case grades K–4.

Each standard is grouped within an *essential element*.

Each *standard title* is a summary of what the student needs to know and understand about a specific set of ideas and approaches.

Each standard explains exactly what the student should know and understand after completing a particular grade level. In this case, at grade 4, there are three knowledge statements.

GEOGRAPHY STANDARD 4 GRADES K–4

Places and Regions

▶ **THE PHYSICAL AND HUMAN CHARACTERISTICS OF PLACES**

. . . .

By the end of the fourth grade, the student knows and understands:

1. **The physical characteristics of places (e.g., landforms, bodies of water, soil, vegetation, and weather and climate)**

2. **The human characteristics of places (e.g., population distributions, settlement patterns, languages, ethnicity, nationality, and religious beliefs)**

3. **How physical and human processes together shape places**

Therefore, the student is able to:

A. **Describe and compare the physical characteristics of places at a variety of scales, local to global, as exemplified by being able to**

Observe and describe the physical characteristics of the local community in words and sketches, using a data-retrieval chart organized by physical features (e.g., landforms, bodies of water, soils, vegetation)

Use a variety of visual materials and data sources (e.g., photographs, satellite-produced images, pictures, tables, charts) to describe the physical characteristics of a region, noting items that have similar distributions (e.g., trees in river valleys)

Use cardboard, wood, clay, or other materials to make a model of a region that shows its physical characteristics (e.g., landforms, bodies of water, vegetation)

B. **Describe and compare the human characteristics of places at a variety of scales, local to global, as exemplified by being able to**

Observe and describe the human characteristics of the local community in words and sketches, using a data-retrieval chart organized by human features (e.g., type of economic activity, type of housing, languages spoken, ethnicity, religion)

113

Use a variety of visual materials, data sources, and narratives (e.g., photographs, pictures, tables, charts, newspaper stories) to describe the human characteristics of a region and to answer such questions as: Where do people live? What kinds of jobs do they have? How do they spend their leisure time?

Use cardboard, wood, clay, or other materials to make a model of a community that shows its human characteristics (e.g., land-use patterns, areas of settlement, locations of community services)

C. **Describe and compare different places at a variety of scales, local to global, as exemplified by being able to**

Observe and describe the physical and human characteristics of the local community and compare them to the characteristics of surrounding communities or of communities in other regions of the country

Use a variety of graphic materials and data sources (e.g., photographs, satellite-produced images, tables, charts) to describe the physical and human characteristics of a region, noting items that have similar distributions (e.g., communities are located on major highways)

Use cardboard, wood, clay, or other materials to make a model of a community that shows its physical and human characteristics (e.g., landforms, bodies of water, vegetation, land-use patterns, areas of settlement)

D. **Describe and explain the physical and human processes that shape the characteristics of places, as exemplified by being able to**

Use maps and other graphic materials to describe the effects of physical and human processes in shaping the landscape (e.g., the effects of erosion and deposition in creating landforms, the effects of agriculture in changing land use and vegetation, the effects of settlement on the building of roads)

Draw maps to show the distribution of population in a region with respect to landforms, climate, vegetation, resources, historic events, or other physical and human characteristics to suggest factors that affect settlement patterns

Keep a daily weather log of wind direction, temperature, precipitation, and general conditions over time to explain some of the factors that affect weather in the local community

Each standard states what the student should be able to do on the basis of this knowledge. In this case, at grade 4, there are four activities, each of which is exemplified by three learning opportunities for students and teachers.

CHAPTER 3

Geographic Skills and Perspectives

GEOGRAPHIC SKILLS

Geographic skills provide the necessary tools and techniques for us to think geographically. They are central to geography's distinctive approach to understanding physical and human patterns and processes on Earth. We use geographic skills when we make decisions important to our well-being—where to buy or rent a home; where to get a job; how to get to work or to a friend's house; where to shop, vacation, or go to school. All of these decisions involve the ability to acquire, arrange, and use geographic information. Daily decisions and community activities are linked to thinking systematically about environmental and societal issues. Community decisions relating to problems of air, water, and land pollution or locational issues, such as where to place industries, schools, and residential areas, also require the skillful use of geographic information. Business and government decisions, from the best site for a supermarket or a regional airport to issues of resource use, or international trade, involve the analysis of geographic data.

Geographic skills help us to make reasoned political decisions. Whether the issues involve the evaluation of foreign affairs and international economic policy or local zoning and land use, the skills enable us to collect and analyze information, come to an informed conclusion, and make reasoned decisions on a course of action. Geographic skills also aid in the development and presentation of effective, persuasive arguments for and against matters of public policy.

Erosion-scalloped, 300-foot cliffs, vegetated by tabletop scrublands, stretch nearly a hundred miles along Australia's southern coast.
DAVID DOUBILET

THE RATIONALE FOR GEOGRAPHIC SKILLS

The geographic skills that a geographically informed person should have consist of five sets adapted from the *Guidelines for Geographic Education: Elementary and Secondary Schools*, prepared by the Joint Committee on Geographic Education and published in 1984 by the Association of American Geographers and the National Council for Geographic Education:

1. ASKING GEOGRAPHIC QUESTIONS

2. ACQUIRING GEOGRAPHIC INFORMATION

3. ORGANIZING GEOGRAPHIC INFORMATION

4. ANALYZING GEOGRAPHIC INFORMATION

5. ANSWERING GEOGRAPHIC QUESTIONS

Following is a brief discussion of the principles underlying the five skill sets, followed by the presentation of skills.

1. ASKING GEOGRAPHIC QUESTIONS

Successful geographic inquiry involves the ability and willingness to ask, speculate on, and answer questions about why things are where they are and how they got there. Students need to be able to pose questions about their surroundings: Where is something located? Why is it there? With what is it associated? What are the consequences of its location and associations? What is this place like?

Students should be asked to speculate about possible answers to questions because speculation leads to the development of hypotheses that link the asking and answering stages of the process. Hypotheses guide the search for information.

Geography is distinguished by the kinds of questions it asks—the "where" and "why there" of a problem. It is important that students develop and practice the skills of asking such questions for themselves. The task can be approached by giving students practice in distinguishing geographic from nongeographic questions and by presenting students with issues and asking them to develop geographic questions. At higher grade levels students can identify geographic problems and ways in which an application of geography can help solve problems or resolve issues.

2. ACQUIRING GEOGRAPHIC INFORMATION

Geographic information is information about locations, the physical and human characteristics of those locations, and the geographic activities and conditions of the people who live in those places. To answer geographic questions, students should start by gathering information from a variety of sources in a variety of ways. They should read and interpret all kinds of maps. They should compile and use primary and secondary information to prepare quantitative and qualitative descriptions. They should collect data from interviews, fieldwork, reference material, and library research.

The skills involved in acquiring geographic information include locating and collecting data, observing and systematically recording information, reading and interpreting maps and other graphic representations of spaces and places, interviewing, and using statistical methods.

Primary sources of information, especially the result of fieldwork performed by the students, are important in geographic inquiry. Fieldwork involves students conducting research in the community by distributing questionnaires, taking photographs, recording observations, interviewing citizens, and collecting samples. Fieldwork helps arouse the students' curiosity and makes the study of geography more enjoyable and relevant. It fosters active learning by enabling students to observe, ask questions, identify problems, and hone their perceptions of physical features and human activities. Fieldwork connects students' school activities with the world in which they live.

Secondary sources of information include texts, maps, statistics, photographs, multimedia, computer databases, newspapers, telephone directories, and government publications.

Tertiary sources such as encyclopedias report information compiled from secondary sources and are important in some research situations.

3. ORGANIZING GEOGRAPHIC INFORMATION

Once collected, the geographic information should be organized and displayed in ways that help analysis and interpretation. Data should be arranged systematically. Different types of data should be separated and classified in visual, graphic forms: photographs, aerial photos, graphs, cross sections, climagraphs, diagrams, tables, cartograms, and maps. Written information from documents or interviews should be organized into pertinent quotes or tabular form.

There are many ways to organize geographic information. Maps play a central role in geographic inquiry, but there are other ways to translate data into visual form, such as by using graphs of all kinds, tables, spreadsheets, and time lines. Such visuals are especially useful when accompanied by clear oral or written summaries. Creativity and skill are needed to arrange geographic information effectively. Decisions about design, color, graphics, scale, and clarity are impor-

tant in developing the kinds of maps, graphs, and charts that best reflect the data.

Geography has been called "the art of the mappable." Making maps should be a common activity for all students. They should read (decode) maps to collect information and analyze geographic patterns and make (encode) maps to organize information. Making maps can mean using sketch maps to make a point in an essay or record field observations. It can mean using symbols to map data on the location of world resources or producing a county-level map of income in a state. It can even mean mapping the distribution of fire-ant mounds in a field or trash on a school playground. For students, making maps should become as common, natural, and easy as writing a paragraph. They should be skilled in interpreting and creating map symbols, finding locations on maps using a variety of reference systems, orienting maps and finding directions, using scales to determine distance, and thinking critically about information on maps.

4. ANALYZING GEOGRAPHIC INFORMATION

Analyzing geographic information involves seeking patterns, relationships, and connections. As students analyze and interpret information, meaningful patterns or processes emerge. Students can then synthesize their observations into a coherent explanation. Students should note associations and similarities between areas, recognize patterns, and draw inferences from maps, graphs, diagrams, tables, and other sources. Using simple statistics students can identify trends, relationships, and sequences.

Geographic analysis involves a variety of activities. It is sometimes difficult to separate the processes involved in organizing geographic information from the procedures used in analyzing it. The two processes go on simultaneously in many cases. But in other instances, analysis follows the manipulation of raw data into an easily understood and usable form. Students should scrutinize maps to discover and compare spatial patterns and relationships; study tables and graphs to determine trends and relationships between and among items; probe data through statistical methods to identify trends, sequences, correlations, and relationships; examine texts and documents to interpret, explain, and synthesize characteristics. Together these analytic processes lead to answers to the questions that first prompted an inquiry and to the development of geographic models and generalizations. These are the analytical skills that all students need to develop.

5. ANSWERING GEOGRAPHIC QUESTIONS

Successful geographic inquiry culminates in the development of generalizations and conclusions based on the data collected, organized, and analyzed. Skills associated with answering geographic questions include the ability to make inferences based on information organized in graphic form (maps, tables, graphs) and in oral and written narratives. These skills involve the ability to distinguish generalizations that apply at the local level from those that apply at the global level (issues of scale are important in developing answers to geographic questions).

Generalizations are the culmination of the process of inquiry, and they help to codify understanding. Developing generalizations requires that students use the information they have collected, processed, and analyzed to make general statements about geography. At other times, however, students use the evidence they have acquired to make decisions, solve problems, or form judgments about a question, issue, or problem.

Geographic generalizations can be made using inductive reasoning or deductive reasoning. Inductive reasoning requires students to synthesize geographic information to answer questions and reach conclusions. Deductive reasoning requires students to identify relevant questions, collect and assess evidence, and decide whether the generalizations are appropriate by testing them against the real world. Students should have experience in both approaches to learning.

Students should also be able to communicate clearly and effectively, especially as they learn to answer geographic questions. It is a skill linked closely to good citizenship. Students can develop a sense of civic responsibility by disseminating the answers they have discovered in geographic inquiry. They can display geographic information in many engaging and effective ways—for example, by using multimedia, such as combinations of pictures, maps, graphs, and narratives, to present a story or illuminate a generalization. Geographic information can also be presented through the use of poems, collages, plays, journals, and essays. Every medium chosen to present geographic information to answer a question or address an issue or problem should stimulate inquiry and communicate clearly. Choosing the best means of presenting answers to geographic questions is an important skill.

Students should also understand that there are alternative ways to reach generalizations and conclusions. There are many types of knowledge, and many levels of reality and meaning. Teachers should encourage students to develop multiple points of view and to seek multiple outcomes to problems. This process should include collecting many kinds of data, including personal, subjective information, from a variety of sources.

The fifth skill set represents the last step in the process of geographic inquiry. But it is not really the end, because the process usually begins again with new questions suggested by the conclusions and generalizations that have been developed. These questions, often posed as hypotheses to be tested, provide a way to review generalizations. Each question answered, decision reached, or problem solved leads to new issues and new problems. Geographic learning is a continuous process that is both empowering and fascinating.

DEVELOPING GEOGRAPHIC SKILLS

I t is essential that students develop the skills that will enable them to observe patterns, associations, and spatial order. Many of the skills that students are expected to learn involve the use of tools and technologies that are part of the process of geographic inquiry. Maps are essential tools of geography because they assist in the visualization of space.

Other tools and technologies, such as satellite-produced images, graphs, sketches, diagrams, and photographs are also integral parts of geographic analysis. The rate of growth of an urban area, for example, can be observed by comparing old and new photographs. Large-scale land-use changes can be made clear by comparing images taken over a period of years.

A new and important tool in geographic analysis is the spatial database, or geographic information system (GIS) (see Appendix E). Geographic information systems make the process of presenting and analyzing geographic information easier, so they accelerate geographic inquiry. Spatial databases also can be developed in the classroom using paper and pencil.

Many of the capabilities that students need to develop geographic skills are termed critical thinking skills. Such skills are not unique to geography and involve a number of generic thinking processes, such as knowing, inferring, analyzing, judging, hypothesizing, generalizing, predicting, and decision-making. These have applications to all levels of geographic inquiry and constitute the bases on which students can build competencies in applying geographic skills to geographic inquiry.

Geographic skills develop over the entire course of the students' school years, and for each of the three successive grade levels discussed. Teachers and other curriculum developers will need to recognize that the students' mastery of geographic skills must be sequenced effectively so that the students retain and build on their understanding.

The Five Sets of Geographic Skills by Grade Level

The geographic skills that all students need to develop are organized by benchmark year (by the end of the fourth, eighth, and twelfth grades).

Geographic Skills to Be Learned by the End of the Fourth Grade

SKILL SET 1

▶ ASKING GEOGRAPHIC QUESTIONS

By the end of the fourth grade, the student should know and understand how to:

1. Ask geographic questions—Where is it located? Why is it there? What is significant about its location? How is its location related to the locations of other people, places, and environments?—as exemplified by being able to

- Ask geographic questions about places in books

- Identify geographic aspects of current news stories

- Pose geographic questions based on the features of the student's own community: Where do my classmates live? How is land used in the area around my school and my home? How far do my classmates travel to school? How long does it take? What mode of transportation do they use? What routes do they follow?

2. Distinguish between geographic and nongeographic questions, as exemplified by being able to

- Classify a list of questions as being geographic or nongeographic

- Pose questions about an issue from the viewpoint of a variety of members of the community and identify which questions are geographic and which are not geographic

SKILL SET 2

▶ ACQUIRING GEOGRAPHIC INFORMATION

By the end of the fourth grade, the student should know and understand how to:

1. Locate, gather, and process information from a variety of primary and secondary sources including maps, as exemplified by being able to

- Apply quantitative skills (e.g., count landforms, cities, lakes, and population characteristics; measure distances)

- Obtain information on the characteristics of places (e.g., climate, elevation, and population density) by interpreting maps

- Determine the distance and compass direction from one place to another on a map

2. Make and record observations about the physical and human characteristics of places, as exemplified by being able to

- Engage in fieldwork to collect information

- Make records of observations systematically in terms of time and place

- Use aerial photographs, satellite images, or topographic maps to identify elements of the physical and human environments

ASK GEOGRAPHIC QUESTIONS	ACQUIRE GEOGRAPHIC INFORMATION	ORGANIZE GEOGRAPHIC INFORMATION	ANALYZE GEOGRAPHIC INFORMATION	ANSWER GEOGRAPHIC QUESTIONS
Ask geographic questions—Where is it located? Why is it there? What is significant about its location? How is its location related to the locations of other people, places, and environments? · · · · · · · · · · · Distinguish between geographic and nongeographic questions	Locate, gather, and process information from a variety of primary and secondary sources including maps · · · · · · · · · · · Make and record observations about the physical and human characteristics of places	Prepare maps to display geographic information · · · · · · · · · · · Construct graphs, tables, and diagrams to display geographic information	Use maps to observe and interpret geographic relationships · · · · · · · · · · · Use tables and graphs to observe and interpret geographic trends and relationships · · · · · · · · · · · Use texts, photographs and documents to observe and interpret geographic trends and relationships · · · · · · · · · · · Use simple mathematics to analyze geographic data	Present geographic information in the form of both oral and written reports accompanied by maps and graphics · · · · · · · · · · · Use methods of geographic inquiry to acquire geographic information, draw conclusions, and make generalizations · · · · · · · · · · · Apply generalizations to solve geographic problems and make reasoned decisions

SKILL SET 3

▶ ORGANIZING GEOGRAPHIC INFORMATION

By the end of the fourth grade, the student should know and understand how to:

1. Prepare maps to display geographic information, as exemplified by being able to

- Map the locations of places on outline maps at a variety of scales, using appropriate symbols (e.g., use point symbols of different sizes to locate the cities, towns, and villages in a state)

- Draw sketch maps to illustrate geographic information (e.g., to provide directions to points in and around the student's community; to map the geographic information of stories; and to locate the distribution of stores in the community)

- Prepare maps as a means of spatially depicting information obtained from graphs (e.g., interpret a bar graph of U. S. exports to other countries and then prepare a map displaying the same information using arrow-shaped lines of varying width)

- Create maps that are labeled appropriately (e.g.,use a self-checking system such as TODALSIGs—Title, Orientation, Date, Author, Legend, Scale, Index, Grid, source)

2. Construct graphs, tables, and diagrams to display geographic information, as exemplified by being able to

- Organize quantitative geographic information into bar graphs, pie graphs, and line graphs

- Keep a daily record of temperature, precipitation, cloud cover, and other weather data in graphic and pictorial forms

- Prepare a diagram to illustrate a written description of a geographic process (e.g., hydrologic cycle, rain shadow, or growth of a settlement)

SKILL SET 4

► ANALYZING GEOGRAPHIC INFORMATION

By the end of the fourth grade, the student should know and understand how to:

1. Use maps to observe and interpret geographic relationships, as exemplified by being able to

- Use maps to draw inferences (e.g., use maps showing migration routes of people at various periods in history to suggest the reasons for the migrations and the particular routes)

- Interpret maps to make decisions (e.g., use maps showing land contours, roads, and land uses to choose good locations for a proposed activity such as a new park, fire station, ski resort, or solid-waste landfill)

- Compare large-scale maps of different places to describe spatial patterns and relationships (e.g., use maps to compare the physical and human characteristics of regions)

2. Use tables and graphs to observe and interpret geographic trends and relationships, as exemplified by being able to

- Prepare explanations of information obtained from tables and graphs (e.g., summarize climagraphs to produce a brief oral or written description of a location's climate and how that climate might influence agriculture, clothing, and other aspects of human life)

- Identify relationships between countries or regions from graphs (e.g., use the data from graphs to compare social and economic indicators from different regions of the world)

- Predict trends based on data in graphic form (e.g., use a graph showing past trends in world consumption of non-renewable resources to predict rates of consumption)

3. Use texts, photographs, and documents to observe and interpret geographic trends and relationships, as exemplified by being able to

- Summarize information obtained from primary and secondary sources (e.g., analyze student-answered questionnaires)

- Compare a variety of media such as photographs, maps, aerial photographs, and field sketches to draw conclusions (e.g., compare field sketches, aerial photographs, and maps to draw conclusions about the transformation of the landscape over time)

- Analyze visual information (e.g., use photographs, cartoons, videos, and CD-ROM images to make geographic inferences about the nature of a place)

4. Use simple mathematics to analyze geographic data, as exemplified by being able to

- Use numerical information to describe the characteristics of a place (e.g., count the number of days of rain and sunshine over a period to determine the average for each category)

- Use numerical information to compare places and discover variations in patterns (e.g., plot average annual rainfall for places in a region)

SKILL SET 5

► ANSWERING GEOGRAPHIC QUESTIONS

By the end of the fourth grade, the student should know and understand how to:

1. Present geographic information in the form of both oral and written reports accompanied by maps and graphics, as exemplified by being able to

- Organize a wall display that integrates maps, graphs, tables, and captions to present a geographic theme or the answers to a geographic question

- Research and make an illustrated oral report to the class or an appropriate public agency on a locational question (e.g., the best place to roller blade, skateboard, ice skate, picnic, or construct a biking-and-hiking trail)

2. Use methods of geographic inquiry to

acquire geographic information, draw conclusions, and make generalizations, as exemplified by being able to

- Make statements summarizing key geography ideas at the conclusion of learning opportunities (e.g., after watching slides of cities around the world, write a paragraph summarizing some major functions of cities)

- Recognize whether a series of statements forms a logical progression that answers geographic questions

3. **Apply generalizations to solve geographic problems and make reasoned decisions, as exemplified by being able to**

- Use maps to find the shortest paths for planning car pools, homework buddies, or babysitting networks (e.g., the "best" [least time, most direct] route from school to a friend's house and home)

- Test generalizations on range (how far individuals are willing to travel for certain goods and services) (e.g., conduct a survey on how far people drive or walk to shop for groceries, and then propose the best location for a new grocery store)

Geographic Skills to Be Learned by the End of the Eighth Grade

. . . .

SKILL SET 1

―――――――――――――――――――

▶ ASKING GEOGRAPHIC QUESTIONS

By the end of the eighth grade, the student should know and understand how to:

1. Identify geographic issues, define geographic problems, and pose geographic questions, as exemplified by being able to

- Analyze newspaper and magazine articles and identify geographic issues and problems evident in the articles

- Develop geographic questions about issues in subjects other than geography (e.g., language arts, history, science, mathematics)

- Ask questions about geographic problems in local issues relating to traffic, the environment, land use, housing, etc., and then summarize these problems by preparing written or oral statements, maps, and graphs

2. Plan how to answer geographic questions, as exemplified by being able to

- Develop questions to obtain information about a place, put the questions to likely informants, and then prepare a short description of their answers

- Identify and organize issues that should be considered in tackling a geographic problem (e.g., identify the factors involved in the location and design of a school playground)

SKILL SET 2

―――――――――――――――――――

▶ ACQUIRING GEOGRAPHIC INFORMATION

By the end of the eighth grade, the student should know and understand how to:

1. Use a variety of research skills to locate and collect geographic data, as exemplified by being able to

- Enter and retrieve population information on a computer, using databases, spreadsheets, and other sources (alternatively, create a handwritten master list of primary sources that could be used to research population issues)

- Know how to find as well as choose appropriate sources of information (e.g., periodicals, Bureau of the Census materials, databases, reference works, interviews, multimedia, etc.)

- Conduct interviews and field surveys in

ASK GEOGRAPHIC QUESTIONS	ACQUIRE GEOGRAPHIC INFORMATION	ORGANIZE GEOGRAPHIC INFORMATION	ANALYZE GEOGRAPHIC INFORMATION	ANSWER GEOGRAPHIC QUESTIONS
Identify geographic issues, define geographic problems, and pose geographic questions · · · · · · · · · · · Plan how to answer geographic questions	Use a variety of research skills to locate and collect geographic data · · · · · · · · · · · Use maps to collect and/or compile geographic information · · · · · · · · · · · Systematically observe the physical and human characteristics of places on the basis of fieldwork	Prepare various forms of maps as a means of organizing geographic information · · · · · · · · · · · Prepare various forms of graphs to organize and display geographic information · · · · · · · · · · · Prepare various forms of diagrams, tables, and charts to organize and display geographic information · · · · · · · · · · · Integrate various types of materials to organize geographic information	Interpret information obtained from maps, aerial photographs, satellite-produced images, and geographic information systems · · · · · · · · · · · Use statistics and other quantitative techniques to evaluate geographic information · · · · · · · · · · · Interpret and synthesize information obtained from a variety of sources— graphs, charts, tables, diagrams, texts, photographs, documents, interviews	Develop and present combinations of geographic information to answer geographic questions · · · · · · · · · · · Make generalizations and assess their validity

the student's local community to collect geographic information

2. Use maps to collect and/or compile geographic information, as exemplified by being able to

- Use cartograms, such as one dealing with petroleum production to prepare a list of major producers

- Read aerial photographs to recognize patterns apparent from the air and identify the patterns on a topographic map of the same area

- Describe phenomena reported on a map (e.g., use dot maps to make statements about population densities in an area in 1910, 1950, and 1990)

3. Systematically observe the physical and human characteristics of places on the basis of fieldwork, as exemplified by being able to

- Conduct field surveys to be able to map information about land use

- Take photographs and/or shoot videos

or prepare sketches of human features (architecture and the urban environment) and physical features (landforms and natural vegetation) of the landscape

- View pictures and video images of a place to collect geographic information (e.g., use slides, video clips, and other visual sources to observe relationships between climate and vegetation)

SKILL SET 3

▶ ORGANIZING GEOGRAPHIC INFORMATION

By the end of the eighth grade, the student should know and understand how to:

1. Prepare various forms of maps as a means of organizing geographic information, as exemplified by being able to

- Use area data to create choropleth maps

(e.g., prepare a map showing areas of food surplus and deficit based on World Bank or Population Reference Bureau data on calories consumed per year per person; use voting data by state to map the vote for Abraham Lincoln in the presidential election of 1860)

- Use maps to plot information contained in graphs (e.g., given a set of graphs showing per capita energy consumption in countries for 1980 and 1990, prepare graduated-circle maps to display the data effectively)

- Use isolines to map information (e.g., physical data, such as elevation and rainfall; demographic data such as number of homicides in urban areas to show regions of greatest and least personal safety; historical data, such as the extent of European settlement in North America at different periods)

2. Prepare various forms of graphs to organize and display geographic information, as exemplified by being able to

- Use weather data to produce climagraphs

- Use population data to produce population pyramids for a variety of countries

- Use computer programs to graph data from geographic databases

3. Prepare various forms of diagrams, tables, and charts to organize and display geographic information, as exemplified by being able to

- Create a table to compare data on a specific topic for different geographic regions (e.g., birth- and death rates for nations in Asia)

- Use flowcharts and diagrams to illustrate inputs, outputs, elements, feedbacks, and other aspects of physical and human systems

- Organize data in tables or diagrams to make decisions or draw conclusions (e.g., use a preference-sorting diagram to organize data regarding places where individuals prefer to live; create a table to summarize data obtained from maps; graphically organize information obtained from questionnaires and surveys)

4. Integrate various types of materials to organize geographic information, as exemplified by being able to

- Prepare overlays of different types of geographic information to create a geographic information system (e.g., a base map, vegetation map, contour map, or land-use map of a region)

- Organize materials for a multimedia report (e.g., maps, graphs, diagrams, and pictures) on a geographic topic

SKILL SET 4

▶ ANALYZING GEOGRAPHIC INFORMATION

By the end of the eighth grade, the student should know and understand how to:

1. Interpret information obtained from maps, aerial photographs, satellite-produced images, and geographic information systems, as exemplified by being able to

- Draw inferences from information presented in maps (e.g., use a variety of maps and other sources to explain the effects a logging operation might have on physical systems)

- Use maps to recognize spatial associations and relationships between locations (e.g., similarities and differences in climate among regions of the world at the same latitude; similarities and differences among urban areas in North America and Africa)

- Interpret information from map overlays to prepare a description of the geography of a region or place

- Evaluate geographic information to identify the possibility of bias (e.g., evaluate map projections to understand the distortions in terms of representing only one viewpoint)

2. Use statistics and other quantitative techniques to evaluate geographic information, as exemplified by being able to

- Use data obtained from quantitative methods of analysis to identify trends and patterns in data (e.g., prepare scatter diagrams to observe relationships between sets of geographic information, such as the number of

Asian food restaurants and the percentage of immigrants from Asia in a U. S. community)

- Produce summaries of geographic information (e.g., use descriptive statistics such as average, median, mode, and range to determine the nature of the distribution of per capita income by nation or snowfall by country)

- Cross-tabulate the occurrences of geographic variables to discover whether they co-vary spatially (e.g., use data on cotton production and length of growing season to demonstrate a relationship)

3. Interpret and synthesize information obtained from a variety of sources—graphs, charts, tables, diagrams, texts, photographs, documents, interviews—as exemplified by being able to

- Analyze and explain geographic themes in texts and documents (e.g., a comparative analysis of a major geographic event—hurricane, volcanic eruption, resource discovery—in different newspapers and news magazines)

- Prepare written and oral explanations of geographic relationships based on synthesis and analysis of information (e.g., write a summary of the geographic diffusion of Islam by using maps, photographs of art and architecture from different regions of the world, and other resources)

- Compare maps of voting patterns, ethnicity, and congressional districts to make inferences about distribution of political power in a U. S. state or region at different periods (e.g., Reconstruction South, era after World War II, and in the 1990s)

▶ ANSWERING GEOGRAPHIC QUESTIONS

By the end of the eighth grade, the student should know and understand how to:

1. Develop and present combinations of geographic information to answer geographic questions, as exemplified by being able to

- Use data from a geographic database to suggest alternative locations for a new road, a park, or a garbage dump

- Develop and present a multimedia report on a geographic topic, making use of maps, graphs, diagrams, videos, and pictures

- Draw sketch maps and graphs to illustrate written and oral summaries of geographic information

2. Make generalizations and assess their validity, as exemplified by being able to

- Prepare a reasoned account about the best locations for a crop by comparing its requirements for moisture with maps of rainfall, temperature, and soil quality

- Select appropriate locations for service industries by using population, transportation, and other kinds of maps (e.g., determine the optimal location for a video-rental store)

- Identify populations at risk for specific natural hazards (e.g., flood-vulnerable houses) by using a topographic map and a map of population distribution

Geographic Skills to Be Learned by the End of the Twelfth Grade

▶ ASKING GEOGRAPHIC QUESTIONS

By the end of the twelfth grade, the student should know and understand how to:

1. Plan and organize a geographic research project (e.g., specify a problem, pose a research question or hypothesis, and identify data sources), as exemplified by being able to

- Examine a series of maps of a region and list geographic questions suggested by the maps (e.g., How do land division systems influence road patterns, the distribution of houses, the efficiency of city services?)

- Study multiple sources of graphic and written information (e.g., databases, graphs, photographs, and firsthand accounts) to list geographic questions and organize a procedure to answer them

▶ ACQUIRING GEOGRAPHIC INFORMATION

By the end of the twelfth grade, the student should know and understand how to:

1. Systematically locate and gather geographic information from a variety of primary and secondary sources, as exemplified by being able to

- Gather data in the field by multiple procedures—observing, identifying, naming, describing, organizing, sketching, interviewing, recording, measuring

- Gather data in the classroom and library from maps, photographs, videos, and other media (e.g., CD-ROM), charts, aerial photographs, and other nonbook sources, and then use the data to identify, name,

describe, organize, sketch, measure, and evaluate items of geographic interest

- Gather data by spatial sampling in both secondary sources and the field (e.g., place a transparent grid of squares on maps to count whether two characteristics—such as corn production and hogs—that are hypothesized to be spatially related do coexist within the grid cells)

- Use quantitative measures (e.g., means, medians, and modes) to describe data (e.g., collect data on social and economic indicators for different nations of the world, conduct simple statistical analysis, and group nations as above or below the average)

2. Systematically assess the value and use of geographic information, as exemplified by being able to

- Contrast the validity and utility of migration data gathered from the field (e.g., a survey) and from secondary sources (e.g., the Census)

- Distinguish the data requirements and appropriate use of choropleth versus isopleth maps

▶ ORGANIZING GEOGRAPHIC INFORMATION

By the end of the twelfth grade, the student should know and understand how to:

1. Select and design appropriate forms of maps to organize geographic information, as exemplified by being able to

- Use various map symbols for particular purposes (e.g., use proportional dot and point symbols to display quantitative data)

- Prepare dot maps, choropleth maps, and isoline maps as appropriate to the level of measurement of the data (nominal, ordinal, interval) and the type of spatial phenomenon (point, line, area)

GRADES 9–12 SKILLS : Students should be given the opportunity to

ASK GEOGRAPHIC QUESTIONS	ACQUIRE GEOGRAPHIC INFORMATION	ORGANIZE GEOGRAPHIC INFORMATION	ANALYZE GEOGRAPHIC INFORMATION	ANSWER GEOGRAPHIC QUESTIONS
Plan and organize a geographic research project (e.g., specify a problem, pose a research question or hypothesis, and identify data sources)	Systematically locate and gather geographic information from a variety of primary and secondary sources · · · · · · · · · · · Systematically assess the value and use of geographic information	Select and design appropriate forms of maps to organize geographic information · · · · · · · · · · · Select and design appropriate forms of graphs, diagrams, tables, and charts to organize geographic information · · · · · · · · · · · Use a variety of media to develop and organize integrated summaries of geographic information	Use quantitative methods of analysis to interpret geographic information · · · · · · · · · · · Make inferences and draw conclusions from maps and other geographic representations · · · · · · · · · · · Use the processes of analysis, synthesis, evaluation, and explanation to interpret geographic information from a variety of sources	Formulate valid generalizations from the results of various kinds of geographic inquiry · · · · · · · · · · · Evaluate the answers to geographic questions · · · · · · · · · · · Apply geographic models, generalizations, and theories to the analysis, interpretation, and presentation of geographic information

- Prepare accurate field maps of small areas using a compass, protractor, plane table, and measuring tape
- Use field data to prepare sketch maps (e.g., map geographic information from the transect of an urban walk or the view from a bus window), noting characteristics of geographic interest such as land use, housing styles, and patterns of neighborhood ethnicity

2. Select and design appropriate forms of graphs, diagrams, tables, and charts to organize geographic information, as exemplified by being able to

- Use scatter graphs—plots of the value of one item against another item—to display the association between two items (e.g., the relationships between land values and distance from the central business district [downtown]; or relation between temperature and rainfall)
- Prepare diagrams that illustrate geographic information (e.g., physical features from topographic maps; landscape sketches from fieldwork; cross sections from topographic maps; or posters with graphic

codes such as ears of corn to represent number of calories consumed)
- Use line graphs to show changing patterns through time (e.g., rural population in the United States from 1890 to 1990; energy consumption in different regions of the world at ten-year intervals from 1950 to the present; telephone connections in the United States, 1890 to 1990)

3. Use a variety of media to develop and organize integrated summaries of geographic information, as exemplified by being able to

- Prepare integrated summaries on geographic issues, featuring texts and documents, audiovisual materials, and maps, and present them in the form of tables, graphs, and diagrams
- Summarize information obtained from questionnaires or field surveys to classify the responses

▶ ANALYZING GEOGRAPHIC INFORMATION

By the end of the twelfth grade, the student should know and understand how to:

1. Use quantitative methods of analysis to interpret geographic information, as exemplified by being able to

- Produce descriptive and analytic statistics to support the development of geographic generalizations (e.g., develop an index of the physical quality of life to support a classification system of world nations by standard-of-living categories)

- Calculate ratios between local measures and national averages of given geographic phenomena

2. Make inferences and draw conclusions from maps and other geographic representations, as exemplified by being able to

- Compare maps of geographic information at different periods to determine relationships (e.g., use maps of the largest urban areas at different periods to compare differences in location and offer explanations on the basis of site, transportation technology, and urban growth)

- Interpret information from several maps simultaneously (e.g., use maps showing family income, transportation networks, resources, and other data to develop ideas on why some regions prosper and others do not)

- Draw conclusions about cause and effect by correlating geographic information (e.g., compare data on soil-nutrient deficiencies and crop yields to determine their relationship)

3. Use the processes of analysis, synthesis, evaluation, and explanation to interpret geographic information from a variety of sources, as exemplified by being able to

- Use a balance sheet to evaluate the costs and benefits of making various decisions about geographic issues (e.g., alternative uses for land located near a freeway exit)

- Determine relationships (areal, cause and effect, chronological, etc.) by analyzing and interpreting geographic data

- Evaluate geographic reasoning (e.g., identify lines of argument and points of view, possible bias, logical flaws in content and perspective, unwarranted assertions, inferences and conclusions)

▶ ANSWERING GEOGRAPHIC QUESTIONS

By the end of the twelfth grade, the student should know and understand how to:

1. Formulate valid generalizations from the results of various kinds of geographic inquiry, as exemplified by being able to

- Use the results of several case-study analyses to speculate about general relationships between geographic variables

- Identify correlations between the locations of different phenomena by examining a variety of maps and atlases

- Use information on natural hazards and people's attitudes toward natural hazards in a specific region to develop generalizations regarding the link between hazards and attitudes toward them

2. Evaluate the answers to geographic questions, as exemplified by being able to

- Synthesize information to support a point of view expressed in written and oral form (e.g., compare various points of view on land use, such as whether to relocate or expand an airport, and present reasons for choosing one point of view)

- Evaluate the feasibility of solutions to problems (e.g., evaluate alternative locations for a visitor center in a wildlife refuge)

3. Apply geographic models, generalizations, and theories to the analysis, interpretation, and presentation of geographic information, as exemplified by being able to

- Use a geographic model to predict consequences on the basis of multiple sources of data (e.g., predict rates of soil erosion from

In amazement, a small boy gains an awe-inspiring perspective of this enormous globe at the Boston Science Museum. Having a geographic perspective means looking at one's world through a lens shaped by personal experience, selective information, and subjective evaluation. GEORGE F MOBLEY

generalizations about the interrelationships of soil, climate, slope, and land use)

- Choose the appropriate model to explain locations of various kinds of industry, recreation, and agriculture patterns in the United States

- Analyze regional political case studies to make generalizations about the forces affecting political stability in a specific region

- Explain the results of geographic inquiry both orally and in writing (e.g., make a presentation to a local government agency on a recycling program researched as part of a class project)

- Identify geographic questions in need of further investigation and develop new hypotheses as the conclusion to a process of inquiry

NATIONAL GEOGRAPHY STANDARDS : 1994

GEOGRAPHIC PERSPECTIVES

A perspective is one point of view among many competing ways of interpreting the meanings of experiences, events, places, persons, cultures, and physical environments. Having a perspective means looking at our world through a lens shaped by personal experience, selective information, and subjective evaluation. A perspective provides a frame of reference for asking and answering questions, identifying and solving problems, and evaluating the consequences of alternative actions. It is essential to be aware that many perspectives exist and that learning to understand the world from many points of view enhances our knowledge and skills. It is also essential to realize that our perspectives incorporate all life experiences and draw upon knowledge from many fields of inquiry. Therefore, people cannot be neatly boxed into specific perspective types regardless of their cultural experiences, ethnic backgrounds, age, gender, or any other characteristic. Geographically informed people know how to contemplate, understand, and apply two specific geographic perspectives, along with complementary disciplinary and personal perspectives.

The two specific geographic perspectives are the spatial perspective and the ecological perspective. Geographic perspectives bring societies and nature under the lens of geography for interpretation and explanation. Geographic perspectives encompass understanding spatial patterns and processes on Earth and comprehending that Earth is composed of living and nonliving elements interacting in complex webs of relationships within nature and between nature and societies. A fully developed set of geographic perspectives, therefore, requires the use of both spatial and ecological points of view.

Knowledge is one fabric woven from many distinctive fields of learning and is organized by different intellectual frameworks. Although each field of study represents distinctive areas of inquiry, specialization, and perspectives, diverse sets of questions are needed to reveal the complexities of nature and societies. Consequently, although spatial and ecological perspectives are hallmarks of the geographic way of looking at the world, additional perspectives are required for us to become fully informed.

THE SPATIAL PERSPECTIVE

As history is concerned with the temporal dimension of human experience (time and chronology), geography is concerned with the spatial dimension of human experience (space and place). The space of Earth's surface is the fundamental characteristic underpinning geography. The essential issue of "whereness"—embodied in specific questions such as, Where is it? Why is it there?—helps humans to contemplate the context of spatial relationships in which the human story is played out.

Understanding spatial patterns and processes is essential to appreciating how people live on Earth. People who approach knowing and doing with a habit of inquiring about whereness possess a spatial perspective.

THE ECOLOGICAL PERSPECTIVE

Earth is composed of living and nonliving elements interacting in complex webs of ecological relationships which occur at multiple levels. Humans are part of the interacting and interdependent relationships in ecosystems and are one among many species that constitute the living part of Earth. Human actions modify physical environments and the viability of ecosystems at local to global scales. The survival of humans and other species requires a viable global ecosystem.

Understanding Earth as a complex set of interacting living and nonliving elements is fundamental to knowing that human societies depend on diverse small and large ecosystems for food, water, and all other resources. People who regularly inquire about connections and relationships among life forms, ecosystems, and human societies possess an ecological perspective.

Complementing the Two Geographic Perspectives

Many perspectives supplement the two geographic perspectives and, when used appropriately, they can expand our understanding of spatial patterns and human–environment interactions. The geographic perspectives can be integrated with other disciplinary perspectives and with our own points of view to enrich and enlarge the understanding of people, places, and environments. Two other perspectives are of particular value to students of geography: the historical perspective and the economic perspective.

THE HISTORICAL PERSPECTIVE

All human events and activities have historic and geographic aspects. Central to historical inquiry are questions concerning chronology, the sequencing of events, relationships within and among societies over time, changes in cultures in various eras, and the changing relationships between civilizations and physical environments. A historical perspective enriches the geographic perspective by adding the essential questions of When? Why then? and Why is the event significant? These questions complement the study of whereness and consequently promote a deepened understanding of past and contemporary events, how and why places and regions form and change, and variations in human use of environments in different cultures and eras.

Understanding temporal patterns is a vital dimension of comprehending human experiences on Earth. People who ask questions about when events occurred and how events are related to each other over time use a historical perspective.

THE ECONOMIC PERSPECTIVE

Economics focuses on how people produce and exchange goods and services to fulfill such needs as food, shelter, transportation, and recreation. Earning a living, developing and trading resources, and inventing, producing, and distributing products and services are central to economics. Previously isolated economies are incorporated into the global economy through difficult transitions from subsistence to commercial activities. Economic transformations promote an increasing interdependence among all societies and cultures on Earth. Technological changes in transportation and communications accelerate and expand economic exchange between the peoples of the world. Local economies may be drastically altered by decisions made in distant places.

Understanding the integration of local, regional, and national economies with the global economy is critical to knowing how people interact. People who ask how diverse peoples earn a living and how peoples are connected through trade in goods and services apply an economic perspective.

Where something occurs is the spatial perspective; how life forms interact with the physical environment is the ecological perspective. We need both perspectives to comprehend Earth as the home of people.

(left) Layers of life in the African rain forest. Each layer—emergent, canopy, understory—is governed by its own climate and is inhabited by a discrete set of plants and animals. (above) A four-level cloverleaf interchange linking Harbor and Santa Monica Freeways in Los Angeles.

BARRON STOREY, LEFT; BRUCE DALE, ABOVE

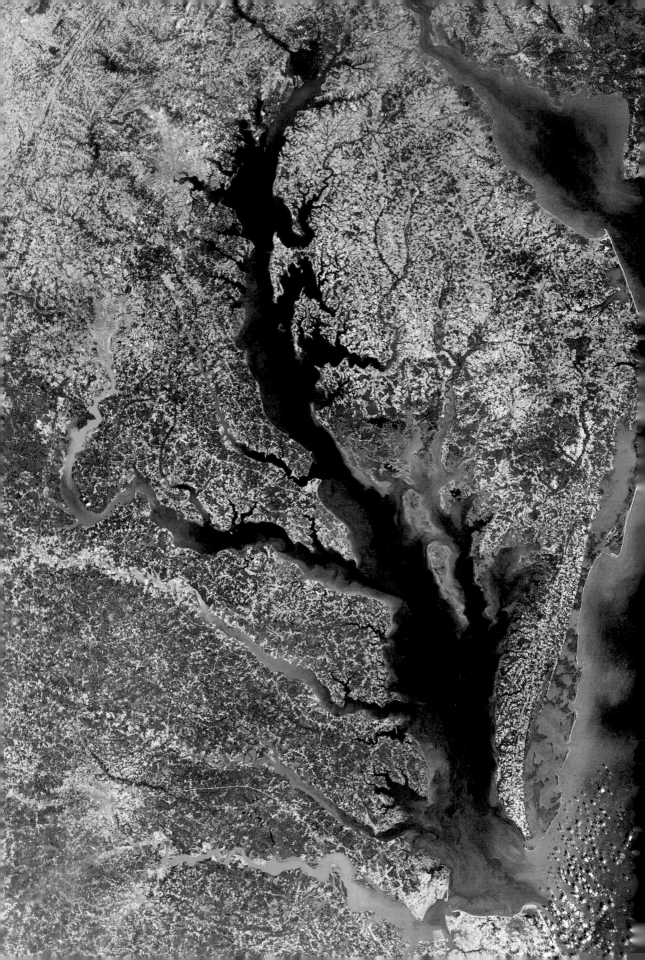

CHAPTER 4

The Subject Matter of Geography

The World in Spatial Terms

GEOGRAPHY STANDARD 1

▶ **HOW TO USE MAPS AND OTHER GEOGRAPHIC REPRESENTATIONS, TOOLS, AND TECHNOLOGIES TO ACQUIRE, PROCESS, AND REPORT INFORMATION FROM A SPATIAL PERSPECTIVE**

Geographic information is compiled, organized, manipulated, stored, and made accessible in a great many ways. It is essential that students develop an understanding of those ways so they can make use of the information and learn the skills associated with developing and communicating information from a spatial perspective.

The study and practice of geography require the use of geographic representations,

The Chesapeake Bay and its surrounding wetlands in a false-color Landsat image. Sediments flowing down the Potomac, Rappahannock, York, and James Rivers glow light blue. Newly harvested and fallow fields on the Delmarva Peninsula appear as pale blue patches. Blue smudges indicate urban areas— Philadelphia, Baltimore, Washington, D.C., and Richmond. EARTH SATELLITE CORPORATION

tools, and technologies. Geographic representations consist primarily of maps, and also include globes, graphs, diagrams, aerial and other photographs, and satellite-produced images. Tools and technologies consist primarily of reference works such as almanacs, gazetteers, geographic dictionaries, statistical abstracts, and other data compilations.

Maps are graphic representations of selected aspects of Earth's surface. They represent compilations of geographic information about selected physical and human features. Using point, line, and area symbols, as well as color, they show how those features are located, arranged, distributed, and related to one another. They range in appearance and purpose from a simple freehand line drawing of how to get to a friend's house to a complex multicolor depiction of atmospheric conditions used in weather forecasting. No single map can show everything, and the features depicted on each map are selected to fit a particular purpose. Maps can depict not only visible surface features such as rivers, seacoasts, roads, and towns but also underground features such as subway systems, tunnels, and geologic formations. They can depict abstract features such as political boundaries, population densities, and lines of latitude and longitude.

In the classroom, maps serve both as repositories of many kinds of geographic infor-

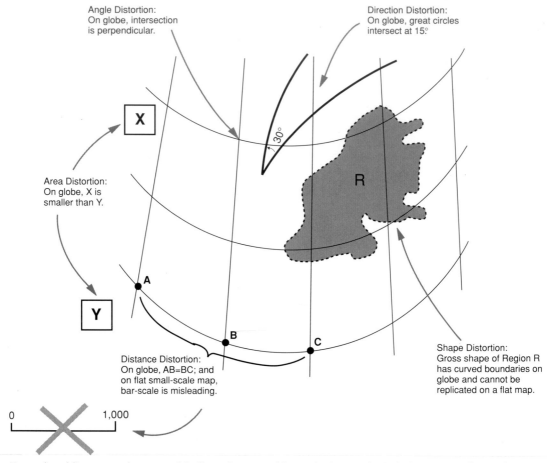

Angle Distortion:
On globe, intersection is perpendicular.

Direction Distortion:
On globe, great circles intersect at 15°

X

30°

R

Area Distortion:
On globe, X is smaller than Y.

Y

A

B

C

Distance Distortion:
On globe, AB=BC; and on flat small-scale map, bar-scale is misleading.

Shape Distortion:
Gross shape of Region R has curved boundaries on globe and cannot be replicated on a flat map.

0   1,000

Examples of five types of cartographic distortion caused by projecting a spherical object onto a flat surface.
SOURCE: *MAP APPRECIATION*, PRENTICE HALL

mation and as an essential means of imparting that information to students. Maps constitute a critical element of geography education. However, they do have limitations. One major limitation is that it is not possible to accurately represent the round Earth on a flat surface without distorting at least one Earth property, such as distance, direction, or size and shape of land and water bodies. Therefore, different map projections are used to depict different Earth properties (e.g., equal area projections show landmasses in correct areal proportion to one another but with distortions of shape). No single map can accurately depict all Earth's properties, so it is essential that students know how to look at a given map and know which properties are rendered correctly and which are distorted.

As scale models, globes constitute the most accurate representation of Earth in terms of the properties of Earth's surface features—area, relative size and shape, scale and distance, and compass direction are proportionately and therefore correctly represented on globes. Globes present an essential overview of Earth, and they can be very useful in the teaching of such concepts as location, spatial patterns, Earth–Sun relationships, and time. However, globes have limitations: They are cumbersome to handle and store, small scale, and only half of Earth can be observed at once.

In addition to maps and globes, graphs, diagrams, aerial and other photographs, and satellite-produced images also provide valuable information about spatial patterns on Earth. They are very diversified in the kinds of information they present and, under certain circumstances, have classroom value as both supplements to and substitutes for globes and maps. However, they also have limitations: For instance, they may not be immediately understandable to students, who may need special instruction in their use.

The tools and technologies used in geography encompass a great variety of reference works, ranging from encyclopedias and other multivolume publications covering many topics to single reports on specialized subjects. Some of these works are in narrative form; some are primarily compilations of data represented in tabular form. Some are easy to understand and use; some are not. Students need to develop an understanding of the kinds of reference works that are available to them, as well as learn how to obtain information from the works, how to gauge the general reliability of that information, and how to convert information from one form to another (e.g., take data from a table and present it in a written narrative).

Traditionally reference works have been available solely in printed form. Currently, however, more and more of them are also being made available in the form of computer-based databases and computer-based information systems. This development is a result of computer systems becoming an essential tool for storing, analyzing, and presenting spatial information. Because of their speed and flexibility, such systems enable the geographically informed person to explore, manipulate, and assess spatial data far more effectively than do conventional printed materials (see Appendix E). Furthermore, current developments in multimedia techniques, such as animation, sound, and interactive learning procedures, promise an even more flexible and creative approach to geographic learning.

Throughout their K–12 schooling, students should continue to have direct experience with a wide variety of geographic representations, especially maps. Maps can become increasingly abstract with each succeeding grade level, reflecting the developmental changes in students' abilities to represent and manipulate spatial and symbolic information. In the early grades, students should come to see maps, like the written word, as a source of information about their world. They should be given opportunities to read and interpret different kinds of maps and to create maps of their classroom, school, and neighborhood using various media (e.g., pencils, cutouts).

Subsequent experiences in map reading and mapmaking should become more sophisticated and abstract as students develop a more comprehensive understanding of the knowledge, skills, and perspectives involved in maps and mapping activities.

In addition, students should be given an opportunity to become familiar with computer systems and computer-based geographic information systems. As such systems become increasingly common in the home, school, and workplace, for many different purposes, people will learn to use them as comfortably and as effectively as they have traditionally used printed materials. Therefore, it is essential that students of geography be exposed to as many forms of geographic data processing as possible and come to understand the role

Meteorologists at McMurdo Station, Victoria Land, Antarctica, study satellite images of that area. Antarctica, the fifth largest continent and the coldest and most desolate place on Earth, serves as a giant laboratory to look at Earth's past and predict its future. GEORGE F. MOBLEY

of computer systems in both the study and practice of geography.

Knowing how to identify, access, evaluate, and use all of these geographic resources will ensure students of a rich school experience in geography and the prospect of having an effective array of problem-solving and decision-making skills for use in both their other educational pursuits and their adult years.

GEOGRAPHY STANDARD 2

▶ HOW TO USE MENTAL MAPS
TO ORGANIZE INFORMATION
ABOUT PEOPLE, PLACES,
AND ENVIRONMENTS IN A
SPATIAL CONTEXT

. . . .

To be geographically informed, a person must keep in mind a lot of information about people, places, and environments, and must be able to organize this information in the appropriate spatial contexts. A very effective way of doing this is to create and use what can be called "mental maps." Such a map is an individual's internalized representation of some aspect or aspects of Earth's surface. It represents what the person knows about the locations and characteristics of places at a variety of scales (local to global), from the layout of the student's bedroom to the distribution of oceans and continents on the surface of Earth. These maps in the mind provide students with an essential means of making sense of the world, and of storing and recalling information about the shapes and patterns of the physical and human features of Earth. Learning how to create and use mental maps, therefore, is a fundamental part of the process of becoming geographically informed.

Mental maps have several distinguishing characteristics:

▶ Mental maps are personal and idiosyncratic and are usually a mixture of both objective knowledge and subjective perceptions. They contain objective and precise knowledge about the location of geographic features such as continents, countries, cities, mountain ranges, and oceans. They also contain more subjective and less precise information, such as impressions of places, rough estimates of relative size, shape, and location, and a general sense of certain connections between places, as well as priorities that reflect the mapmaker's own predilections.

▶ Mental maps are used in some form by all people throughout their lives. Such maps enable people to know what routes to take when traveling, comprehend what others say or write about various places, and develop an understanding of the world.

▶ Mental maps represent ever changing summaries of spatial knowledge and serve as indicators of how well people know the spatial characteristics of places. People develop and refine their mental maps both through personal experience and through learning from teachers and the media. They refine at least some of their maps to ever higher levels of completeness and accuracy, and they continue to add information so that the maps reflect a growing understanding of a changing world. Critical geographic observation is essential to this development and refinement process, because mental maps reflect people's skill in observing and thinking about the world in spatial terms (and have nothing to do with their ability to draw).

As students read, hear, observe, and think more about the world around them, they can add more detail and structure to their maps. As students get older, their mental maps accumulate multiple layers of useful information, and this growth in complexity and utility can provide them with a sense of satisfaction as more places and events in the world can be placed into meaningful spatial contexts.

If geography is to be useful in creating a framework for understanding the world—

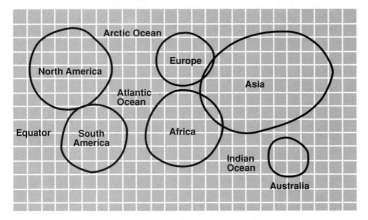

How to Draw the World in 30 Seconds

Six quickly sketched circles, roughly in the right places and in roughly proportionate sizes, make a working map of the continents. Asia is the biggest, Australia the smallest.

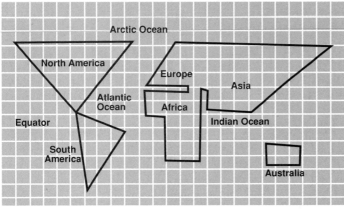

Turn the continents into squares, rectangles, and triangles. Remember that the Africa bulge is over the Equator, the Tropic of Cancer underpins Asia, and the Tropic of Capricorn cuts Australia in half.

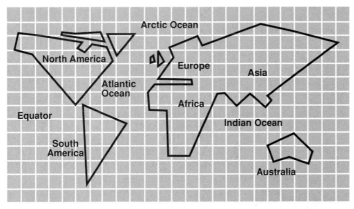

With a few more lines regional and national identities emerge. India is one more triangle, Scandinavia the beak of Europe. Here is a valid map for making political and economic points.

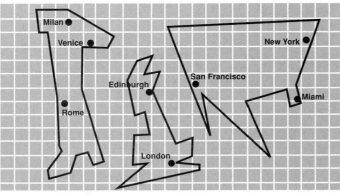

For everyday use, reduce your own country to a simple shape. With important cities as spatial markers you have the working outline for most nontechnical geographic needs. SOURCE: *THE REAL WORLD*, HOUGHTON MIFFLIN COMPANY

past, present, and future—then coherent mental maps must take shape and become increasingly refined as students progress through their school years. Students should be encouraged to develop and update their mental maps to ensure that they continue to have essential knowledge of place location, place characteristics, and other information that will assist them in personal decision-making and in establishing a broad-based perception of Earth from a local to a global perspective. In addition, they need to understand that developing mental maps is a basic skill for everyone who wants to engage in a lifetime of geographic understanding.

GEOGRAPHY STANDARD 3

▶ HOW TO ANALYZE THE SPATIAL
ORGANIZATION OF PEOPLE,
PLACES, AND ENVIRONMENTS
ON EARTH'S SURFACE

· ·

Thinking in spatial terms is essential to knowing and applying geography. It enables students to take an active, questioning approach to the world around them, and to ask what, where, when, and why questions about people, places, and environments. Thinking spatially enables students to formulate answers to critical questions about past, present, and future patterns of spatial organization, to anticipate the results of events in different locations, and to predict what might happen given specific conditions. Spatial concepts and generalizations are powerful tools for explaining the world at all scales, local to global. They are the building blocks on which geographic understanding develops.

Thinking in spatial terms means having the ability to describe and analyze the spatial organization of people, places, and environments on Earth's surface. It is an ability that is central to a person being geographically literate.

Geographers refer to both the features of Earth's surface and activities that take place on Earth's surface as phenomena. The phenomena may be physical (topography, streams and rivers, climates, vegetation types, soils), human (towns and cities, population, highways, trade flows, the spread of a disease, national parks), or physical and human taken together (beach resorts in relation to climate,

topography, or major population centers). The location and arrangement of both physical and human phenomena form regular and recurring patterns.

The description of a pattern of spatial organization begins by breaking it into its simplest components: points, lines, areas, and volumes. These four elements describe the spatial properties of objects: a school can be thought of as a point connected by roads (which are lines) leading to nearby parks and neighborhoods (which are areas), whereas a lake in a park can be thought of as a volume. The next step in the descriptive process is to use such concepts as location, distance, direction, density, and arrangement (linear, grid-like, random) to capture the relationships between the elements of the pattern. Thus the U.S. interstate highway system can be described as lines connecting points over an area—the arrangement is partly grid-like (with north–south and east–west routes as in the central United States) and partly radial or star-shaped (as in the highways centered on Atlanta)—and the pattern of interstates is denser in the East than it is in the West.

The analysis of a pattern of spatial organization proceeds with the use of such concepts as movement and flow, diffusion, cost of distance, hierarchy, linkage, and accessibility to explain the reasons for patterns and the functioning of the world. In the case of a physical pattern, such as a river system, there is a complex hierarchical arrangement linking small streams with small drainage basins and large rivers with drainage basins that are the sum total of all of the smaller drainage basins. There are proportional spatial relationships between stream and river length, width, volume, speed, and drainage basin area. The

Irregular fields of infinitely varied size and shape are characteristic of many long-settled areas. Boundaries are typically oriented to natural features, such as streams and hills or human creations such as roads. Modern agricultural machinery usually demands larger fields, which means that ancient hedgerows, sometimes hundreds of years old, are uprooted.

Long lots in North America are of French origin; strip fields reach back from the riverfront. Some of the longest were laid out in Quebec, along the St. Lawrence River. Most have since been subdivided into shorter parcels, although some have been joined to their neighbors to create wider fields.

Plowing that ignores slopes can lead to gullying and erosion. Contour plowing, where the plow travels around the hill at the same level, reduces runoff and conserves soil.

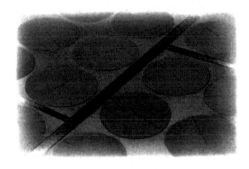

Circular field shapes result when land in dry parts of the world is irrigated by rotating sprinklers.

gradual changes that can occur in these properties of a river system are related to climate, topography, and geology.

Central to geography is the belief that there is pattern, regularity, and reason to the locations of physical and human phenomena on Earth's surface and that there are spatial structures and spatial processes that give rise to them. Students must be encouraged to think about all aspects of the spatial organization of their world. Understanding the distribution and arrangement of Earth's physical and human features depends on analyzing data gathered from observation and field study, working with maps and other geographic representations, and posing geographic questions and deriving geographic answers.

Spatial relationships, spatial structures, and spatial processes are simple to understand, despite their apparent unfamiliarity. For example, the spatial organization of human settlement on Earth's surface is generally a pattern of a few large cities, which are widely spaced and many smaller towns, which are closer together. A comparative analysis of those cities and towns shows that cities offer a wide range of goods and services whereas small towns offer fewer goods and services. Taken together, the description and the analysis explain why consumers shop where they do, why they often buy different products at different locations, and also why changes occur in this spatial pattern.

Understanding patterns of spatial organization enables the geographically informed

Eisenhüttenstadt, former East Germany, 1973. The consequences of emissions from factories like this one—acid rain, decrease in the ozone layer, and other pollution—are worldwide. GORDON GAHAN

person to answer three fundamental geographic questions: Why are these phenomena located in these places? How did they get there? Why is this pattern significant? Description and analysis of patterns of spatial organization must occur at scales ranging from local to global.

Students confront a world that is increasingly interdependent. Widely separated places are interconnected as a consequence of improved transportation and communication networks. Human decisions at one location have physical impacts at another location. (For example, the decision to burn coal rather than oil in a power plant may result in acid rain damaging vegetation hundreds of miles away.)

Understanding such spatial linkages requires that students become familiar with a range of spatial concepts and models that can be used to describe and analyze patterns of spatial organization. This knowledge can be grounded in the students' own immediate experiences, and yet it will give the students the power to understand the arrangement of physical and human geographic phenomena anywhere on Earth.

Places and Regions

∙∙

GEOGRAPHY STANDARD 4

▶ **THE PHYSICAL AND HUMAN CHARACTERISTICS OF PLACES**

∙∙∙∙∙∙∙∙∙∙∙∙∙∙∙∙∙∙∙∙∙∙∙∙∙∙∙∙∙∙∙∙∙∙∙∙∙∙∙

People's lives are grounded in particular places. We come from a place, we live in a place, and we preserve and exhibit fierce pride over places. Our sense of self is intimately entwined with that of place. Who we are is often inseparable from where we are. Places are human creations and the geographically informed person must understand the genesis, evolution, and meaning of places.

Places are parts of Earth's space, large or small, that have been endowed with meaning by humans. They include continents, islands, countries, regions, states, cities, neighborhoods, villages, rural areas, and uninhabited areas. They usually have names and boundaries. Each place possesses a distinctive set of tangible and intangible characteristics that helps to distinguish it from other places. Places are characterized by their physical and human properties. Their physical characteristics include climate, landforms, soils, hydrology, vegetation, and animal life. Their human characteristics include language, religion, political systems, economic systems, population distribution, and quality of life.

Places change over time as both physical and human processes operate to modify Earth's surface. Few places remain unchanged for long and these changes have a wide range of consequences. As knowledge, ideologies, values, resources, and technologies change, people make place-altering decisions about how to use land, how to organize society, and ways in which to relate (such as economically or politically) to nearby and distant places. Out of these processes emerge new places, with existing places being reorganized and expanded, other places declining, and some places disappearing. Places change in size and complexity and in economic, polit-

ical, and cultural importance as networks of relationships between places are altered through population expansion, the rise and fall of empires, changes in climate and other physical systems, and changes in transportation and communication technologies. A place can be dramatically altered by events both near and far.

Knowing how and why places change enables people to understand the need for knowledgeable and collaborative decision-making about where to locate schools, factories, and other things and how to make wise use of features of the physical environment such as soil, air, water, and vegetation. Knowing the physical and human characteris-

In Bangladesh as in the rest of southern Asia the inhabitants must cope with the results of monsoons. STEVE MCCURRY

In Luzon, the Philippines, rice can be raised on the mountain slopes because farmers terraced the slopes to prevent erosion and to permit flooding to provide adequate water. STEVE MCCURRY

tics of their own places influences how people think about who they are, because their identity is inextricably bound up with their place in life and the world. Personal identity, community identity, and national identity are rooted in place and attachment to place. Knowing about other places influences how people understand other peoples, cultures, and regions of the world. Knowledge of places at all scales, local to global, is incorporated into people's mental maps of the world.

Students need an understanding of why places are the way they are, because it can enrich their own sense of identity with a particular place and enable them to comprehend and appreciate both the similarities and differences of places around their own community, state, country, and planet.

GEOGRAPHY STANDARD 5

▶ **THAT PEOPLE CREATE REGIONS TO INTERPRET EARTH'S COMPLEXITY**

. . . .

Region is a concept that is used to identify and organize areas of Earth's surface for various purposes. A region has certain characteristics that give it a measure of cohesiveness and distinctiveness and that set it apart from other regions. As worlds within worlds, regions can be used to simplify the whole by organizing Earth's surface on the basis of the presence or absence of selected physical and human characteristics. As a result, regions are human constructs whose boundaries and characteristics are derived from sets of specific criteria. They can vary in scale from local to global; overlap or be mutually exclusive; exhaustively partition the entire world or capture only selected portions of it. They can nest within one another, forming a multilevel mosaic. Understanding the idea of region and the process of regionalization is fundamental to being geographically informed.

Understanding the nature of regions requires a flexible approach to the world. The criteria used to define and delimit regions can be as spatially precise as coastlines and political boundaries, or as spatially amorphous as suggesting the general location of people with allegiances to a particular professional athletic team or identifying a market area for distributing the recordings of a specific genre of music. Regions can be as small as a neighborhood or as vast as a territorial expanse covering thousands of square miles in which the inhabitants speak the same language. They can be areas joining people in common causes or they can become areas for conflict, both internal and external. Geographers define regions in three basic ways:

The first type is the formal region. It is characterized by a common human property, such as the presence of people who share a particular language, religion, nationality, political identity or culture, or by a common physical property, such as the presence of a particular type of climate, landform, or vegetation. Political entities such as counties, states, countries, and provinces are formal regions because they are defined by a common political identity. Other formal regions include climate regions (e.g., areas with a Mediterranean climate), landform regions (e.g., the Ridge and Valley and Piedmont regions of Pennsylvania), and economic regions (e.g., the wheat belt of Kansas, the citrus-growing areas of south Texas, and the irrigated farmlands of the Central Valley of California). Formal regions can be defined by measures of population, per capita income, ethnic background, crop production, population density and distribution, or industrial production, or by mapping physical characteristics such as temperature, rainfall, growing season, and average date of first and last frost.

The second type of region is the functional region. It is organized around a node or focal point, with the surrounding areas linked to that node by transportation systems, communication systems, or other economic associations involving such activities as manufacturing and retail trading. A typical functional region is a metropolitan area (MA) as defined by the Bureau of the Census. For example, the New York MA is a functional region that covers parts of several states. It is linked by commuting patterns, trade flows, television and radio broadcasts, newspapers, travel for recreation and entertainment. Other functional regions include shopping areas centered on malls or supermarkets, areas served by branch banks, and ports and their hinterlands.

The third type of region is the perceptual region. It is a construct that reflects human feelings and attitudes about areas and is therefore defined by people's shared subjective images of those areas. It tends to reflect the elements of people's mental maps, and, although it may help to impose a personal sense of order and structure on the world, it often does so on the basis of stereotypes that may be inappropriate or incorrect. Thus southern California, Dixie, and the upper Midwest are perceptual regions that are thought of as being spatial units, although they do not have precise borders or even commonly accepted regional characteristics and names.

Some regions, especially formal regions, tend to be stable in spatial definition, but may undergo change in character. Others, especial-

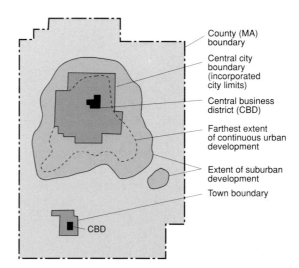

An example of a metropolitan area (MA)—a central city that is an employment center surrounded by bedroom communities. The definition of such terms as MA and central business district (CBD) is dynamic and represents attempts to derive statistical units meaningful for public policy and economic decisions. SOURCE: *HUMAN GEOGRAPHY*, WILLIAM BROWN PUBLISHERS

The Red River Valley, North Dakota. Its rich, flat prairie became a formal region when defined by climate, soil, and agriculture. ANNIE GRIFFITHS BELT

ly functional regions, may retain certain basic characteristics, but may undergo spatial redefinition over time. Yet other regions, particularly perceptual regions, are likely to vary over time in both spatial extent and character.

Regional change, in the context of the human spatial organization of Earth's surface, is an area of study that provides students with opportunities to examine and learn about the complex web of demographic and economic changes that occur.

Regions serve as a valuable organizing technique for framing detailed knowledge of the world and for asking geographic questions. Because regions are examples of geographic generalizations, students can learn about the characteristics of other regions of the world by knowing about one region. Knowing about the physical processes that create the Mediterranean climate and vegeta-

tion of southern California, for example, can serve as an analogue for learning about other regions with Mediterranean climates and vegetation in Australia, Europe, South America, and Africa. Regions provide a context for discussing similarities and differences between parts of the world.

Through understanding the idea of region, students can apply geographic knowledge, skills, and perspectives to solving problems as immediate as making an informed decision about a neighborhood zoning issue, or as long-range as predicting the reconfiguration of political and economic alliances owing to resource shortages or changes in the global ecosystem. Most importantly, studying regions enables students to synthesize their understanding of the physical and human properties of Earth's surface at scales that range from local to global.

▶ HOW CULTURE AND EXPERIENCE INFLUENCE PEOPLE'S PERCEPTIONS OF PLACES AND REGIONS

. . . .

People's perception of places and regions is not uniform. Rather, their view of a particular place or region is their interpretation of its location, extent, characteristics, and significance as influenced by their own culture and experience. It is sometimes said that there is no reality, only perception. In geography there is always a mixture of both the objective and the subjective realms, and that is why the geographically informed person needs to understand both realms and needs to see how they relate to each other.

Individuals have singular life histories and experiences, which are reflected in their having singular mental maps of the world that may change from day to day and from experience to experience. As a consequence, individuals endow places and regions with rich, diverse, and varying meanings. In explaining their beliefs and actions, individuals routinely refer to age, sex, class, language, ethnicity, race, and religion as part of their cultural identity, although some of their actions may be at least partly a result of sharing values with others. Those shared beliefs and values reflect the fact that individuals live in social and cultural groups or sets of groups. The values of these groups are usually complex and cover such subjects as ideology, religion, politics, social structure, and economic structure. They influence how the people in a particular group perceive both themselves and other groups.

The significance that an individual or group attaches to a specific place or region may be influenced by feelings of belonging or alienation, a sense of being an insider or outsider, a sense of history and tradition or of novelty and unfamiliarity. People's perception of Earth's surface is strongly linked to the concept of place utility—the significance that a place has to a particular function or people. For example, a wilderness area may be seen as a haven by a backpacker or as an economic threat by a farming family trying to hold back forest growth at the edges of its fields. The physical reality of the wilderness area is the same in both cases, but the perceptual frameworks that assign meaning to it are powerfully distinct. A place or region can be exciting and dynamic, or boring and dull depending on an individual's experience, expectations, frame of mind, or need to interact with that particular landscape. The range, therefore, of perceptual responses to a place or region is not only vast, but is also continually changing.

Some places and regions are imbued with great significance by certain groups of people, but not by others. For example, for Muslims the city of Mecca is the most holy of religious places, whereas for non-Muslims it has only historical significance. For foreign tourists Rio de Janeiro is a city of historical richness that evokes images of grandness, energy, and festiveness, but for many local street youths it is a harsh environment where they have to struggle for daily survival. Around the world the names of such places as Hiroshima, Auschwitz, Bhopal, and Chernobyl convey profoundly sad and horrific collective images, but

Hadj pilgrims pray before the Great Mosque in the holy city of Mecca, Saudi Arabia. MEHMET BIBER

This once-flourishing farm in Texas was one of many Dust Bowl farms that fell victim to the consequences of an influx of immigrants, unrestricted grazing, overstocking, and poor management combined with severe drought. STEVEN C. WILSON / ENTHEOS

The human consequences of the Dust Bowl (migration to the west) are exemplified by this woman and her children on the road in Tulelake, California, September 1939. LIBRARY OF CONGRESS

for the people who live there, the reality of life tends to be how best to earn a living, raise a family, educate children, and enjoy one's leisure time. At another level, Disneyland or "my hometown" may evoke equally strong but positive and idiosyncratic images among local inhabitants. People's group perceptions of places and regions may change over time. For instance, as settlement and knowledge spread westward during the nineteenth century, parts of what are now Oklahoma, Kansas, and Nebraska went from being labeled as within the Great American Desert to being likened to the Garden of Eden. Then during the drought years of the 1930s, these same areas changed character yet again, becoming the heart of what was known as the Dust Bowl.

Culture and experience shape belief systems, which in turn influence people's perceptions of places and regions throughout their lives. So it is essential that students understand the factors that influence their own perception of places and regions, paying special attention to the effects that personal and group points of view can have on their understanding of other groups and cultures. Accordingly, it may be possible for students to avoid the dangers of egocentric and ethnocentric stereotyping, to appreciate the diverse values of others in a multicultural world, and to engage in accurate and sensitive analysis of people, places, and environments.

Physical Systems

GEOGRAPHY STANDARD 7

▶ **THE PHYSICAL PROCESSES
THAT SHAPE THE PATTERNS
OF EARTH'S SURFACE**

Physical processes create, maintain, and modify Earth's physical features and environments. Because the physical environment is the essential background for all human activity on Earth, the geographically informed person must understand the processes that produce those features.

Physical processes can be grouped into four categories: those operating in the atmosphere (i.e., climate and meteorology), those operating in the lithosphere (e.g., plate tectonics, erosion, and soil formation), those operating in the hydrosphere (e.g., the circulation of the oceans and the hydrologic cycle), and those operating in the biosphere (e.g., plant and animal communities and ecosystems).

By understanding the interactions within and between these categories of physical processes, the geographically informed person can pose and answer certain fundamental questions: What does the surface of Earth look like? How have its features been formed? What is the nature of these features and how do they interact? How and why are they changing? What are the spatially distinct combinations of environmental features? How are these environmental features related to past, present, and prospective human uses of Earth? The answers to these questions lead to an understanding of how Earth serves as the home of all plants and animals, including humans.

Processes shape and maintain the physical environment. Therefore it is vital that students appreciate the complex relationships between processes and resultant features, and how these relationships give rise to patterns of spatial organization. For example, in a region such as southern California, the physical landscape is constantly reshaped by a complex set of interacting physical processes: earthquakes, coastal erosion, land subsidence owing to subsurface oil and water extraction, flash floods and landslides caused by heavy rainfall in the spring, and drought and the loss of chaparral vegetation from fire in the dry summer weeks. In turn, these processes show chains of interaction: the chaparral vegetation is the biosphere's response to the climate and soil. Given the expected variations in rainfall in this Mediterranean climate regime, the chaparral becomes dormant and is prone to fire; however, clearance of the chaparral vegetation, especially in the canyons of steep hills, exposes the surface to flash flooding and soil erosion.

Five basic ideas help to explain the interactions and effects of physical processes. These are known as system, boundary, force, state of

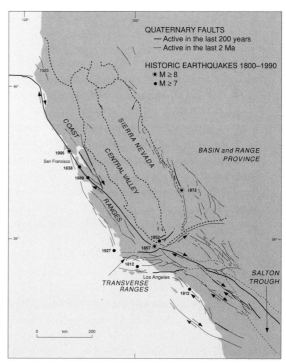

The San Andreas Fault system, other Quaternary faults, and historic earthquakes in California. Inset shows present relationships of the San Andreas transform margin. SNAPSHOTS OF NORTH AMERICA

Paria Canyon on the Arizona–Utah border. Sandstorms, a physical process, shifted huge sand dunes some 200 million years ago, and iron oxide cemented them in place. TOM BEAN/DRK PHOTO

equilibrium, and threshold. A system is a collection of elements that are mutually connected and therefore influence one another to form a unified whole (e.g., the hydrologic cycle). Each system has boundaries, either real or arbitrary, within which it operates. Some forces, such as gravity and weather, activate and drive processes; other forces, such as friction, resist change and act to maintain the status quo. Systems exist in different states. When a system is in equilibrium, driving forces such as gravity and resisting forces such as friction are in balance. However, when a threshold—the point at which change may occur—is reached adjustment takes place. For example, an avalanche occurs when gravity, acting on deep layers of snow, overcomes the friction that was holding the snow mass in place (i.e., a state of equilibrium gives way when a threshold is reached). After the avalanche a new state of equilibrium is established.

It is essential that students understand the physical processes that act upon Earth and that such processes affect the choices made by people in different regions of the United States. Knowledge of these processes is required for dealing with such commonplace issues as: evaluating locations of relative safety in an earthquake-prone region; purchasing a home in a floodplain; coping with the threat of sinkholes and subsidence in a landscape underlain by limestone deposits; building a house in an area that has shrink–swell clay soils.

It is also essential that students learn to make intelligent predictions about future events and evaluate the short- and long-term effects of physical events on places and regions. Evaluating reports of world climate change requires knowing the factors that affect climate and weather in general and how the natural environment functions in particular regions. Climate and weather affect more than just personal decision-making on a daily basis. They are major factors in understanding world economic conditions over longer periods. Many important natural resources are formed by physical processes that occur in relatively few places on Earth. Understanding physical processes and the patterns of resources they produce is vital to understanding not only the physical geography of Earth's surface but also the strategic relationships between nations and world trade patterns.

Understanding physical processes enables the geographically informed person to link the personal with the societal, the short term with the long term, and the local with the global dimensions of Earth.

GEOGRAPHY STANDARD 8

► THE CHARACTERISTICS AND SPATIAL DISTRIBUTION OF ECOSYSTEMS ON EARTH'S SURFACE

. . . .

Ecosystems are a key element in the viability of planet Earth as human home. Populations of different plants and animals that live and interact together are called a community. When such a community interacts with the other three components of the physical environment—atmosphere, hydrosphere, and lithosphere—the result is an ecosystem. The cycles of flows and interconnections—physical, chemical, and biological—between the parts of ecosystems form the mosaic of Earth's environments. The geographically informed person needs to understand the spatial distribution, origins, functioning, and maintenance of different ecosystems and to comprehend how humans have intentionally or inadvertently modified these ecosystems.

Ecosystems form distinct regions on Earth's surface, which vary in size, shape, and complexity. They exist at a variety of scales, from small and very localized areas (e.g., a single

Coral islands, like the Maldives, absorb rainfall; freshwater is less dense than seawater so the two do not mix and islanders have ready access to freshwater under the island. The current influx of tourists promises to unbalance this system. JAMES STANFIELD

From a human perspective, the ecosystems of Antarctica are some of the most inhospitable and also the most fragile.
GEORGE F. MOBLEY

stand of oak trees or a clump of xerophytic grasses) to larger areas with precise geographic boundaries (e.g., a pond, desert biome, island, or beach). Larger scale ecosystems can form continent-wide belts, such as the tundra, taiga, and steppe of northern Asia. The largest ecosystem is the planet itself.

All elements of the environment, physical and human, are part of several different but nested ecosystems. Ecosystems, powered by solar energy, are dynamic and ever-changing. Changes in one ecosystem ripple through others with varying degrees of impact. As self-regulating open systems that maintain flows of energy and matter, they naturally move toward maturity, stability, and balance in the absence of major disturbances. In ecological terms, the physical environment can be seen as an interdependent web of production and consumption cycles. The atmosphere keeps plants and animals alive through solar energy, chemical exchanges (e.g., nitrogen-fixing and photosynthesis), and the provision of water. Through evapotranspiration the atmosphere and plants help to purify water. Plants provide the energy to keep animals alive either directly through consumption or indirectly through their death and decay into the soil,

where the resultant chemicals are taken up by new plants. Soils keep plants and animals alive and work to cleanse water. The root systems of plants and the mechanical and chemical effects of water percolating through bedrock create new soil layers. Ecosystems therefore help to recycle chemicals needed by living things to survive, redistribute waste products, control many of the pests that cause disease in both humans and plants, and offer a huge pool of resources for humans and other living creatures.

However, the stability and balance of ecosystems can be altered by large-scale natural events such as El Niño, volcanic eruptions, fire, or drought. But ecosystems are more drastically transformed by human activities. The web of ecological interdependency is fragile. Human intervention can shatter the balance of energy production and consumption. For example, the overgrazing of pasturelands, coupled with a period of drought, can lead to vegetation loss, the exposure of topsoil layers, and massive soil erosion (as occurred in the 1930s Dust Bowl); tropical forest clear-cutting can lead to soil erosion and ecological breakdown, as is currently occurring in Amazonia; the construction of oil pipelines in tundra environments can threaten the movements of the caribou herds on which indigenous Inuit populations depend.

By knowing how ecosystems operate and change, students are able to understand the basic principles that should guide programs for environmental management. Students can understand the ways in which they are dependent on the living and nonliving systems of Earth for their survival. Knowing about ecosystems will enable them to learn how to make reasoned decisions, anticipate the consequences of their choices, and assume responsibility for the outcomes of their choices about the use of the physical environment. It is important that students become well-informed regarding ecosystem issues so they can evaluate conflicting points of view on the use of natural resources. The degree to which present and future generations understand their critical role in the natural functioning of ecosystems will determine in large measure the quality of human life on Earth.

Human Systems

· ·

GEOGRAPHY STANDARD 9

▶ **THE CHARACTERISTICS, DISTRIBUTION, AND MIGRATION OF HUMAN POPULATIONS ON EARTH'S SURFACE**

· ·

Human population has increased dramatically over the last few centuries. In 1830, more than 900 million people inhabited Earth. As the twenty-first century approaches, Earth's population is nearly six billion. At the same time, extraordinarily large and dense clusters of people are growing: Tokyo has already reached a population in excess of 25 million. The geographically informed person must understand that the growth, distribution, and movements of people on Earth's surface are the driving forces behind not only human events—social, cultural, political, and economic—but also certain physical events—large-scale flooding, resource depletion, and ecological breakdown.

Students need to develop an understanding of the interaction of the human and environmental factors that help to explain the characteristics of human populations, as well as their distribution and movements. The distribution and density of Earth's population reflect the planet's topography, soils, vegetation, and climate types (ecosystems); available resources; and level of economic development. Population growth rates are influenced by such factors as education (especially of women), religion, telecommunications, urbanization, and employment opportunities. Mortality rates are influenced by the availability of medical services, food, shelter, health services, and the overall age and sex distribution of the population.

Another key population characteristic is growth, which may be described in terms of fertility and mortality, crude birth- and death rates, natural increase and doubling time, and

population structure (age and sex distribution). These basic demographic concepts help bring focus to the human factors that explain population distributions and densities, growth patterns, and population projections. Population pyramids, for example, indicate the differential effects of past events, such as wars, disease, famine, improved sanitation, and vaccination programs, on birth- and death rates and gender. An analysis of specific age cohorts enables predictions to be made. For example, a large proportion zero to 15 years old suggests rapid population growth, whereas a large proportion 45 to 60 years old suggests a mature population, which will soon require significant resources to support the elderly. Both predictions could have significant geographic implications for a community; for example, a young population could create a need for more housing and schools, whereas an older population could create a need for more retirement and medical facilities. Such demographic analyses can be performed at all scales.

Almost every country is experiencing in-

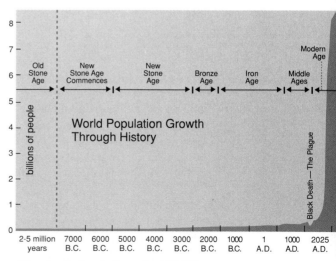

The advent of agriculture about 10,000 years ago permitted population to increase. More recently improved sanitation and better nutrition have caused a population explosion.

SOURCE: KIMBERLEY A. CREWS AND PATRICIA CANCELLIER, THE POPULATION REFERENCE BUREAU, INC.

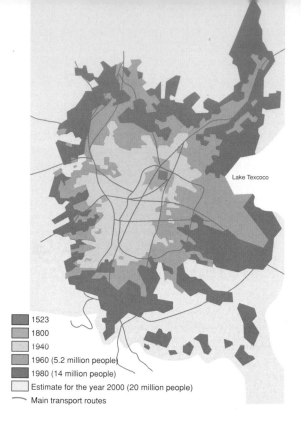

1523
1800
1940
1960 (5.2 million people)
1980 (14 million people)
Estimate for the year 2000 (20 million people)
Main transport routes

Lake Texcoco

Mexico City. In 1325 the Aztecs built a village of reed huts on the island of Tlateloco in Lake Texcoco as a refuge and defense against their neighbors. Within 200 years Tenochtitlan (Place of the Prickly Pear Cactus) had been transformed into a lavish imperial city covering nearly five square miles. Within another 500 years (by the year 2025) Mexico's capital is expected to house about 20 million people (right). As Mexico City grows, so do neighboring cities like Netza. SOURCE: THE REAL WORLD, HOUGHTON MIFFLIN COMPANY; PHOTO: STEPHANIE MAZE

creased urbanization. Across Earth peasant and pastoral life is giving way to the more economically promising lure of life in cities, as people seeking better jobs or more income move to areas where opportunities are better. The majority of the world's people are moving toward a way of life that only a minority of people experienced less than a century ago. Population geographers predict that Tokyo, São Paulo, Bombay, Shanghai, Lagos, and Mexico City will be the next century's most massive population centers. However, people in some developed countries are giving up the economic advantages of city life for the ease and attractions of suburbs and small towns, especially those with access to employment in metropolitan areas.

Migration is one of the most distinctive and visible characteristics of human populations, and it leads to significant reshaping of population distribution and character. It is a dynamic process that is constantly changing Earth's landscapes and modifying its cultures. It takes place at a variety of scales and in different contexts. At international scales geographers track the flows of immigrants and emigrants. At national scales they consider net regional balances of in- and out-migrants or the flows from rural to urban areas, which are a principal cause of urbanization. At a local scale they consider the continuous mobility of college students, retirees, and tourists or the changes of address that occur without necessarily resulting in a job change or change in friendship patterns.

The context of migration varies from voluntary and discretionary (the search for a better place to live), to voluntary but unavoidable (the search for a place to live), to involuntary and unavoidable (the denial of the right to choose a place to live).

In the two voluntary contexts, migration often results from the weighing of factors at the point of origin and at potential destinations against the costs (financial and emotional) of moving. "Pull" factors may make another place seem more attractive and therefore influence the decision to move. Other factors are unpleasant enough to "push" the migrant out of the local setting and toward another area. These factors reflect people's objective knowledge of places and also their secondhand impressions. As a consequence, many countries have experienced waves of people going from settled areas to new lands in the interior (e.g., the westward movement in the United States in the nineteenth century and the move from the southeast coast to the interior of Brazil starting in the 1960s, when the new capital city of Brasilia was built).

Voluntary and unavoidable migration occurs when much of a region's or country's population is impelled into migration streams, such as the millions of Irish who fled to the United States in the 1840s because of the potato famine or the millions of Somalis, Sudanese, and Rwandans who moved in the 1990s because of drought, famine, and civil war. However, some migrations are forced and involuntary. Such was the case with African Americans

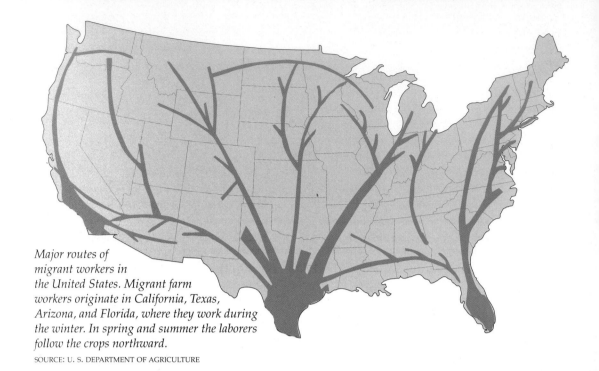

Major routes of migrant workers in the United States. Migrant farm workers originate in California, Texas, Arizona, and Florida, where they work during the winter. In spring and summer the laborers follow the crops northward.

SOURCE: U. S. DEPARTMENT OF AGRICULTURE

who were taken to North and South America in the seventeenth, eighteenth, and nineteenth centuries to work as slave laborers on sugar, cotton, and tobacco plantations.

Demographic shifts rearrange patterns of population and create new human landscapes. Natural increase, war, famine, and disease play decisive roles in influencing why many people live where they do. Migration sets people in motion as they leave one place, strike out for a second, and possibly settle in a third. Intervening obstacles influence the pattern of migra-tion. Physical barriers such as deserts, mountains, rivers, and seas or cultural barriers such as political boundaries, languages, economic conditions, and cultural traditions determine how people move and where they settle.

It is essential that students develop an understanding of the dynamics of population characteristics, distribution, and migration, and in particular of how population distribution (in terms of size and characteristics) is linked to the components of fertility, mortality, and mobility.

GEOGRAPHY STANDARD 10

▶ THE CHARACTERISTICS, DISTRIBUTION, AND COMPLEXITY OF EARTH'S CULTURAL MOSAICS

. . . .

Culture is a complex, multifaceted concept. It is a term used to cover the social structure, languages, belief systems, institutions, technology, art, foods, and traditions of particular groups of humans. The term is used to define each group's way of life and its own view of itself and of other groups, as well as to define the material goods it creates and uses, the skills it has developed, and the behaviors it transmits to each successive generation.

The human world is composed of culture groups, each of which has its distinctive way of life as reflected in the group's land-use practices, economic activities, organization and layout of settlements, attitudes toward the role of women in society, education system, and observance of traditional customs and holidays. These ways of life result in landscapes and regions with a distinctive appearance. Landscapes often overlap, thus forming elaborate mosaics of peoples and places.

These cultural mosaics can be approached from a variety of spatial scales. At one scale, for example, Western Europe's inhabitants can be seen as a single culture group; at another scale they consist of distinctive national culture groups (e.g., the French and the Spanish); and at yet another scale each national culture group can be subdivided into smaller, regionally clustered culture groups (e.g., the Flemings and Walloons in Belgium).

As Earth evolves into an increasingly interdependent world in which different culture groups come into contact more than ever before, it becomes more important that people have an understanding of the nature, complexity, and spatial distribution of cultural mosaics.

Given the complexity of culture, it is often useful—especially when studying the subject from a geographic point of view—to focus on the languages, beliefs, institutions, and technologies that are characteristic of a culture. The geographically informed person, therefore, is an individual who has a thorough grasp of the nature and distribution of culture groups.

Language both represents and reflects many aspects of a culture. It stands as an important symbol of culture. It is seen as a sign of the unity of a particular culture group. It can be analyzed—in terms of vocabulary and structure—for clues about the values and beliefs of a culture group. Language is also a visible marker that provides a way of tracing the history of a culture. The complex and often tense relations between French-speaking and English-speaking people in Quebec illustrate and reflect the importance of language to culture groups and also the value of studying the geography of language.

Beliefs include religion, customs, values, attitudes, ideals, and world views. A person's point of view on issues is influenced by cultural beliefs, which in turn influence decisions about resources, land use, settlement patterns, and a host of other geographically important concerns. The complicated and often difficult relations of Hindus and Muslims in India demonstrate how the spatial organization of a country can be shaped by the geography of religion.

Switzerland grew out of a defense pact among the valley communities of Uri, Unterwalden, and Schwyz in the thirteenth century. Today the culture groups of this country of four languages remain bound together by their belief in a strong democratic tradition and unflagging neutrality. SOURCE: NATIONAL GEOGRAPHIC SOCIETY

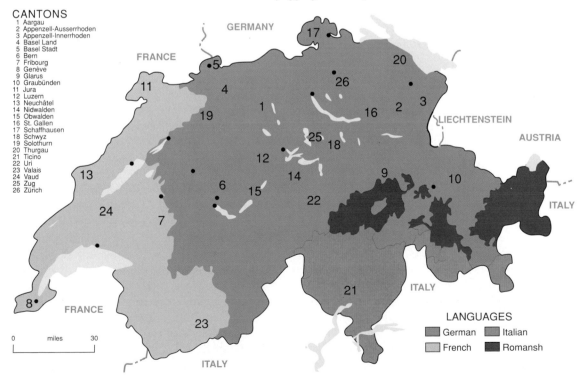

CANTONS
1 Aargau
2 Appenzell-Ausserrhoden
3 Appenzell-Innerrhoden
4 Basel Land
5 Basel Stadt
6 Bern
7 Fribourg
8 Genève
9 Glarus
10 Graubünden
11 Jura
12 Luzern
13 Neuchâtel
14 Nidwalden
15 Obwalden
16 St. Gallen
17 Schaffhausen
18 Schwyz
19 Solothurn
20 Thurgau
21 Ticino
22 Uri
23 Valais
24 Vaud
25 Zug
26 Zürich

LANGUAGES
German   Italian
French   Romansh

0   miles   30

Men of Appenzell–Innerrhoden, Switzerland, gather for the Landsgemeinde, the annual vote by show of hands. Although Switzerland granted suffrage to women in 1971, the right to vote in the two Appenzell cantons extends only to men. COTTON COULSON

Institutions shape the ways in which people organize the world around them; for example, sets of laws, educational systems, political arrangements, and the structure of the family shape a culture region. The Mormon culture region of the western United States shows how institutions are embodied in a distinctive place, demarcating it and influencing practically every aspect of daily life.

Technology includes the tools and skills a group of people use to satisfy their needs and wants. Levels of technology range from the simplest tools used by hunters and gatherers to the most complex machines and information systems used in modern industrial societies. Technologies can be usefully understood as either hardware—the tools themselves—or software—the skilled ways in which a society uses tools. The Amish of south-central Pennsylvania have created a distinctive landscape that is simultaneously an expression of technology, institutions, beliefs, and language.

Whatever characteristic of culture is con-

sidered, it is clear that the mosaics of Earth's cultural landscapes are not static. Culture changes as a result of a variety of human processes, migration and the spread (diffusion) of new cultural traits—language, music, and technology—to existing culture groups. The processes of cultural change accelerate with improvements in transportation and communication. Each culture in the world has borrowed attributes from other cultures whether knowingly or not, willingly or not.

Students should be exposed to a rich appreciation of the nature of culture so they can understand the ways in which people choose to live in different regions of the world. Such an understanding will enable them to appreciate the role culture plays in the spatial organization of modern society. Rivalry and tension between cultures contribute much to world conflict. As members of a multicultural society in a multicultural world, students must understand the diverse spatial expressions of culture.

▶ **THE PATTERNS AND NETWORKS OF ECONOMIC INTERDEPENDENCE ON EARTH'S SURFACE**

. . . .

Resources are unevenly scattered across the surface of Earth, and no country has all of the resources it needs to survive and grow. Thus each country must trade with others, and Earth is a world of increasing global economic interdependence. Accordingly, the geographically informed person understands the spatial organization of economic, transportation, and communication systems, which produce and exchange the great variety of commodities—raw materials, manufactured goods, capital, and services—which constitute the global economy.

The spatial dimensions of economic activity and global interdependence are visible everywhere. Trucks haul frozen vegetables to markets hundreds of miles from growing areas and processing plants. Airplanes move large numbers of business passengers or vacationers. Highways, especially in developed countries, carry the cars of many commuters, tourists, and other travelers. The labels on products sold in American supermarkets typically identify the products as coming from other U. S. states and from other countries.

The spatial dimensions of economic activity are more and more complex. For example, petroleum is shipped from Southwest Asia, Africa, and Latin America to major energy-importing regions such as the United States, Japan, and Western Europe. Raw materials and food from tropical areas are exchanged for the processed or fabricated products of the mid-latitude developed countries. Components for vehicles and electronics equipment are made in Japan and the United States, shipped to South Korea and Mexico for partial assembly, returned to Japan and the United States for final assembly into finished products, and then shipped all over the world.

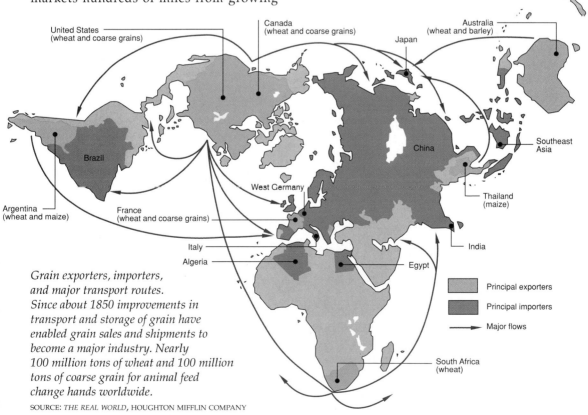

Grain exporters, importers, and major transport routes. Since about 1850 improvements in transport and storage of grain have enabled grain sales and shipments to become a major industry. Nearly 100 million tons of wheat and 100 million tons of coarse grain for animal feed change hands worldwide.

SOURCE: *THE REAL WORLD*, HOUGHTON MIFFLIN COMPANY

Coffee beans dry in the sun near Matagalpa, Nicaragua. Coffee beans are of major economic importance in Central and South America and Africa. JAMES NACHTWEY

Economic activities depend upon capital, resources, power supplies, labor, information, and land. The spatial patterns of industrial labor systems have changed over time. In much of Western Europe, for example, small-scale and spatially dispersed cottage industry was displaced by large-scale and concentrated factory industry after 1760. This change caused rural emigration, the growth of cities, and changes in gender and age roles. The factory has now been replaced by the office as the principal workplace in developed countries. In turn, telecommunications are diminishing the need for a person's physical presence in an office. Economic, social, and therefore spatial relationships change continuously.

The world economy has core areas where the availability of advanced technology and investment capital are central to economic development. In addition, it has semi-peri-pheries where lesser amounts of value are added to industry or agriculture, and peripheries where resource extraction or basic export agriculture are dominant. Local and world economies intermesh to create networks, movement patterns, transportation routes, market areas, and hinterlands.

In the developed countries of the world's core areas, business leaders are concerned with such issues as accessibility, connectivity, location, networks, functional regions, and spatial efficiency—factors that play an essential role in economic development and also reflect the spatial and economic interdependence of places on Earth.

In developing countries, such as Bangladesh and Guatemala, economic activities tend to be at a more basic level, with a substantial proportion of the population being engaged in the production of food and raw materials. Nonetheless, systems of interdependence have developed at the local, regional, and national levels. Subsistence farming often exists side by side with commercial agriculture. In China, for example, a government-regulated farming system provides for structured production and tight economic links of the rural population to nearby cities. In Latin America and Africa, rural people are leaving the land and migrating to large cities, in part to search for jobs and economic prosperity and in part as a response to overpopulation in marginal agricultural regions. Another important trend is industrialized countries continuing to export their labor-intensive processing and fabrication to developing countries. The recipient countries also profit from the arrangement financially but at a social price. The arrangement can put great strains on centuries-old societal structures in the recipient countries.

As world population grows, as energy costs increase, as time becomes more valuable, and as resources become depleted or discovered, societies need economic systems that are more efficient and responsive. It is particularly important, therefore, for students to understand world patterns and networks of economic interdependence and to realize that traditional patterns of trade, human migration, and cultural and political alliances are being altered as a consequence of global interdependence.

▶ **THE PROCESSES, PATTERNS, AND FUNCTIONS OF HUMAN SETTLEMENT**

· ·

People seldom live in isolation. Most reside in settlements, which vary greatly in size, composition, location, arrangement, and function. These organized groupings of human habitation are the focus of most aspects of human life: economic activities, transportation systems, communications media, political and administrative systems, culture and entertainment. Therefore, to be geographically competent—to appreciate the significance of geography's central theme that Earth is the home of people—a person must understand settlement processes and functions and the patterns of settlements across Earth's surface.

Settlements exercise a powerful influence in shaping the world's different cultural, political, and economic systems. They reflect the values of cultural groups and the kinds of political structure and economic activity engaged in by a society. Accordingly, the patterns of settlement across Earth's surface differ markedly from region to region and place to place. Of great importance to human existence, therefore, are the spatial relationships between settlements of different sizes: their spacing, their arrangement, their functional differences, and their economic specialties. These spatial relationships are shaped by trade and the movements of raw materials, finished products, people, and ideas.

Cities, the largest and densest human settlements, are the nodes of human society. Almost half of the world's people now live in cities, and the proportion is even higher in the developed regions of the world. In the United States, more than three-quarters of the people live in urban areas. More than two-thirds of the people of Europe, Russia, Japan, and Australia live in such areas.

Cities throughout the world are growing rapidly, but none so rapidly as those in developing regions. For example, the ten largest cities in the world in the year 2000 will include such Latin American cities as São Paulo and Mexico City. In some regions of the world there are concentrations of interconnected cities and urban areas, which are known as megalopoli. In Japan, the three adjacent and continuous cities of Tokyo–Kawasaki–Yokohama make up such a megalopolis. In Germany there is another, consisting of the Rhine River Valley and the cities of Essen, Düsseldorf, Dortmund, and Wuppertal. The corridor from Boston to Washington, D.C., is also a megalopolis (sometimes called Megalopolis because it was the first one to be designated).

Cities are not the same all over the world. North American cities, for example, differ from European cities in shape and size, density of population, transportation networks, and the patterns in which people live and work within the city. The same contrast is true of cities in Africa, Latin America, and Asia. For example, in North American cities wealthy people tend to live in the outskirts or suburban areas, whereas lower income residents tend to live in inner-city areas. In Latin America the spatial pattern is reversed: wealthy people live close to the city centers, and poor people live in slums or barrios found at the edges of urban areas.

In North America, Europe, and Japan urban areas are linked to one another by well-integrated, efficient, and reliable transportation and communications systems. In these

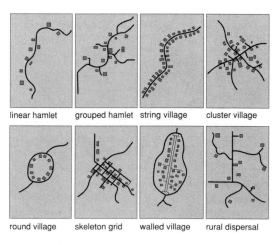

linear hamlet   grouped hamlet   string village   cluster village

round village   skeleton grid   walled village   rural dispersal

Basic settlement forms. SOURCE: *HUMAN GEOGRAPHY,* WILLIAM BROWN PUBLISHERS

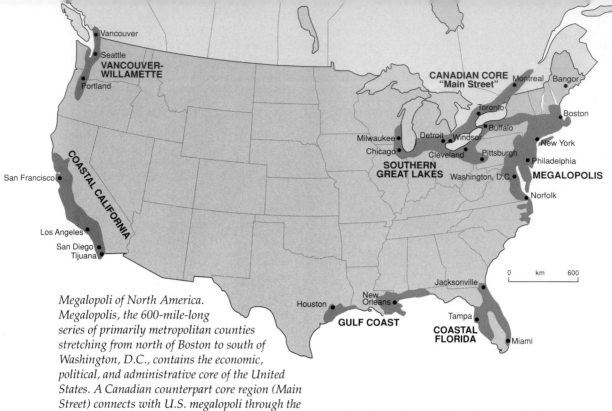

Megalopoli of North America. Megalopolis, the 600-mile-long series of primarily metropolitan counties stretching from north of Boston to south of Washington, D.C., contains the economic, political, and administrative core of the United States. A Canadian counterpart core region (Main Street) connects with U.S. megalopoli through the cities of Buffalo and Detroit. SOURCE: *HUMAN GEOGRAPHY,* WILLIAM BROWN PUBLISHERS

(opposite) The walled city of Datong in Shanxi province, northern China. GEORG GERSTER

regions, even the smallest villages are linked in a web of trade, transportation, and communication networks. In contrast, in developing regions such as Latin America and Southeast Asia, a single primate city often dominates the life of the country. A primate city such as Buenos Aires or Manila is preeminent in its influence on the culture, politics, and economic activities of its country. Nevertheless, in terms of transportation and communications links it may be better connected to the outside world than it is to other regions of the country it serves.

Settlements and the patterns they etch on Earth's surface provide not only data on current economic and social aspects of human existence but also a historical record. Today's settlement patterns, evident on a map, provide information about past settlement patterns and processes, and the boundaries of counties and other political entities indicate how people organized the land as they settled it. In all such cases, the surviving evidence of past settlements can and should be amplified by the students' use of research materials to develop a fuller understanding of how settlements relate to their physical settings over time. It is

valuable, for example, to know about life in a German medieval town and the town's relationship to the surrounding countryside; life in a typical North Dakota settlement along a railroad line in the 1890s; and life in the walled city of Xian and the city's importance in north China in the second century B.C.

Students must develop an understanding of the fundamental processes, patterns, and functions of human settlement across Earth's surface, and thereby come to appreciate the spatially ordered ways in which Earth has become the home of people. They need to acquire a working knowledge of such topics as: the nature and functions of cities, the processes that cause cities to grow and decline, how cities are related to their market areas or hinterlands; the patterns of land use and value, population density, housing type, ethnicity, socioeconomic status, and age distribution in urban areas; the patterns of change, growth, and decline within urban areas; the process of suburbanization; and how new types of urban nodes develop. Geographers ask these questions to make sense of the distribution and concentrations of human populations.

▶ HOW THE FORCES OF COOPERA-
TION AND CONFLICT AMONG
PEOPLE INFLUENCE THE DIVISION
AND CONTROL OF EARTH'S
SURFACE

· ·

Competing for control of large and
small areas of Earth's surface is a
universal trait among societies and
has resulted in both productive
cooperation and destructive conflict between groups over time. The geographically
informed person has a general understanding
of the nature and history of the forces of cooperation and conflict on Earth and the spatial
manifestation of these forces in political and
other kinds of divisions of Earth's surface.
This understanding enables the individual to
perceive how and why different groups have
divided, organized, and unified areas of
Earth's surface.

Divisions are regions of Earth's surface
over which groups of people establish control
for purposes of politics, administration, religion, and economics. Each such region usually has an area, a name, and a boundary. In the
past even small groups inhabiting vast territo-
ries divided space in accordance with their
cultural values and life-sustaining activities.
For them some spaces were sacred, others
were devoted to hunting or gathering, and
still others were intended for shelter and
socializing. In present-day urban, industrial
societies, earning a livelihood, owning or
renting a home in a safe neighborhood, getting a drink of clean water, buying food,
being able to travel safely within one's own
community—all of these activities are linked
to how Earth is divided by different groups
for different purposes.

Often, conflicts over how to divide and
organize parts of Earth's space have involved
control of resources (e.g., Antarctica or the
ocean floor), control of strategic routes (e.g.,
the Panama or Suez Canals or the Darda-
nelles), or the domination of other peoples
(e.g., European colonialism in Africa). Language, religion, political ideologies, national
origins, and race motivate conflicts over how
territory and resources will be developed,
used, and distributed. Conflicts over trade,
human migration and settlement, and exploitation of marine and land environments
reflect how Earth's surface is divided into
fragments controlled by different political and
economic interest groups.

The primary political division of Earth is
by state sovereignty—a particular government is recognized by others as having
supreme authority over a carefully delimited
territory and the population and resources
within that space. With the exception of
Antarctica, Earth's surface is exhaustively
partitioned by state sovereignty. These political divisions are recognized by the United
Nations and its member states, which discuss
and act on issues of mutual interest, especially international peace and security. However,
the partitioning is not mutually exclusive.
Some nations exert competing claims to certain areas (e.g., the islands in the South Atlantic Ocean, which are claimed by Great Britain
as the Falkland Islands and by Argentina as
the Malvinas).

Regional alliances among nations for military, political, cultural, or economic reasons
constitute another form of the division of
Earth's surface. Among these many alliances
are the North Atlantic Treaty Organization,
the Caribbean Community and Common
Market, the Council of Arab Economic Unity,
and the European Union. In addition, numer-
ous multinational corporations divide Earth's
space and compete with each other for resource development, manufacturing, and the
distribution of goods and services. And non-
governmental organizations such as the International Red Cross and various worldwide
religious groups divide space to administer
their programs.

Events of the twentieth century illustrate
that the division of Earth's surface among different groups pursuing diverse goals continues
unabated at all scales of human activity. World
wars, regional wars, civil wars, and urban riots
often are manifestations of the intensity of feel-

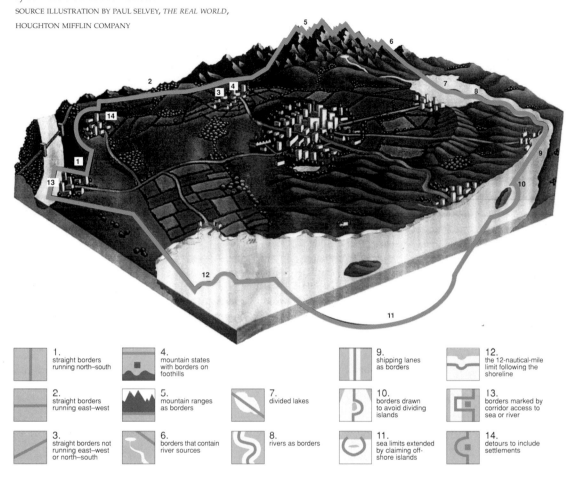

Hypothetical landscape illustrating lines commonly chosen to delineate various kinds of borders enumerated below.

SOURCE ILLUSTRATION BY PAUL SELVEY, *THE REAL WORLD*, HOUGHTON MIFFLIN COMPANY

1. straight borders running north–south

2. straight borders running east–west

3. straight borders not running east–west or north–south

4. mountain states with borders on foothills

5. mountain ranges as borders

6. borders that contain river sources

7. divided lakes

8. rivers as borders

9. shipping lanes as borders

10. borders drawn to avoid dividing islands

11. sea limits extended by claiming off-shore islands

12. the 12-nautical-mile limit following the shoreline

13. borders marked by corridor access to sea or river

14. detours to include settlements

ing humans hold for the right to divide Earth according to their particular perceptions and values. Traditionally, most territorial disputes have been over the land surface, but with the increasing value of resources in the oceans and even outer space, political division of these spaces has become a topic of international debate. Cooperation and conflict will occur in all of these spatial contexts.

At smaller spatial scales, land-use zones in municipalities, administrative districts for airports and other essential services such as water supply and garbage disposal, and school districting within counties, states, and provinces are all examples of the local division of space. Franchise areas, regional divisions of national and multinational corporations, and

free-trade zones indicate the economic division of space. City neighborhood associations, suburban homeowners' associations, civic and volunteer organization districts, and the divisions of neighborhood space by youth gangs on the basis of socioeconomic status, race, or national origin illustrate the power of social and cultural divisions of space.

The interlocking systems for dividing and controlling Earth's space influence all dimensions of people's lives, including trade, culture, citizenship and voting, travel, and self-identity. Students must understand the genesis, structure, power, and pervasiveness of these divisions to appreciate their role within a world that is both globally interdependent and locally controlled.

Environment and Society

. . . .

GEOGRAPHY STANDARD 14

▶ **HOW HUMAN ACTIONS MODIFY THE PHYSICAL ENVIRONMENT**

. . . .

Many of the important issues facing modern society are the consequences—intended and unintended, positive and negative—of human modifications of the physical environment. So it is that the daily news media chronicle such things as the building of dams and aqueducts to bring water to semiarid areas, the loss of wildlife habitat, the reforestation of denuded hills, the depletion of the ozone layer, the ecological effects of acid rain, the reduction of air pollution in certain urban areas, and the intensification of agricultural production through irrigation.

Environmental modifications have economic, social, and political implications for most of the world's people. Therefore, the geographically informed person must understand the reasons for and consequences of human modifications of the environment in different parts of the world.

Human adaptation to and modification of physical systems are influenced by the geographic context in which people live, their understanding of that context, and their technological ability and inclination to modify the physical environment. To survive people depend on the physical environment. They adapt to it and modify it to suit their changing need for things such as food, clothing, water, shelter, energy, and recreational facilities. In meeting their needs, they bring knowledge and technology to bear on physical systems.

Consequently, humans have altered the balance of nature in ways that have brought economic prosperity to some areas and created environmental dilemmas and crises in others. Clearing land for settlement, mining, and agriculture provides homes and livelihoods for some but alters physical systems and trans-forms human populations, wildlife, and vegetation. The inevitable by-products—garbage, air and water pollution, hazardous waste, the overburden from strip mining—place enormous demands on the capacity of physical systems to absorb and accommodate them.

The intended and unintended impacts on physical systems vary in scope and scale. They can be local and small-scale (e.g., the terracing of hillsides for rice growing in the Philippines and acid stream pollution from strip mining in eastern Pennsylvania), regional and medium scale (e.g., the creation of agricultural polderlands in the Netherlands and of an urban heat island with its microclimatic effects in Chicago), or global and large-scale (e.g., the clearing of the forests of North America for agriculture or the depletion of the ozone layer by chlorofluorocarbons).

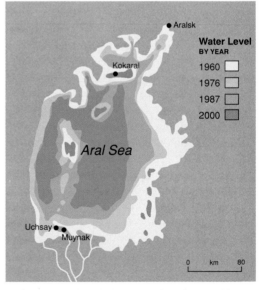

Environmental degradation has been hastened by the view that people can subdue nature (or geography). The Aral Sea is an example of this view—since 1960 it has lost more than 40 percent of its surface area, exposing thousands of square miles of sea bottom and increasing the salinity of the remaining water so that many native species can no longer live in it. SOURCE: *THE REAL WORLD*, HOUGHTON MIFFLIN COMPANY

Some 11,000 square miles of former seabed in the Aral Sea has become a desert of sand and salt, like this area along the southern shore. DAVID C. TURNLEY

Students must understand both the potential of a physical environment to meet human needs and the limitations of that same environment. They must be aware of and understand the causes and implications of different kinds of pollution, resource depletion, and land degradation and the effects of agriculture and manufacturing on the environment. They must know the locations of regions vulnerable to desertification, deforestation, and salinization, and be aware of the spatial impacts of technological hazards such as photochemical smog and acid rain. Students must be aware that current distribution patterns for many plant and animal species are a result of relocation diffusion by humans.

In addition, students must learn to pay careful attention to the relationships between population growth, urbanization, and the resultant stress on physical systems. The process of urbanization affects wildlife habitats, natural vegetation, and drainage patterns. Cities create their own microclimates and pro-duce large amounts of solid waste, photochemical smog, and sewage. A growing world population stimulates increases in agriculture, urbanization, and industrialization. These processes expand demands on water resources, resulting in unintended environmental consequences that can alter water quality and quantity.

Understanding global interdependence begins with an understanding of global dependence—the modification of Earth's surface to meet human needs. When successful the relationship between people and the physical environment is adaptive; when the modifications are excessive the relationship is maladaptive. Increasingly, students will be required to make decisions about relationships between human needs and the physical environment. They will need to be able to understand the opportunities and limitations presented by the geographical context and to set those contexts within the local to global continuum.

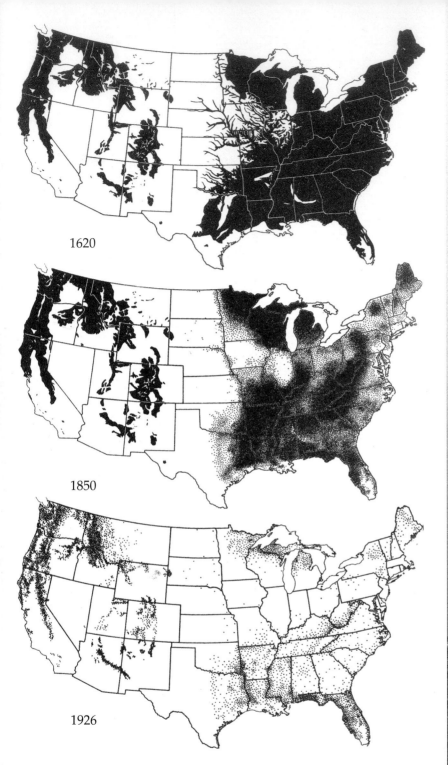

1620

1850

1926

Virgin forest in the United States disappeared, principally through land clearing, at an increasing rate for 300 years after Europeans arrived. In the twentieth century replanting has countered this trend, but at the same time various forms of pollution—toxic chemicals, ozone, acid rain—have become a major cause of deforestation. STEVE ADAMS

Land clearing in the Olympic Mountains, Washington.
JAMES P. BLAIR

▶ HOW PHYSICAL SYSTEMS
AFFECT HUMAN SYSTEMS

No matter what the spatial scale, Earth's surface presents a picture of physical diversity in terms of soils, climates, vegetation, and topography. That diversity offers a range of environmental contexts for people. The geographically informed person must understand how humans are able to live in various kinds of physical environments—not only those of the familiar mid-latitudes but also those that seem less conducive to intensive settlement such as the Arctic tundra and the Equatorial rain forest—and the role physical features of those environments play in shaping human activities.

To live in any given physical environment humans must develop patterns of spatial organization, which take advantage of opportunities offered and avoid or minimize the effects of limitations. Physical systems and environmental characteristics do not, by themselves, determine the pattern of human activity. If the incentives are great enough settlement is possible, although at great cost and risk. The trans-Alaska oil pipeline and construction techniques used in tundra-area settlements are evidence of the extent of human ingenuity. However, the environment does place limitations on human societies (e.g., a glaciated region with its com-

plex of features—thin, rocky water-logged soils and unique landforms—offers few opportunities for commercial agriculture).

A central concept is the idea of carrying capacity—the maximum, sustained level of use of an environment that is possible without incurring significant environmental deterioration, which would eventually lead to environmental destruction. Environments vary in their carrying capacity, and people's failure to understand it—or their inability to live within it—can lead to environmental disaster. Cyclical environmental change, especially in semiarid environments, can pose particular problems for human use of that environment and can lead to desertification, famine, and mass migration, as has occurred in the Sahel of north-central Africa. The relationship between any environment and its inhabitants is mediated by decisions about how much to consume and in what ways to consume. Energy conservation, water conservation, and recycling can have significant effects on patterns of environmental use.

In modern times humans have used technology as a means of reducing the potential effect of physical systems on human activity. In the United States, for example, the widespread introduction of air-conditioning has allowed people to relocate to the South and Southwest, regions previously considered less suited to settlement. And in various regions of Earth, use of the airplane has made it possible to establish settlements and industries in hitherto inaccessible places. However, the use of technology to overcome physical impediments to human activity can also have wide-ranging and sometimes unexpected consequences. For instance, the attempt to control rivers by building dams and dredging waterways to prevent destructive and life-threatening floods can also lead to diminished soil replenishment, increased water salinity, reduced flow of sediment to oceans, and increased riverbank erosion.

In addition to carrying-capacity limitations, the physical environment often im-

Spiral cloud bands characteristic of a hurricane, photographed from a satellite.
NUCLEAR REGULATORY COMMISSION

poses significant costs on human society. Natural hazards are defined as processes or events in the physical environment that are not caused by humans but whose consequences can be harmful. They cost the United States billions of dollars each year. Hurricanes, earthquakes, tornadoes, volcanoes, storms, floods, forest fires, and insect infestations are events that are not preventable and whose precise location, timing, and magnitude are not predictable. Their negative consequences can be reduced by understanding the potential vulnerability of different groups of people and by implementing a variety of strategies such as improved building design, land-use regulation, warning systems, and public education.

Whether the issue is the mitigation of a natural hazard or recognition of carrying capacity, students need to understand the characteristics and spatial properties of the physical environment. It is essential that they be able to translate an understanding of the physical processes and patterns that shape Earth's surface into a picture of that surface as a potential home for people. That home can hold only so many people or be used only in certain ways without incurring costs. Judgment as to the acceptability of those costs requires an understanding of environmental opportunities and constraints.

Dauphin Island, Alabama. Hurricane winds of some 120 miles per hour and high seas have battered beach houses their owners persistently build along the shore.
PAUL CHESLEY/PHOTOGRAPHERS ASPEN

Outer Banks, North Carolina. RANDY TAYLOR

▶ **THE CHANGES THAT OCCUR IN THE MEANING, USE, DISTRIBUTION, AND IMPORTANCE OF RESOURCES**

• •

A resource is any physical material that constitutes part of Earth and which people need and value. There are three basic resources—land, water, and air—that are essential to human survival. However, any other natural material also becomes a resource if and when it becomes valuable to humans. The geographically informed person must develop an understanding of this concept and of the changes in the spatial distribution, quantity, and quality of resources on Earth's surface.

Those changes occur because a resource is a cultural concept, with the value attached to any given resource varying from culture to culture and period to period. Value can be expressed in economic or monetary terms, in legal terms (as in the Clean Air Act), in terms of risk assessment, or in terms of ethics (the responsibility to preserve our National Parks for future generations). The value of a resource depends on human needs and the technology available for its extraction and use. Rock oil seeping from rocks in northwestern Pennsylvania was of only minor value as a medicine until a technology was developed in the mid-nineteenth century that enabled it to be refined into a lamp illuminant. Some resources that were once valuable are no longer important. For example, it was the availability of pine tar and tall timber—strategic materials valued by the English navy—that in the seventeenth century helped spur settlement in northern New England, but that region now uses its vegetative cover (and natural beauty) as a different type of resource—for recreation and tourism. Resources, therefore, are the result of people seeing a need and perceiving an opportunity to meet that need.

The quantity and quality of a resource is determined by whether it is a renewable, non-renewable, or a flow resource. Renewable resources, such as plants and animals, can replenish themselves after they have been used if their physical environment has not been destroyed. If trees are harvested care-

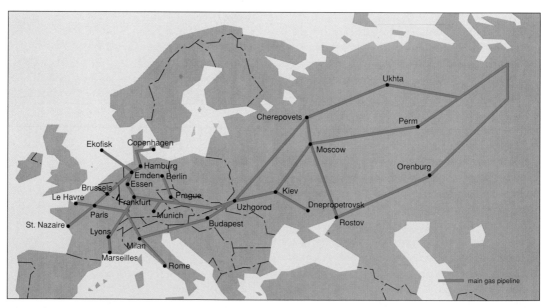

Natural gas routes to Europe. In addition to its own sources, notably those in the North Sea, Europe receives natural gas from Asia and North Africa via pipeline and specially adapted vessels. Pipelines from Siberia supply 15 percent of Europe's natural gas. SOURCE: *THE REAL WORLD*, HOUGHTON MIFFLIN COMPANY

Aquaculture promises stability for Maine's chronically cyclic, and now declining, fishing industry. Here, an aquaculturist shovels salmon chow (pellets containing vitamin-enriched fish-meal and ground herring) to Atlantic salmon being raised in pens in Eastport, Maine, where netting protects the fish from sea and sky predators. KEVIN FLEMING

fully, a new forest will grow to replace the one that was cut. If animals eat grass in a pasture to a certain level, grass will grow again and provide food for animals in the future, as long as the carrying capacity of the land is not exceeded by the pressure of too many animals. Nonrenewable resources, such as minerals and fossil fuels (coal, oil, and natural gas), can be extracted and used only once. Flow resources, such as water, wind, and sunlight, are neither renewable nor nonrenewable because they must be used as, when, and where they occur. The energy in a river can be used to generate electricity, which can be transmitted over great distances. However, that energy must be captured by turbines as the water flows past or it will be lost.

The location of resources influences the distribution of people and their activities on Earth. People live where they can earn a living. Human migration and settlement are linked to the availability of resources, ranging from fertile soils and supplies of freshwater to deposits of metals or pools of natural gas. The patterns of population distribution that result from the relationship between resources and employment change as needs and technologies change. In Colorado, for example, abandoned mining towns reflect the exhaustion of nonrenewable resources (silver and lead deposits), whereas ski resorts reflect the exploitation of renewable resources (snow and scenery).

Technology changes the ways in which humans appraise resources, and it may modify economic systems and population distributions. Changes in technology bring into play new ranges of resources from Earth's stock. Since the industrial revolution, for example, technology has shifted from waterpower to coal-generated steam to petroleum-powered engines, and different resources and their

In Eastern Europe, workers in out-of-date factories such as this one try to keep pace with demand.
JAMES NACHTWEY

source locations have become important. The population of the Ruhr Valley in Germany, for example, grew rapidly in response to the new importance of coal and minerals in industrial ventures. Similarly, each innovation in the manufacture of steel brought a new resource to prominence in the United States, and resulted in locational shifts in steel production and population growth.

Demands for resources vary spatially. More resources are used by economically developed countries than by developing countries. For example, the United States uses petroleum at a rate that is five times the world average. As countries develop economically, their demand for resources increases faster than their population grows. The wealth that accompanies economic development enables people to consume more. The consumption of a resource does not necessarily occur where the resource is produced or where the largest reserves of the resource are located. Most of the petroleum produced in Southwest Asia, for example, is consumed in the United States, Europe, and Japan.

Sometimes, users of resources feel insecure when they have to depend on other places to supply them with materials that are so important to their economy and standard of living. This feeling of insecurity can become especially strong if two interdependent countries do not have good political relations, share the same values, or understand each other. In some situations, conflict over resources breaks out into warfare. One factor in Japan's involvement in World War II, for example, was that Japan lacked petroleum resources of its own and coveted oil fields elsewhere in Asia, especially after the United States threatened to cut off its petroleum exports to Japan.

Conflicts over resources are likely to increase as demand increases. Globally, the increase in demand tends to keep pace with the increase in population. More people on Earth means more need for fertilizers, building materials, food, energy, and everything else produced from resources. Accordingly, if the people of the world are to coexist, Earth's resources must be managed to guarantee adequate supplies for everyone. That means reserves of renewable resources need to be sustained at a productive level, new reserves of nonrenewable resources need to be found and exploited, new applications for flow resources need to be developed, and, wherever possible, cost-effective substitutes—especially for nonrenewable resources—need to be developed.

It is essential that students have a solid grasp of the different kinds of resources, of the ways in which humans value and use (and compete over) resources, and of the distribution of resources across Earth's surface.

The Uses of Geography

▶ **HOW TO APPLY GEOGRAPHY TO INTERPRET THE PAST**

Geographers and historians agree that the human story must be told within the context of three intertwined points of view—space, environment, and chronology. The geographically informed person understands the importance of bringing the spatial and environmental focus of geography to bear on the events of history and vice versa, and the value of learning about the geographies of the past.

An understanding of geography can inform an understanding of history in two important ways. First, the events of history take place within geographic contexts. Second, those events are motivated by people's perceptions, correct or otherwise, of geographic contexts. By exploring what the world was like and how it was perceived at a given place at a given time, the geographically informed person is able to interpret major historical issues. For example, why did the land invasions of Russia by Sweden under Charles XII, France under Napoleon, and Germany under Hitler all fail? And why

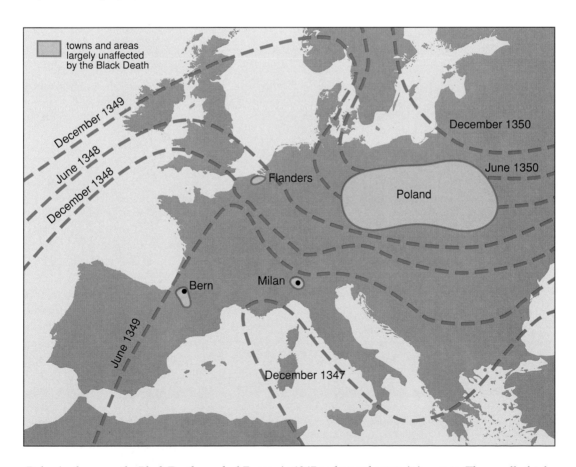

Bubonic plague, or the Black Death, reached Europe in 1347 and spread across it in waves. The usually fatal disease spread most rapidly in cities and wiped out whole villages. But for reasons that remain unclear, cities such as Milan, Italy and Bern, Switzerland escaped. SOURCE: *THE REAL WORLD*, HOUGHTON MIFFLIN COMPANY

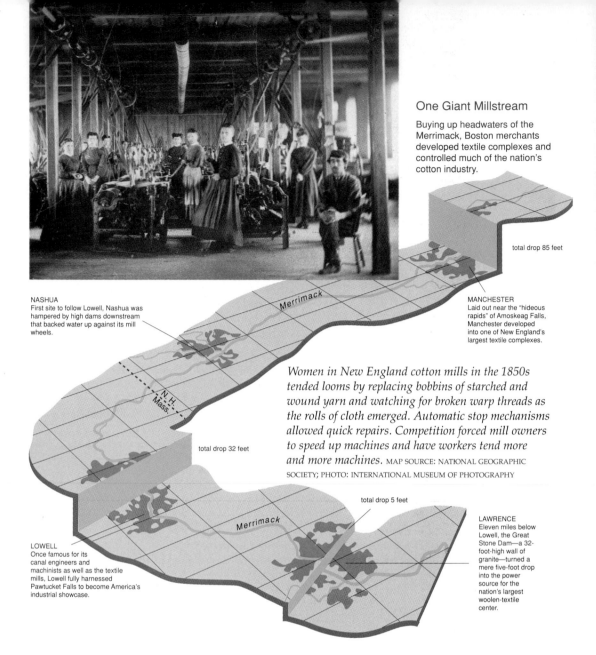

One Giant Millstream

Buying up headwaters of the Merrimack, Boston merchants developed textile complexes and controlled much of the nation's cotton industry.

total drop 85 feet

NASHUA
First site to follow Lowell, Nashua was hampered by high dams downstream that backed water up against its mill wheels.

MANCHESTER
Laid out near the "hideous rapids" of Amoskeag Falls, Manchester developed into one of New England's largest textile complexes.

Merrimack

N. H.
Mass.

total drop 32 feet

Women in New England cotton mills in the 1850s tended looms by replacing bobbins of starched and wound yarn and watching for broken warp threads as the rolls of cloth emerged. Automatic stop mechanisms allowed quick repairs. Competition forced mill owners to speed up machines and have workers tend more and more machines. MAP SOURCE: NATIONAL GEOGRAPHIC SOCIETY; PHOTO: INTERNATIONAL MUSEUM OF PHOTOGRAPHY

total drop 5 feet

Merrimack

LOWELL
Once famous for its canal engineers and machinists as well as the textile mills, Lowell fully harnessed Pawtucket Falls to become America's industrial showcase.

LAWRENCE
Eleven miles below Lowell, the Great Stone Dam—a 32-foot-high wall of granite—turned a mere five-foot drop into the power source for the nation's largest woolen-textile center.

did people want to build the Panama and Suez Canals?

Answering such questions requires a geographic approach to the spatial organization of the world as it existed then and as that world was seen by the people of those times. In the case of the land invasions of Russia, the failure of the invaders can be linked to the dimensions, conditions, and constraints of the physical and human environments involved: the harsh weather conditions to be endured, the prevalence of rivers and marshes to be crossed, the vehicle-impeding mud to be overcome, the vast distances to be traversed,

the shortages of food and other supplies, and the hostility, determination, and home-ground advantage of the defenders. As all three invasions demonstrated, space and environment form a context within which people make choices.

The geographic approach to the past also requires looking at the ways in which different people understood and assessed the physical and human geographical features of their spatial and environmental contexts. In the case of the Panama and Suez Canals, the geographic approach involves an assessment of how people and governments perceived and valued transportation costs in terms of both money and time, the topography and geology of the area, the available technology and labor force, the political forces operating in Central America, Europe, and Southwest Asia, and the economic returns that would ensue. Such an assessment leads to understanding that the canals were constructed because it was determined that the efforts and costs would be worthwhile in terms of the resulting economic and political gains.

Looking at the past geographically requires that attention be given to the beliefs and attitudes of the peoples of bygone times regarding the environment, human migration, land use, and especially their own rights and privileges versus those of others. Such information can be obtained through the use of contemporary newspapers and other firsthand accounts. It also can be obtained through the study of visible remains of buildings and other facilities, which offer clues to what occurred and why. A careful geographical analysis of today's cultural and physical landscapes is a valuable resource for learning about the past.

The geographies of past times carry important messages for today's people. The events of human history have been played out on a vast and complex geographic stage, and countless generations have had to make the best of what Earth has provided in the form of climate, land and water resources, plants and animals, and transportation routes; all of these things are shaped by the ongoing interactions of physical and human systems and have created the contexts in which history has unfolded. The study of history, without these rich contexts, is one-dimensional. In like fashion, the study of geography, without an appreciation of history, is one-dimensional. Understanding the geographies of past times, therefore, is as important as understanding the geography of the present. Students must appreciate that viewing the past from both spatial and chronological points of view can lead to a greater awareness and depth of understanding of physical and human events, and is an essential ingredient in the interpretation of the world of today. Students must also understand that the geographic approach helps to explain why events did happen in a particular way but not necessarily why they must have happened in that way.

GEOGRAPHY STANDARD 18

▶ HOW TO APPLY GEOGRAPHY TO INTERPRET THE PRESENT AND PLAN FOR THE FUTURE

Geography is for life and not simply an exercise for its own sake. As the world becomes both more complex and more interconnected—as a result of economic development, population growth, technological advancement, and increased cooperation (and, to some extent, conflict)—the need for geographic knowledge, skills, and perspectives increases among the world's peoples. Geography is the key to nations, peoples, and individuals being able to develop a coherent understanding of the causes, meanings, and effects of the physical and human events that occur—and are likely to occur—on Earth's surface.

Consequently, the practical applications of geography (along with other aspects of geographic literacy) need to be fostered in all students in preparation for life as the responsible citizens and leaders of tomorrow.

Through its spatial emphasis, geography enables students to comprehend spatial patterns and spatial contexts; connections and movements between places; the integration of local, regional, national, and global scales; diversity; and systems. Through its ecological emphasis, geography enables students to comprehend physical processes and patterns; ecosystems; the physical interconnections between local and global environments; and the impact of people on the physical environment.

Taken together, these sets of understandings enable students to pose and answer geographic questions about the spatial organization of the world in which they live. At a local

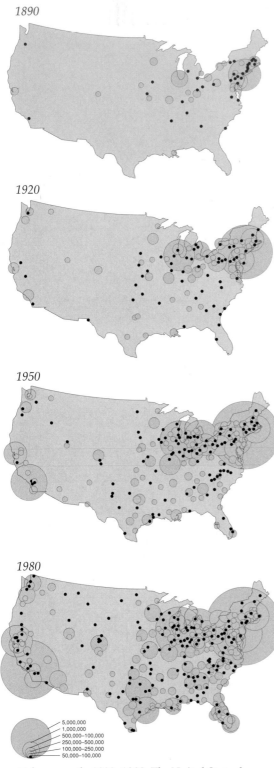

1890

1920

1950

1980

5,000,000
1,000,000
500,000–100,000
250,000–500,000
100,000–250,000
50,000–100,000

Urban growth, 1890–1980. The United States has shifted its center of gravity from the snow belt to the Sunbelt. Will West Coast cities continue to grow rapidly, reinforcing the importance of the Sunbelt? Will cities of the North continue to grow slowly, mainly at their fringes? SOURCE: NATIONAL GEOGRAPHIC SOCIETY

and personal level students need to understand the reasons for and implications of decisions about such issues as community recycling programs, the loss of agricultural land to new housing, the choice between spending tax dollars on a sewage treatment plant or housing for senior citizens, the expansion of the runways of a local airport, or the introduction of air quality standards. They also need to be aware of the impact of such decision-making on their own lives and the lives of others, and that eventually, as community members and voting citizens, they will be asked to participate in the decision-making process. Such participation demands the knowledge and judgment of geographically informed people who know where to find relevant information, how to evaluate it, how to analyze it, and how to represent it.

Geographic literacy also has great significance at a more global and less personally immediate level. With a solid foundation in the interlinked knowledge, skills, and perspectives of geography, students will be better able to analyze and reach informed opinions about a variety of issues—ranging from the implications of resource depletion and the economic and social tensions caused by exponential population growth to what will happen within the family of nations as old political structures change, new alliances are formed, and realignments cause mass migration of refugees seeking asylum, security, and economic opportunity.

With a solid understanding of geography, people are better able to decide where to live and work, how and where to travel, and how to assess the world in spatial terms. In a world where people are competing for territory, resources, markets, and economic positions, knowing too little about geography is a liability, which compromises the capacity of people to function successfully at home or abroad. Creating effective and lasting solutions to the world's pressing problems requires that today's students mature into adults who can make skilled and informed use of geographic knowledge, skills, and perspectives to identify possible solutions, predict their consequences, and implement the best solutions. That is why it is imperative that all students in the United States achieve geographic literacy.

CHAPTER 5

National Geography Standards

Grades K–4

GEOGRAPHY STANDARD 1 GRADES K–4

The World in Spatial Terms

▶ HOW TO USE MAPS AND OTHER GEOGRAPHIC REPRESENTATIONS, TOOLS, AND TECHNOLOGIES TO ACQUIRE, PROCESS, AND REPORT INFORMATION FROM A SPATIAL PERSPECTIVE

. . . .

By the end of the fourth grade, the student knows and understands:

1. **The characteristics and purposes of geographic representations—such as maps, globes, graphs, diagrams, aerial and other photographs, and satellite-produced images**

2. **The characteristics and purposes of tools and technologies—such as reference works and computer-based geographic information systems**

3. **How to display spatial information on maps and other geographic representations**

4. **How to use appropriate geographic tools and technologies**

Therefore, the student is able to:

A. **Identify and describe the characteristics and purposes of geographic representations, tools, and technologies, as exemplified by being able to**

Examine a variety of maps to identify and describe their basic elements (e.g., title, legend, cardinal and intermediate directions, scale, grid, principal parallels, meridians)

Interpret aerial photographs or satellite-produced images to locate and identify physical and human features (e.g., mountain ranges, rivers, vegetation regions, cities, dams, reservoirs)

Design a map that displays information selected by the student, using symbols explained in a key

A Washington, D.C., child draws a map to his friend's house, using notes he took when surveying the neighborhood. JOSEPH H. BAILEY

B. Show spatial information on geographic representations, as exemplified by being able to

Read a narrative and then create a sketch map to illustrate the narrative (e.g., make a map showing the movement of a family of ducks as described in *Make Way for Ducklings*; or after reading the *Little House* series by Laura Ingalls Wilder make a map of where the Ingalls family lived)

Report regional data in both a two-dimensional format (e.g., by using proportional symbols drawn on a map) and a three-dimensional format (e.g., stacking a proportionate number of counters on each region)

Construct diagrams or charts to display spatial information (e.g., construct a bar graph that compares the populations of the five largest cities in a U. S. state)

C. Use geographic representations, tools, and technologies to answer geographic questions, as exemplified by being able to

Use a map grid (e.g., latitude and longitude or alphanumeric system) to answer the question—What is this location?—as applied to places chosen by the teacher and student

Use thematic maps to answer questions about human distributions (e.g., What explains the distribution of the human population on Earth?)

Use different types of map scales (linear, fractional, and word scale) to measure the distance between two places in response to the question—How far is location A from location B?

The World in Spatial Terms

▶ **HOW TO USE MENTAL MAPS TO ORGANIZE INFORMATION ABOUT PEOPLE, PLACES, AND ENVIRONMENTS IN A SPATIAL CONTEXT**

. . . .

By the end of the fourth grade, the student knows and understands:

1. **The locations of places within the local community and in nearby communities**

2. **The location of Earth's continents and oceans in relation to each other and to principal parallels and meridians**

3. **The location of major physical and human features in the United States and on Earth**

Therefore, the student is able to:

A. **Identify major physical and human features at a variety of scales (local to global) using maps, globes, and other sources of graphic information, as exemplified by being able to**

Use symbols to locate, identify, and mark features of the local community (e.g., shopping areas, restaurants, fire stations, schools, post offices) on a prepared base map

Use labels and symbols to locate and identify physical and human features (e.g., largest cities, rivers, recreation areas, historic sites, landforms, power plants) on a prepared base map of the state or United States

Identify physical and human features along a great circle route between two places (e.g., Los Angeles and Moscow, Singapore and Buenos Aires) using a globe, maps, and other sources of graphic information

B. **Use a mental map to identify the locations of places, as exemplified by being able to**

Draw a sketch map from memory of the local community showing the route to and from school, to and from stores, and to and from recreational facilities

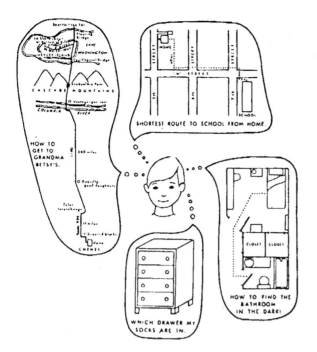

SHORTEST ROUTE TO SCHOOL FROM HOME.

HOW TO GET TO GRANDMA BETSY'S.

WHICH DRAWER MY SOCKS ARE IN.

HOW TO FIND THE BATHROOM IN THE DARK!

A mental map is our idea of where something is and how to get to it. We all store these geographic images in our minds. JOURNAL OF GEOGRAPHY

Prepare a sketch map to indicate the approximate locations of places, both local and global, featured in a newspaper or television news story

Answer questions about the locations of places (e.g., Is Maine farther east than Florida? Is Singapore closer to Europe or North America? The Suez Canal connects the Red Sea with what other sea?)

C. **Sketch an accurate map to answer questions about the locations of physical and human features, as exemplified by being able to**

Sketch a map showing the location of the local community in relation to major landmarks (e.g., a major river, city, or landform)

Use a sketch map indicating the approximate location of major mountain ranges in the world to illustrate a geographic idea (e.g., to explain the rain-shadow effect of mountains, or to show how mountains can affect transportation routes)

Mark and label the locations of places discussed in history, language arts, science, and other school subjects (e.g., use sketch maps regularly, as a matter of habit, to place historic events in their spatial contexts or depict countries or regions read about in language arts)

D. **Describe selected geographic features on the basis of using mental maps, as exemplified by being able to**

Write a short account from memory illustrated with a sketch map, describing the location of a shopping mall, a neighboring city, the downtown area of the community, and other important features of the local region

Write a description from memory of the physical and human characteristics of the state in which the student lives and create a sketch map to illustrate the account

Write a brief summary from memory of the distribution of physical and human features in different regions of the United States and world (e.g., the distribution of population in mid-latitude regions of the world)

The World in Spatial Terms

▶ HOW TO ANALYZE THE SPATIAL
ORGANIZATION OF PEOPLE, PLACES, AND
ENVIRONMENTS ON EARTH'S SURFACE

. . . .

By the end of the fourth grade, the student knows and understands:

1. **The spatial elements of point, line, area, and volume**

2. **The spatial concepts of location, distance, direction, scale, movement, and region**

3. **That places and features are distributed spatially across Earth's surface**

4. **The causes and consequences of spatial interaction on Earth's surface**

Therefore, the student is able to:

A. **Analyze Earth's surface in terms of its spatial elements of point, line, area, and volume, as exemplified by being able to**

Use a simple map to identify physical and human features in terms of the four spatial elements (e.g., locations [point], transportation and communication routes [line], regions [area], lakes filled with water [volume])

Prepare simple diagrams of various places, using the four spatial elements (e.g., a diagram showing the school and student homes [points], roads that connect them [lines], and the school attendance region [area])

Use a map of the local region that shows transportation links between communities to decide the best routes for getting to each community, the easiest community to get to, and the most difficult community to get to

B. **Use the spatial concepts of location, distance, direction, scale, movement, and region to describe the spatial organization of places, as exemplified by being able to**

Write descriptions of the spatial organization of places featured in stories (e.g., use a children's story such as "Little Red Riding Hood" to examine concepts of distance, direction, and location—the relative location of the two houses, the distance between them, and the direction and movement of the wolf and Little Red Riding Hood)

Locate the homes of classmates and the school on a map, measure the distance from each home to school, determine the direction from each home to school, identify the route traveled by each student, and outline on the map the region created by the locations of the homes

Measure the distance between two locations in miles, kilometers, time, cost, and perception, and draw conclusions about different ways of measuring distance (e.g., contrast the amount of time and the cost of traveling from one location to other locations using different means of transportation)

c. **Observe and compare the patterns and densities of places on Earth's surface, as exemplified by being able to**

Observe the distribution of features on maps or aerial photographs to identify spatial patterns and associations (e.g., the relationships between fast-food locations and accessibility)

Calculate the density of specific features within a grid placed over a map (e.g., use a grid to plot and count the locations of students' homes and color each grid square according to density)

	Point	Line	Area
Point	Air Traffic among Cities	Stops along a Mail Route	School and School District
Line		Road Network	River Drainage Basin
Area		*The dimensional primitives of geography. Points are concentrations or foci. Lines are paths of movement or boundaries. Together with areas that show the extent of things, they are the primitives upon which the logical structures of geography are built.* © BELL & HOWELL COMPANY	City's Trade Areas

Lake Nasser, in southern Egypt and northern Sudan, was formed in the 1960s as a result of the construction of the Aswan High Dam. This photograph was taken from a manned spacecraft. NASA

Use maps of physical features to observe patterns produced by physical processes (e.g., the drainage basin of a river system, the ridge-and-valley pattern of the Appalachians, or vegetation on the windward and leeward sides of a mountain range)

D. Analyze the locations of places and suggest why particular locations are used for certain human activities, as exemplified by being able to

Create a sketch map or scale model of the community locating key places and explain the locations of service and commercial activities, housing, public utilities, fire stations, and schools using the concept of accessibility

Identify why some locations are better than others for specific activities (e.g., why gas stations and convenience stores are often at the intersections of major streets and doctors' offices near hospitals)

Observe and map the locations of essential services in the community (e.g., street-lights, phone booths, mailboxes, fire hydrants), and suggest reasons for the locations of the services

E. Identify connections among places and explain the causes and consequences of spatial interaction, as exemplified by being able to

Identify cultural characteristics that originated in other cultures and trace the spread of each characteristic and the means by which it spread (e.g., trace the movement from Africa to America of cultural characteristics such as foods, language, music, and customs as a result of the slave trade between the seventeenth and nineteenth centuries)

Use labels on clothing, canned goods, and other consumer items to map links with locations in different regions of the country and world and then write a brief account suggesting reasons for the patterns observed on the map

Write a story or play about the consequences of a community being cut off from interaction with the outside world for three days—an account of life in the community without fuel, fresh fruits and vegetables, truck deliveries, mail service, and other forms of community-to-outside-world interaction

GEOGRAPHY STANDARD 4 GRADES K–4

Places and Regions

▶ THE PHYSICAL AND HUMAN
CHARACTERISTICS OF PLACES

. . . .

By the end of the fourth grade, the student knows and understands:

1. **The physical characteristics of places (e.g., landforms, bodies of water, soil, vegetation, and weather and climate)**

2. **The human characteristics of places (e.g., population distributions, settlement patterns, languages, ethnicity, nationality, and religious beliefs)**

3. **How physical and human processes together shape places**

Therefore, the student is able to:

A. **Describe and compare the physical characteristics of places at a variety of scales, local to global, as exemplified by being able to**

Observe and describe the physical characteristics of the local community in words and sketches, using a data-retrieval chart organized by physical features (e.g., landforms, bodies of water, soils, vegetation)

Use a variety of visual materials and data sources (e.g., photographs, satellite-produced images, pictures, tables, charts) to describe the physical characteristics of a region, noting items that have similar distributions (e.g., trees in river valleys)

Use cardboard, wood, clay, or other materials to make a model of a region that shows its physical characteristics (e.g., landforms, bodies of water, vegetation)

B. **Describe and compare the human characteristics of places at a variety of scales, local to global, as exemplified by being able to**

Observe and describe the human characteristics of the local community in words and sketches, using a data-retrieval chart organized by human features (e.g., type of economic activity, type of housing, languages spoken, ethnicity, religion)

Use a variety of visual materials, data sources, and narratives (e.g., photographs, pictures, tables, charts, newspaper stories) to describe the human characteristics of a region and to answer such questions as: Where do people live? What kinds of jobs do they have? How do they spend their leisure time?

Erosion caused by deforestation, Switzerland. RINGIER DOKUMENTATIONSZENTRUM

Use cardboard, wood, clay, or other materials to make a model of a community that shows its human characteristics (e.g., land-use patterns, areas of settlement, locations of community services)

C. **Describe and compare different places at a variety of scales, local to global, as exemplified by being able to**

Observe and describe the physical and human characteristics of the local community and compare them to the characteristics of surrounding communities or of communities in other regions of the country

Use a variety of graphic materials and data sources (e.g., photographs, satellite-produced images, tables, charts) to describe the physical and human characteristics of a region, noting items that have similar distributions (e.g., communities are located on major highways)

Use cardboard, wood, clay, or other materials to make a model of a community that shows its physical and human characteristics (e.g., landforms, bodies of water, vegetation, land-use patterns, areas of settlement)

D. **Describe and explain the physical and human processes that shape the characteristics of places, as exemplified by being able to**

Use maps and other graphic materials to describe the effects of physical and human processes in shaping the landscape (e.g., the effects of erosion and deposition in creating landforms, the effects of agriculture in changing land use and vegetation, the effects of settlement on the building of roads)

Draw maps to show the distribution of population in a region with respect to landforms, climate, vegetation, resources, historic events, or other physical and human characteristics to suggest factors that affect settlement patterns

Keep a daily weather log of wind direction, temperature, precipitation, and general conditions over time to explain some of the factors that affect weather in the local community

Places and Regions

▶ THAT PEOPLE CREATE REGIONS TO
INTERPRET EARTH'S COMPLEXITY

. . . .

By the end of the fourth grade, the student knows and understands:

1. **The concept of region as an area of Earth's surface with unifying geographic characteristics**

2. **The similarities and differences among regions**

3. **The ways in which regions change**

Therefore, the student is able to:

A. **Define regions by being able to use physical and human criteria, as exemplified by being able to**

Identify and demarcate areas that are alike and different and form regions from these areas (e.g., residential neighborhoods, parks, industrial areas, regions of dense and less dense settlement)

Identify and describe a variety of regions that result from spatial patterns of human activity or human characteristics (e.g., political regions, population regions, economic regions, language or other regions)

Identify and describe physical regions (e.g., landform regions, soil regions, vegetation regions, climate regions, water basins) by studying the physical environment at a variety of scales and using field notes, maps, and other sources

B. **Compare and contrast regions, as exemplified by being able to**

Compare the ways in which one neighborhood is similar to and different from another neighborhood (e.g., house size, style of streetlight, presence of sidewalks, vegetation type, and at least one population characteristic, such as age of residents) and explain why both neighborhoods can be defined as regions

Compare the student's own region with a region on another continent and explain how they are similar and different

Use graphic materials, primary documents, narratives, and data sources to compare the geographic characteristics of regions of the world at similar latitudes (e.g., Gulf

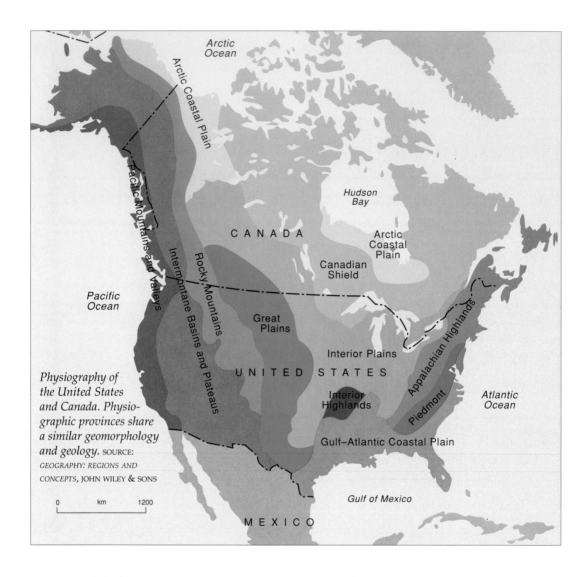

Physiography of the United States and Canada. Physiographic provinces share a similar geomorphology and geology. SOURCE: GEOGRAPHY: REGIONS AND CONCEPTS, JOHN WILEY & SONS

Coastal plain in the New Orleans area, the Nile River Valley in the Cairo area, and the Yangtze River Valley in the Shanghai area)

c. Describe changes in the physical and human characteristics of regions that occur over time and identify the consequences of such changes, as exemplified by being able to

Prepare a display contrasting life in a region in the past with life in the same region in the present—in terms of population size, ethnic composition, cultural characteristics such as language, economic activities, transportation, cuisine, or means of recreation—to identify ways in which the region has changed

Identify changes in the internal structure or function of a region (e.g., construction of a new shopping center, new hospital, or new manufacturing plant)

Develop a set of questions to ask senior citizens about regional change during their lifetimes (e.g., changes in transportation, shopping, habits, how people earn a living, environmental conditions) and write a summary of the answers

GEOGRAPHY STANDARD 6 GRADES K–4

Places and Regions

▶ HOW CULTURE AND EXPERIENCE INFLUENCE
PEOPLE'S PERCEPTIONS OF PLACES AND REGIONS

. . . .

By the end of the fourth grade, the student knows and understands:

1. **How to describe the student's own community and region from different perspectives**

2. **Ways in which different people perceive places and regions**

Therefore, the student is able to:

A. **Describe places and regions in different ways, as exemplified by being able to**

Make a poster or collage or use another mode of expression that reflects the student's perception (mental map) of a place or region (e.g., my home town, historic sites, recreation areas)

Make and exchange drawings and sketch maps with a classmate to compare and contrast perceptions of the same place (e.g., similarities and differences in details remembered, emphases depicted, positive or negative reactions)

Write a historical account of the local community as seen from the student's own perspective, with emphasis on how the student's views and values have changed over time

B. **Compare the different ways in which people view and relate to places and regions, as exemplified by being able to**

Describe how different people perceive places and regions (e.g., how children, mothers, joggers, and city-park workers view a park) through the use of role playing, simulations, and other activities

Conduct interviews to collect information on how people of different age, sex, or ethnicity view the same place or region and then organize the information by subject (e.g., medical facilities), type of interviewee (e.g., African-American male teenager, middle-aged female Chicano, elderly white female), and response (e.g., like/dislike, important/unimportant)

Analyze songs, poems, and stories about places to make inferences about people's feelings regarding the places featured in those works

Physical Systems

▶ THE PHYSICAL PROCESSES THAT SHAPE THE
PATTERNS OF EARTH'S SURFACE

. . . .

By the end of the fourth grade, the student knows and understands:

1. **The components of Earth's physical systems: the atmosphere, lithosphere, hydrosphere, and biosphere**

2. **How patterns (location, distribution, and association) of features on Earth's surface are shaped by physical processes**

3. **How Earth–Sun relations affect conditions on Earth**

Therefore, the student is able to:

A. **Identify and describe the physical components of Earth's atmosphere, lithosphere, hydrosphere, and biosphere, as exemplified by being able to**

Use pictures from instructional materials and hand-drawn sketches to distinguish between different components of Earth's physical systems (e.g., lithospheric features [landforms] such as mountains, hills, plateaus, plains, river valleys, and peninsulas and hydrospheric features such as oceans, lakes, and rivers)

Describe different climates in terms of precipitation and temperature and the types of plants and animals associated with each, using pictures, maps, and graphs

Construct a model of the hydrologic cycle focusing on surface and subsurface water features (e.g., rivers, lakes, oceans, runoff, groundwater, aquifers, water tables)

B. **Explain how physical processes help to shape features and patterns on Earth's surface, as exemplified by being able to**

Describe the physical environment of the student's own region and the physical processes that act on it (e.g., weather, tectonic forces, wave action, freezing and thawing, gravity, soil-building processes)

Compare and interpret maps and photographs to explain how physical processes affect features of Earth's surface (e.g., the effects of climate and weather on vegetation, erosion and deposition on landforms, mud slides on hills)

The biosphere is Earth's thin layer of life, which extends from the land areas (lithosphere) and water areas (hydrosphere) into the air (atmosphere). The cycling molecules of water (H_2O), oxygen (O_2), and carbon dioxide (CO_2) through the biosphere make it a self-sustaining ecosystem. © NATIONAL GEOGRAPHIC SOCIETY

Compare climatic conditions in different regions of the world, taking into consideration factors such as distance from the Equator, elevation, and distance from cold and warm ocean currents

c. Describe how Earth's position relative to the Sun affects events and conditions on Earth, as exemplified by being able to

Prepare a model or design a demonstration to show the tilt of Earth in relation to the Sun in order to explain seasons at different locations on Earth

Explain how the length of day can influence human activities in different regions of the world (e.g., use of daylight savings time, school schedules in the United States, summer and winter activities in areas north of the Arctic Circle)

Relate seed and garden catalog descriptions of growing seasons to the United States Department of Agriculture hardiness zone maps

Physical Systems

▶ **THE CHARACTERISTICS AND SPATIAL DISTRIBUTION OF ECOSYSTEMS ON EARTH'S SURFACE**

. . . .

By the end of the fourth grade, the student knows and understands:

1. **The components of ecosystems**

2. **The distribution and patterns of ecosystems**

3. **How humans interact with ecosystems**

Therefore, the student is able to:

A. **Describe and illustrate the components of ecosystems at a variety of scales, as exemplified by being able to**

Collect samples of components of a local ecosystem and arrange them in a diorama model of the ecosystem

Illustrate a food chain or webs of food chains by sequentially ordering pictures or samples of a variety of living things (e.g., fungi, insects, plants, animals)

Identify and compare communities of plants and animals and the physical environments in which they live (e.g., fish and marine vegetation in coastal zones; grasses, birds, and insects in grassland areas)

B. **Identify and explain the distribution and patterns of ecosystems, as exemplified by being able to**

Write descriptions of groups of plants and animals associated with vegetation and climatic regions on Earth (e.g., the plant and animal life supported in a mid-latitude forest in North America and the kinds of plants and animals found in a tropical rain forest in Africa) and illustrate them with pictures and other visual images

Place pictures of different vegetation regions on the appropriate portions of a world climate map, a world temperature map, and world precipitation map

Use sketch maps of the student's region and state to show the locations of different associations of plants and animals (e.g., animals that live in forests, animals and

Tropical broadleaf forest in Honduras. DAVID ALAN HARVEY

trees that thrive in cities, animals and plants that live near the coast, a lake, or a
river)

c. Explain how humans interact with ecosystems, as exemplified by being able to

Compile a list of the resources used by the student in a typical day and trace the
resources back to their original niche in an ecosystem to understand how humans
interact with and depend upon ecosystems

List ways in which humans can change ecosystems (e.g., clearing forests, widening
channels of waterways, draining wetlands, setting or suppressing fires)

Describe how vegetation and soil can affect human settlement (e.g., good sites for
building or farming) and ways in which humans can affect vegetation and soil (e.g.,
changing vegetation or practicing soil conservation)

Human Systems

▶ THE CHARACTERISTICS, DISTRIBUTION, AND MIGRATION OF HUMAN POPULATIONS ON EARTH'S SURFACE

. . . .

By the end of the fourth grade, the student knows and understands:

1. **The spatial distribution of population**

2. **The characteristics of populations at different scales (local to global)**

3. **The causes and effects of human migration**

Therefore, the student is able to:

A. **Describe the spatial distribution of population, as exemplified by being able to**

Study the distribution of population on a map of the student's local community or state and suggest reasons for the patterns observed (e.g., more people live closer to downtown than far away, perhaps because they want to be close to where they work; and more people live in one part of the state than another, perhaps because it has more resources and job opportunities)

Study a map of the United States showing population densities and then write an account suggesting how differences in density are related to location (e.g., population density is higher east of the Mississippi River than west of it and higher on the East Coast and West Coast than in the mountains and deserts of the western part of the country)

Suggest reasons for the distribution of people on Earth (e.g., few people live where it is very dry or very cold) by comparing maps of population distribution with maps that show climate, precipitation, length of growing season, natural resources, and other physical features

B. **Describe and compare the characteristics of populations at a variety of scales, as exemplified by being able to**

Create graphs and maps of the local community showing population characteristics (e.g., ethnicity, age distribution, number of families and single households, number of employed and unemployed, males and females)

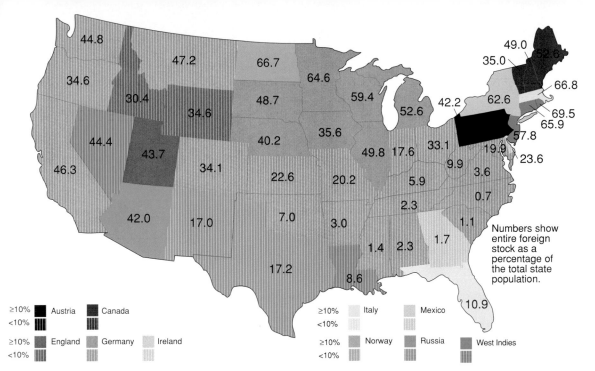

Snapshot of a nation just beginning to absorb its greatest influx of immigrants. The 1920 census counted
Americans of "foreign stock"—those either born abroad or with at least one parent born in a foreign country.
SOURCE: NATIONAL GEOGRAPHIC SOCIETY

Develop a census questionnaire featuring population characteristics of interest to the
student (e.g., number of sisters and brothers, distance traveled to school, place of birth,
month of birth, favorite sport, types of pets, ages of parents and grandparents), collect
the data from students in two classes, and describe and compare the two populations

Use data, graphs, and maps of population characteristics to compare the population characteristics (e.g., life expectancy, infant mortality, urban population, and per
capita gross domestic product) of two places (e.g., two states, two countries, two
different world regions such as Latin America and Africa, or two subregions within
a single region such as Southeast Asia or East Asia)

c. **Compare the causes and effects of human migration, as exemplified by
being able to**

Read narratives describing a variety of migrations in different regions of the world
and then discuss the reasons for each migration (e.g., a voluntary move such as the
move of a family to a larger apartment closer to a school, landless Easterners pulled
to homesteads in the Great Plains, or an involuntary move such as Africans being
transported to North and South America or refugees from the potato famine fleeing
starvation in Ireland)

Write a diary entry or short play describing the reasons why an individual or family would be involved in a voluntary or involuntary migration (e.g., a family deciding to leave Europe to settle in the United States in the 1890s, a man in China deciding to go to the United States to work in railroad construction in the 1860s, or a
Turk deciding to go to Germany to seek employment in the 1980s)

Write an account and draw a sketch map to suggest ways in which physical geography affects the routes, flows, and destinations of migrations (e.g., rivers channeling
migrating people along valleys, mountains acting as barriers, mountain passes acting
as funnels, long distances impeding the flow of information about destinations)

Human Systems

▶ THE CHARACTERISTICS, DISTRIBUTION, AND
COMPLEXITY OF EARTH'S CULTURAL MOSAICS

· ·

By the end of the fourth grade, the student knows and understands:

1. **How the characteristics of culture affect the ways in which people live**

2. **How patterns of culture vary across Earth's surface**

3. **How cultures change**

Therefore, the student is able to:

A. **Identify and compare the cultural characteristics of different regions and people, as exemplified by being able to**

Identify the components of culture (e.g., language, social organization, beliefs and customs, forms of shelter, economic activities, education systems) and write a brief description of the student's culture, including at least one statement about each component

Distinguish between the ways of life of different people living in the same region (e.g., the cultural differences between Native Americans and Europeans living along the eastern seaboard in the seventeenth century or among Sikhs, Hindus, and Muslims living in India today)

Use components of culture to compare how children live in different regions (e.g., similarities and differences in terms of environment and resources, technology, food, shelter, social organization, beliefs and customs, schooling, what girls and boys are allowed to do)

B. **Describe and compare patterns of culture across Earth, as exemplified by being able to**

Write an account, using thematic maps, briefly describing the world's culture regions (e.g., ethnic origin, language, religion, political systems, food preferences)

Prepare a visual display featuring graphs, maps, and pictures to compare the ways in which people earn a living or support themselves in different regions of the world (e.g., by subsistence farming versus wage-earning in Mexico or ranching in Central America versus ranching in the United States)

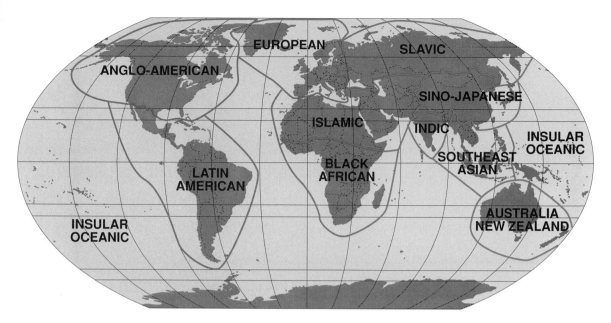

Cultural realms of the world. Culture is the sum of all learned patterns of behavior, institutions, values, and belief systems of the population. Each cultural realm has economic, political, religious, linguistic, and ethnic similarities that distinguish it from other cultural realms. SOURCE: BELL & HOWELL COMPANY

Understand how cultures differ in their use of similar environments and resources by comparing one culture with another (e.g., compare how people live in Phoenix, Arizona, with how people live in Riyadh, Saudi Arabia)

c. Describe changes in culture, as exemplified by being able to

Use interviews with parents and grandparents to understand cultural change (e.g., how the role of women in society has changed and how that has affected life in the United States and other regions of the world; how radio and then television changed leisure activities in the United States)

Use a variety of instructional materials to describe the current and former types of work done by women in developed and developing countries and then suggest reasons for any changes (e.g., changes in the role of women in providing food in sub-Saharan Africa and in the United States)

Use historical data, primary and secondary documents, illustrations, and other sources of information to describe changes in a cultural characteristic (e.g., the role of children in society, clothing styles, modes of transportation, food preferences, types of housing, attitudes toward the environment and resources)

Human Systems

▶ THE PATTERNS AND NETWORKS OF ECONOMIC
INTERDEPENDENCE ON EARTH'S SURFACE

· ·

By the end of the fourth grade, the student knows and understands:

1. **The location and spatial distribution of economic activities**

2. **The factors that influence the location and spatial distribution of economic activities**

3. **The transportation and communication networks used in daily life**

Therefore, the student is able to:

A. **Explain how people in different parts of the world earn their living, as exemplified by being able to**

Describe and compare the ways in which people satisfy their basic needs and wants through the production of goods and services in different regions of the world (e.g., growing food versus shopping for food in a developing and developed society and economic activities in a rural region versus those of an urban region in the same U. S. state)

Use a map to show economic links between regions and write a general account of how trade affects the way people earn their living in each region (e.g., the flow of fuels from Southwest Asia to industrialized, energy-poor regions of the world; the flow of electronic goods from Pacific rim nations to the United States)

Describe how people in different places earn a living, by creating a map to show the places producing food, clothing, and household items and the places of origin for the raw materials used to make those goods

B. **Locate and classify economic activities, as exemplified by being able to**

Classify land in a community by types of economic activity and prepare a map showing the different uses (e.g., industrial, recreational, commercial, residential)

Use maps to understand the patterns of economic activity in an urban area and suggest reasons for the patterns (e.g., central business districts, industrial areas, shopping malls, places for entertainment and recreation, government service centers)

Locate economic activities that use natural resources in the local region, state, and nation (e.g., agriculture, mining, fishing, forestry) and describe the importance of the activities to these areas

c. **Identify factors important in the location of economic activities, as exemplified by being able to**

Use a phone book and map of the local community to locate clusters of related businesses or other economic activities and then suggest why they are located where they are (e.g., medical supply and uniform stores, laboratories, and doctors' offices near a hospital; warehouses and industries near major transportation routes; clusters of car dealerships on major highways; fast-food restaurants in highly accessible locations close to population concentrations)

Prepare a list of consumer products (e.g., soft drinks, bread, compact discs, baseball bats), identify the raw materials and manufacturing and processing needed to produce each one, and decide whether the products are made close to the sources of their raw materials or close to the consumers who buy them

List agricultural products produced in the student's region, identify where they are processed, and map how they are distributed

d. **Identify the modes of transportation and communication used to move people, products, and ideas from place to place, as exemplified by being able to**

Compare the importance of automobile transportation in the United States, relative to other countries, by preparing graphs and maps that show the number of automobiles per capita in countries in different parts of the world

List and describe the advantages and disadvantages of different modes of transportation for specific products and purposes (e.g., barges and trains for bulky heavy items; airplanes for high-cost perishables; pipelines for liquids and gases; bicycles, light-rail systems, and cars for urban commuting)

Prepare a time line and maps showing how transportation and communication have changed and have affected trade and economic activities (e.g., regions can specialize economically; with improved roads and refrigerated trucking, more fresh fruits and vegetables are available out of season; regional, national, and global markets expand as transportation and communication systems improve)

Human Systems

▶ THE PROCESSES, PATTERNS, AND FUNCTIONS OF
HUMAN SETTLEMENT

. . . .

By the end of the fourth grade, the student knows and understands:

1. **The types and spatial patterns of settlement**

2. **The factors that affect where people settle**

3. **How spatial patterns of human settlement change**

4. **The spatial characteristics of cities**

Therefore, the student is able to:

A. **Describe the types of settlement and patterns of land use in the United States and world regions, as exemplified by being able to**

Prepare written comparisons of past and present types of settlements in the United States and other countries (e.g., describe the sequence of settlement formation and growth from a hamlet to a village, town, and city)

Compare housing and land use in urban and suburban areas, noting similarities and differences (e.g., where people live, where services are provided, where products are made, types of housing, yard size, population density, transportation facilities, presence of infrastructure elements such as sidewalks and streetlights)

Read narratives and poems about a type of community unlike that of the student (e.g., an urban community if the student lives in a rural area) and then summarize the similarities and differences in a chart

B. **Locate clusters of settlement and suggest the reasons for their distribution, as exemplified by being able to**

Use maps to identify clusters of dense settlement and relate them to reasons for settlement (e.g., fertile soil, good transportation, and availability of water in the Ganges River Valley and the availability of coal, iron, and other natural resources and river transportation in the Ruhr)

Read accounts by past and present settlers in different regions of the United States to explain why people have chosen to settle and live in those places (e.g., job opportunities, available land, climate)

Compare two or more regions to suggest probable reasons for similarities and differences in population size and density (e.g., length of settlement, environment and resources, cultural traditions, historic events, accessibility)

C. **Explain patterns of settlement at different periods, as exemplified by being able to**

Analyze the similarities and differences among the world's culture hearths (culture groups' places of origin) and suggest why humans settled in those places and why these settlements persist today (e.g., as centers of innovation and cultural, social, economic, and political development that attract people from other places)

Describe the settlement patterns that characterize the development of the student's local community or state (e.g., from the movement of people into an area previously unoccupied, to the spread of settlements to fill the area, to hamlet and village formation, to competition among villages for economic dominance and growth; from a small number of dispersed settlers with few services to concentrations of settlers in a village, town, or city with many more services and then to the modern pattern of suburbanization and decentralization)

Trace the reasons for the growth and decline of settlements (e.g., boomtowns to ghost towns in mining areas; the rise or decline of towns linked or not linked by highways or railroads; the history of company or single-industry towns in periods of prosperity or recession)

D. **Describe the characteristics and locations of cities, as exemplified by being able to**

Use maps and other graphics to locate major cities in North America and explain the processes that have caused them to grow (e.g., location along transportation routes, availability of resources that have attracted settlers and economic activities, continued access to other cities and resources)

Describe changes in cities in the United States over time using maps, pictures, statistics, and personal recollections (e.g., the movement of industry from downtown to the edge of cities; suburban growth; changes in the shapes of urban areas)

Use telephone books from towns, small cities, and large cities to identify and describe the differences between settlements of different sizes (e.g., differences in the availability of goods and services, cultural and recreational opportunities, and specialized medical services)

Human Systems

▶ **HOW THE FORCES OF COOPERATION AND CONFLICT AMONG PEOPLE INFLUENCE THE DIVISION AND CONTROL OF EARTH'S SURFACE**

* *

By the end of the fourth grade, the student knows and understands:

1. **The types of territorial units**

2. **The extent and characteristics of political, social, and economic units at different scales (local to global)**

3. **How people divide Earth's surface**

4. **How cooperation and conflict affect places in the local community**

Therefore, the student is able to:

A. **Identify and describe types of territorial units, as exemplified by being able to**

Use layers of colored paper, transparencies, and other graphics to identify political units at different scales, local to global (e.g., precinct, census district, school attendance zone, township, metropolitan area, county, state, and nation)

Prepare a chart, diagram, or map that lists public services offered to citizens by government agencies and identifies the area served by each (e.g., the hierarchy of police protection from local station to county sheriff to state police department to national agency; the hierarchy of justice involving municipal courts, county courts, state courts, and federal district courts)

Prepare an atlas that shows a variety of territorial units (e.g., county maps of the state; state maps of the United States and Mexico; province maps of Canada; country maps of North and South America; world maps of regional trade groups, countries linked in cooperative relationships [e.g., the European Union])

B. **Describe the characteristics of political units at different scales, as exemplified by being able to**

East Germans first breached the Berlin Wall on November 9, 1989. Economically and culturally profound consequences followed the opening of the border between East and West Germany after nearly thirty years of separation.
ANTHONY SUAU / BLACK STAR

Describe the common characteristics of political regions (e.g., boundaries, laws, functions, degree of autonomy, jurisdictional span)

Prepare a chart that compares the size and population of ten large countries and ten small countries

Describe the functions of political units (e.g., law-making, law enforcement, provision of services, powers of taxation) and how they differ on the basis of scale (e.g., municipality, county, state, country)

C. Explain how and why people compete for control of Earth's surface , as exemplified by being able to

Identify a recent change in the political or economic system of a country (e.g., breakup of former Czechoslovakia, civil war in former Yugoslavia, end of apartheid in South Africa) and suggest reasons for the change (e.g., ethnic or national differences, competition for political control, economic inequalities)

Prepare a series of maps to illustrate how the United States expanded its territory to reach its current shape and size

Research, write, and illustrate a geographic history of a state that focuses on how the state got its present boundaries

D. Analyze current events as examples of cooperation, conflict, or both, as exemplified by being able to

Identify a local issue (in the student's community) that has been a point of conflict, analyze the situation, and find ways in which it illustrates the idea of cooperation and conflict

Use events in the local community or in communities in other regions to write stories about ways in which people solve problems by cooperating (e.g., working in groups to pick up trash along a road, participating in a neighborhood crime-watch group, or participating in community house-building projects)

Use current events to map incidents of cooperation and conflict between countries

Environment and Society

▶ HOW HUMAN ACTIONS MODIFY
THE PHYSICAL ENVIRONMENT

. . . .

By the end of the fourth grade, the student knows and understands:

1. **How people depend on the physical environment**

2. **How people modify the physical environment**

3. **That the physical environment can both accommodate and be endangered by human activities**

Therefore, the student is able to:

A. **Describe ways in which people depend on the physical environment, as exemplified by being able to**

Prepare an illustrated chart to show how the atmosphere, biosphere, lithosphere, and hydrosphere contribute to the student's daily life

Make a list of things that people need, want, and obtain from the physical environment (e.g., food, clean air, water, and mineral resources) and identify those obtained from the physical environment in the student's community, region, state, and from other countries

Write an account comparing how people in the local community and people elsewhere in the state depend on the physical environment

B. **Identify ways in which humans alter the physical environment, as exemplified by being able to**

List examples of changes in land use in the local community (e.g., changing from open land to farmland, from one type of farming to another, from farms to houses and stores, from factories and other industrial uses to abandonment)

Use maps and graphs to illustrate changes in the physical environment of the local community or region brought about by processes such as urban growth, the development of transportation and agriculture, and the introduction of new species of plants and animals

Terraced rice fields on mountain slopes in Bali, Indonesia. GILBERT M. GROSVENOR

Prepare an illustrated booklet that shows how and why people alter the physical environment (e.g., by creating irrigation projects, clearing the land to make room for houses and shopping centers, planting crops, building roads)

c. Assess the impact of human activities on the physical environment, as exemplified by being able to

Develop a chart that compares the plants and animals that used to be found in the local community with those now found there and suggest reasons for any changes (e.g., changes in climate, air pollution, water pollution, expanding human settlement)

Write an account that gives examples of how human activities have increased the ability of the physical environment to support human life in the local community, state, United States, and other countries (e.g., use of irrigation and dry-land farming techniques to improve crop yields, reforestation to prevent erosion, flood-control projects to make land habitable)

Identify examples in the local community of ways in which the physical environment is stressed by human activities

Environment and Society

▶ HOW PHYSICAL SYSTEMS AFFECT HUMAN SYSTEMS

. . . .

By the end of the fourth grade, the student knows and understands:

1. **How variations within the physical environment produce spatial patterns that affect human adaptation**

2. **The ways in which the physical environment provides opportunities for people**

3. **The ways in which the physical environment constrains human activities**

Therefore, the student is able to:

A. **Describe how humans adapt to variations in the physical environment, as exemplified by being able to**

List ways in which people adapt to the physical environment (e.g., choices of clothing, housing styles, agricultural practices, recreational activities, food, daily and seasonal patterns of life)

Describe and compare the traditional ways of life of different groups of Native Americans who lived in the student's community, region, or state to draw conclusions about how they adapted to the natural resources available (e.g., dependence of Plains people on bison, dependence of Iroquois on crops produced by fertile soil of the Great Lakes region, dependence on fishing of people in the Northeast and Pacific Northwest)

Use pictures of housing in the student's community, region, or in other parts of the United States at different periods of time to describe how the physical environment can influence the choice of building material and style of construction, and how people adapt building styles to the availability of building materials (e.g., sod houses in the Great Plains, dugouts in early Texas settlements, log cabins in wooded areas of the eastern United States)

B. **Identify opportunities that the physical environment provides for people, as exemplified by being able to**

Describe how the student's community benefits from the physical environment (e.g., people make their living by farming on fertile land, fishing in local water, or working in mines; the community is a port located on a natural harbor, a tourist center located in a scenic or historic area, or an industrial center with good access to natural resources)

Evaluate the effects of weather and climate (temperature range, distribution of rainfall, length of growing season, periods of storms, and hours of sunshine) on agricultural activities, types of housing, fuel consumption, and other activities in the student's community and state

Describe the characteristics of the community's physical environment that first attracted settlers, and the opportunities that the environment offers today to reach conclusions about how people's views of the environment can change with changes in technology and culture

c. Identify ways in which human activities are constrained by the physical environment, as exemplified by being able to

Describe how the physical environment constrains activities in the student's community, region, and state on a daily, seasonal, and permanent basis (e.g., the effects of weather and climate on agriculture, recreational activities, availability of water, expansion of settlement)

Describe the characteristics of climates in different regions of the world and how they affect the lives of people who live there (e.g., how people are affected by living in an area of permafrost, in an area that gets over 200 inches of rainfall a year, or in an area that gets almost no rain)

Explain how landforms can limit human activities (e.g., mountains, cliffs, and swamps impeding migration and transportation, subsurface rock being unsuitable as a building foundation, slopes being too steep for agriculture or settlement)

d. Describe and locate natural hazards in the physical environment, as exemplified by being able to

Define and give examples of natural hazards (e.g., floods, wind storms, tornadoes, or earthquakes) that occur in the student's community, region, and state

Compare the natural hazards that occur in the student's physical environment with those that occur in similar environments elsewhere in terms of their location, magnitude, frequency, and effect on people

Collect data on the occurrence of natural hazards in the student's state and elsewhere in the United States over a period to create a map entitled: Location of Types of Natural Hazards in the State/Nation from Month to Month

Environment and Society

▶ **THE CHANGES THAT OCCUR IN THE MEANING, USE, DISTRIBUTION, AND IMPORTANCE OF RESOURCES**

By the end of the fourth grade, the student knows and understands:

1. **The characteristics of renewable, nonrenewable, and flow resources**

2. **The spatial distribution of resources**

3. **The role of resources in daily life**

Therefore, the student is able to:

A. **Locate and differentiate between renewable, nonrenewable, and flow resources, as exemplified by being able to**

Put symbols on a base map to identify the locations of sources of nonrenewable resources (e.g., fossil fuels, minerals) and explain how each resource is used

Design and conduct a survey of students, family, and other members of the community to measure resource use in the school, home, and community on a typical day and classify the resources as renewable (e.g., timber), nonrenewable (e.g., petroleum), or flow (e.g., running water or wind)

Write a script for a documentary aimed at other students that explains the characteristics of different types of resources and where the resources come from

B. **Explain the relationships between the locations of resources and patterns of population distribution, as exemplified by being able to**

Describe the relationships between economic activities and resources by using maps to identify major industrial districts and the sources of iron ore, coal, and other natural resources

Describe, by using maps, major transportation routes that link resources with consumers and identify the transportation modes used (e.g., ship, pipeline, barge, or railroad)

Use historical case studies to explain how settlement patterns are influenced by the discovery and use of resources (e.g., Colorado mining towns as centers of settlement in the late nineteenth century or the growth of industry and cities along the fall line of the Appalachians starting in the eighteenth century)

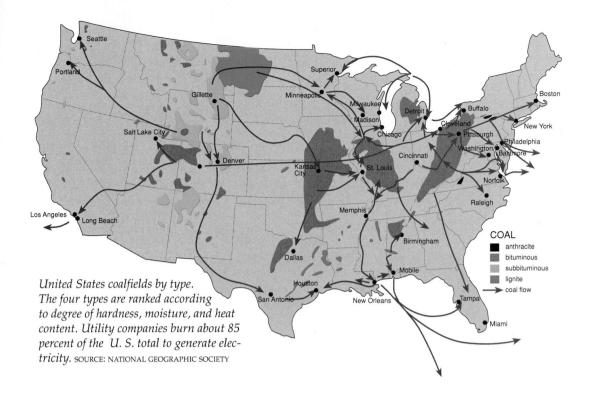

United States coalfields by type.
The four types are ranked according
to degree of hardness, moisture, and heat
content. Utility companies burn about 85
percent of the U. S. total to generate electricity. SOURCE: NATIONAL GEOGRAPHIC SOCIETY

COAL
- anthracite
- bituminous
- subbituminous
- lignite
- → coal flow

C. **Describe the meaning and role of resources in the student's daily life, as exemplified by being able to**

Describe how and where electricity is generated for the local community, using a sketch map to show the sources of the raw materials

Identify on a base map the source locations of resources for the manufacture of items commonly used in the local community (e.g., automobiles, medicines, clothing, and food)

Write a short account comparing the resources for other regions of the world with resources used in the student's region, with emphasis on differences in the ways in which resources are used and valued (e.g., use of wood in the United States for construction compared to use of wood in the Dominican Republic for fuel)

D. **Identify and evaluate critical present-day issues related to the use of resources, as exemplified by being able to**

List the advantages and disadvantages of recycling and reusing different types of materials

Write a play or poem that focuses on ways to conserve natural resources

Develop a plan to conserve a local resource, such as water or wildlife (e.g., that of a power-boat owner or a fisherman; that of a hunter or a wildlife photographer)

The Uses of Geography

▶ HOW TO APPLY GEOGRAPHY TO
INTERPRET THE PAST

. . . .

By the end of the fourth grade, the student knows and understands:

1. **How places and geographic contexts change over time**

2. **That people's perceptions of places and geographic contexts change over time**

3. **That geographic contexts influence people and events over time**

Therefore, the student is able to:

A. **Describe how the physical and human characteristics of places change over time, as exemplified by being able to**

Arrange in chronological order pictures of types of houses built in the student's region and explain why the size and style of such homes have changed over time (e.g., migration patterns, demographic changes, economic conditions)

Use graphs of major employment categories to trace changes that have occurred in how people have earned a living in the student's state (e.g., industry, farming, fishing, retail trade, government)

Prepare a time line illustrating changes in the vegetation and animal population in a region (e.g., trace successive changes in vegetation caused by human occupance and agriculture in a region)

B. **Show how the student's community has changed, as exemplified by being able to**

Use maps, illustrations, and aerial photographs from different time periods to identify and describe factors that have contributed to changing land use in the community (e.g., street and road development, population shifts, regulations governing land use)

Use primary and secondary documents to identify groups of people who have affected the growth, development, culture, and patterns of land use of the community

Interview older community members as a basis for writing a "this is how it was" story of the community and illustrate the story with maps and pictures

C. **Describe ways in which changes in people's perceptions of environments have influenced human migration and settlement, as exemplified by being able to**

Explain how the discovery or depletion of a resource or technology may influence human perceptions of environments and migration patterns (e.g., the history of oil in different United States regions such as Pennsylvania, Louisiana, and Texas or changes in attitude toward the Great American Desert)

Use primary and secondary documents to trace how people's perception of an environment has changed with length of settlement and familiarity with the area

Read stories about children living in the past, describe their attitudes toward the physical environment, and compare those attitudes with the attitudes of children today

D. **Describe the geographic context that has influenced people and events in the past, as exemplified by being able to**

Use maps and narratives to trace historic events in a spatial context (e.g., read accounts of Paul Revere's ride and follow the route at an appropriate scale, or locate the site of a major Civil War battle and describe the influence of the site on the course of the conflict)

Use maps to compare trade routes with wind patterns and ocean currents, and suggest how they were related in previous centuries (e.g., the trade routes followed by early European colonists were linked to the trade winds; Muslim trading vessels used monsoon winds to cross the Indian Ocean in the eighth century)

Prepare visual materials (maps, charts, graphs) and written descriptions of the physical and human characteristics of places that answer the question, What was it like to live in place X in time Y? (e.g., prepare maps showing settlements and transportation routes of the student's state at the turn of the twentieth century)

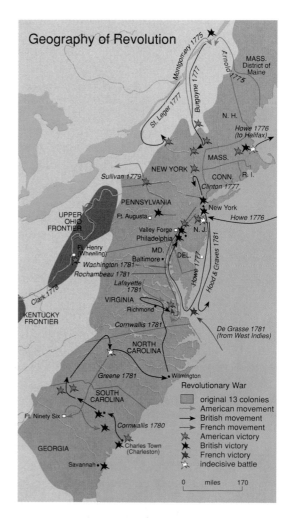

After the 1775 failed British offensive in Massachusetts and disastrous American forays into Canada, the Revolutionary War shifted to the mid-Atlantic region. By 1778 George Washington acknowledged a standoff. By the end of 1778 Lord Cornwallis faced guerrilla war and mounting casualties. His surrender at Yorktown ended Britain's southern strategy and effectively ended the war.
© NATIONAL GEOGRAPHIC SOCIETY

The Uses of Geography

▶ HOW TO APPLY GEOGRAPHY TO INTERPRET
THE PRESENT AND PLAN FOR THE FUTURE

. . . .

By the end of the fourth grade, the student knows and understands:

1. **The dynamic character of geographic contexts**

2. **How people's perceptions affect their interpretation of the world**

3. **The spatial dimensions of social and environmental problems**

Therefore, the student is able to:

A. **Identify ways in which geographic conditions change, as exemplified by being able to**

Describe the relationship between population growth and resource use by interpreting a graph containing information on both topics

Draw cartoon strips or make storybooks to illustrate ways in which resources can be managed and to explain why it is important to do so (e.g., soil conservation practices can preserve agricultural productivity for future generations, and recycling nonrenewable resources helps provide resources for future generations)

Prepare a time line and visual display to show the projected increases in world population

B. **Describe how differences in perception affect people's views of the world, as exemplified by being able to**

Use a data-retrieval chart to organize information on how different groups of people perceive the same place, environment, or event (e.g., examine a variety of maps with different perspectives to understand different images of the world)

Compare the lives of children in different societies of the world in terms of their attitudes and feelings about personal life, education, aspirations, and the differences between girls and boys

Develop a defensible answer to the following questions: Is there a global environmental crisis? If so, what caused it?

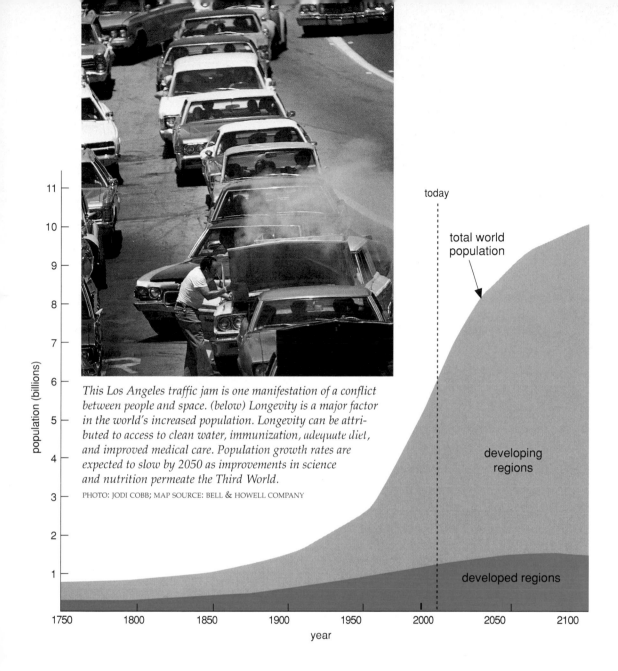

This Los Angeles traffic jam is one manifestation of a conflict between people and space. (below) Longevity is a major factor in the world's increased population. Longevity can be attributed to access to clean water, immunization, adequate diet, and improved medical care. Population growth rates are expected to slow by 2050 as improvements in science and nutrition permeate the Third World.

PHOTO: JODI COBB; MAP SOURCE: BELL & HOWELL COMPANY

C. **Make informed decisions regarding nature–society issues, as exemplified by being able to**

Describe some human-induced changes that are taking place in different parts of the United States and speculate on their future impacts (e.g., development and conservation issues in terms of the wetland of coastal New Jersey)

Propose and discuss alternative solutions to an environmental problem and the likely consequences of each solution, and then decide on the best solution (e.g., the best way to recycle plastic milk cartons in the local community)

Analyze the spatial aspects of a social problem by mapping it (e.g., look at the distribution of family income in an urban area and draw conclusions about unemployment rates in the area)

CHAPTER 6

National Geography Standards

Grades 5–8

Belize rain forest. NASA/JPL

The World in Spatial Terms

▶ HOW TO USE MAPS AND OTHER GEOGRAPHIC
REPRESENTATIONS, TOOLS, AND TECHNOLOGIES
TO ACQUIRE, PROCESS, AND REPORT INFORM-
ATION FROM A SPATIAL PERSPECTIVE

. . . .

By the end of the eighth grade, the student knows and understands:

1. **The characteristics, functions, and applications of maps, globes, aerial
   and other photographs, satellite-produced images, and models**

2. **How to make and use maps, globes, graphs, charts, models, and databases
   to analyze spatial distributions and patterns**

3. **The relative advantages and disadvantages of using maps, globes,
   aerial and other photographs, satellite-produced images, and models
   to solve geographic problems**

Therefore, the student is able to:

A. **Describe the essential characteristics and functions of maps and
   geographic representations, tools, and technologies, as exemplified
   by being able to**

   Describe the purposes and distinguishing characteristics of selected map
   projections and globes, aerial photographs, and satellite-produced images

   Explain map essentials (e.g., scale, directional indicators, symbols)

   Explain the characteristics and purposes of geographic databases (e.g., databases
   containing census data, land-use data, topographic information)

B. **Develop and use different kinds of maps, globes, graphs, charts,
   databases, and models, as exemplified by being able to**

   Use data and a variety of symbols and colors to create thematic maps and graphs
   of various aspects of the student's local community, state, country, and the world
   (e.g., patterns of population, disease, economic features, rainfall, vegetation)

   Use data to develop maps and flowcharts showing major patterns of movement of
   people and commodities (e.g., international trade in petroleum, wheat, cacao)

Construct a model depicting Earth–Sun relationships and use it to explain such concepts as Earth's axis, seasons, rotation, revolution, and principal lines of latitude and longitude

C. **Evaluate the relative merits of maps and other geographic representations, tools, and technologies in terms of their value in solving geographic problems, as exemplified by being able to**

Choose the most appropriate maps and graphics in an atlas to answer specific questions about geographic issues (e.g., topography and transportation routes)

Evaluate the advantages and disadvantages of using a map or a cartogram to illustrate a data set (e.g., data on population distribution, language-use patterns, energy consumption at different times of year)

Evaluate the merits of using specific map projections for specific purposes (e.g., use of the Mercator projection for navigation and the Robinson projection for depicting areal distributions)

D. **Use geographic tools and technologies to pose and answer questions about spatial distributions and patterns on Earth, as exemplified by being able to**

Develop criteria to draw regional service boundaries on maps (e.g., assign students to schools in a rapidly growing suburban area)

Use maps to understand patterns of movement in space and time (e.g., mapping hurricane tracks over several seasons; mapping the spread of influenza throughout the world)

Use maps to make and justify decisions about the best location for facilities (e.g., a place to build a restaurant, locate a recycling center, or select and develop a factory site)

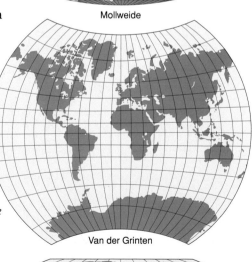

Mollweide

Van der Grinten

Robinson

Projections that have been used to depict a round Earth on flat paper. The Mollweide, developed in 1805, accurately represents relative size of landmasses but distorts their shape; the Van der Grinten, 1922, represents shapes of landmasses more accurately but distorts their relative size; and the Robinson, 1988, is a compromise in representing both shape and size.

SOURCE: AMERICAN CARTOGRAPHIC ASSOCIATION

The World in Spatial Terms

▶ HOW TO USE MENTAL MAPS TO ORGANIZE
INFORMATION ABOUT PEOPLE, PLACES, AND
ENVIRONMENTS IN A SPATIAL CONTEXT

· ·

By the end of the eighth grade, the student knows and understands:

1. **The distribution of major physical and human features at different scales (local to global)**

2. **How to translate mental maps into appropriate graphics to display geographic information and answer geographic questions**

3. **How perception influences people's mental maps and attitudes about places**

Therefore, the student is able to:

A. **Identify the locations of certain physical and human features and events on maps and globes and answer related geographic questions, as exemplified by being able to**

Identify the locations of culture hearths (e.g., Mesopotamia, Huang Ho, the Yucatán Peninsula, the Nile Valley)

Identify the largest urban areas in the United States now and in the past

Mark major ocean currents, wind patterns, landforms, and climate regions on a map

B. **Use mental maps to answer geographic questions, as exemplified by being able to**

Describe how current events relate to their physical and human geographic contexts

Draw sketch maps of different regions and compare them with atlas maps to determine the accuracy of place location and knowledge (e.g., political maps of Canada, the United States, and Europe)

Use mental maps of place location to list the countries through which a person would travel between two points (e.g., Paris to Moscow, Cairo to Nairobi, Rio de Janeiro to Lima)

C. Draw sketch maps from memory and analyze them, as exemplified by being able to

Translate a mental map into sketch form to illustrate relative location of, size of, and distances between places (e.g., major urban centers in the United States)

Prepare a sketch map of the student's local community to demonstrate knowledge of the transportation infrastructure that links the community with other places (e.g., approximate locations of major highways, rivers, airports, railroads)

Draw a world map from memory and explain why some countries are included (and others not), why some countries are too large (and others too small)

D. Analyze ways in which people's mental maps reflect an individual's attitudes toward places, as exemplified by being able to

Identify and compare the different criteria that people use for rating places (e.g., environmental amenities, economic opportunity, crime rate)

Analyze sketch maps produced by different people on the basis of their mental maps and draw inferences about the factors (e.g., culture, education, age, sex, occupation, experience) that influence those people's perceptions of places

Compare passages from fiction to reach conclusions about the human perception of places (e.g., Las Vegas as exciting, Paris as romantic, Calcutta as densely settled)

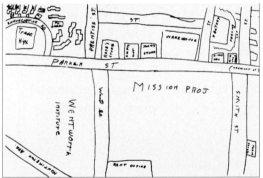

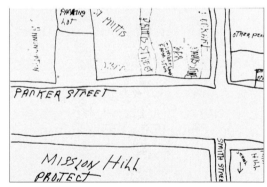

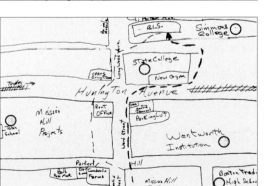

Three African-American students drew mental maps of their neighborhood in Boston: one (top left) knows only that the Mission Hill project is where white children live; he has never gone near it. The second (top right) has reduced the size of the project but increased the width of Parker Street, the division between the black and white neighborhoods. Both attend neighborhood schools; the third attends the well-known Boston Latin School. He has reduced the scale of the project but located five educational institutions, indicating the importance of education for him. SOURCE: MENTAL MAPS

The World in Spatial Terms

▶ HOW TO ANALYZE THE SPATIAL
ORGANIZATION OF PEOPLE, PLACES, AND
ENVIRONMENTS ON EARTH'S SURFACE

· ·

By the end of the eighth grade, the student knows and understands:

1. **How to use the elements of space to describe spatial patterns**

2. **How to use spatial concepts to explain spatial structure**

3. **How spatial processes shape patterns of spatial organization**

4. **How to model spatial organization**

Therefore, the student is able to:

A. **Analyze and explain distributions of physical and human phenomena with respect to spatial patterns, arrangements, and associations, as exemplified by being able to**

Analyze distribution maps to discover phenomena (e.g., resources, terrain, climate, water, cultural hearths) that are related to the distribution of people

Use dot distribution maps to determine the patterns of agricultural production (e.g., wheat, hogs, potatoes, soybeans) in the United States and the world and relate these patterns to such physical phenomena as climate, topography, and soil

Analyze the distribution of urban places to determine how they are linked together, with particular emphasis on links between places of different sizes (e.g., commuter flows between central cities, surrounding suburbs, and small towns)

B. **Analyze and explain patterns of land use in urban, suburban, and rural areas using terms such as distance, accessibility, and connections, as exemplified by being able to**

Map urban land use and compare dominant land-use patterns (e.g., finance versus retail, light industry versus residential) in city centers and peripheral areas

Use telephone books and maps to identify and compare land uses that are frequently near each other and others that are frequently far apart (e.g., hotels and restaurants, schools or churches and bars)

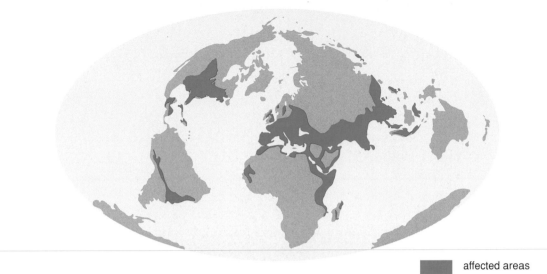

affected areas

Cholera was a major affliction throughout the world in the nineteenth century (this map shows the affected areas from 1865–1875). SOURCE: AMERICAN GEOGRAPHICAL SOCIETY

Describe and analyze the spatial arrangement of urban land-use patterns (e.g., commercial, residential, industrial) in the student's local community or in a nearby community

C. **Explain the different ways in which places are connected and how these connections demonstrate interdependence and accessibility, as exemplified by being able to**

Compile a table summarizing links between places and draw conclusions regarding distance, accessibility, and frequency of interaction (e.g., where classmates were born and now live, where sports teams travel to play)

Develop time lines, maps, and graphs to determine how changing transportation and communication technology has affected relationships between places

Develop a list of places in the world that Americans depend on for imported resources and manufactured goods (e.g., petroleum from Southwest Asia, copper from South America, diamonds from South Africa) and explain such dependence

D. **Describe the patterns and processes of migration and diffusion, as exemplified by being able to**

Trace the spread of language, religion, and customs from one culture to another (e.g., Chinese restaurants to San Francisco, the German language to the Midwest in the nineteenth century, Islam to New York City in the twentieth century)

Diagram the spatial spread of a contagious disease through a population (e.g., the spread of cholera in England in the mid-nineteenth century, AIDS in Asia in the 1990s)

Trace global migration patterns of plants and animals, as well as the diffusion of culture traits from points of origin to destination, and draw general conclusions about the speed and direction of such movements

Places and Regions

▶ **THE PHYSICAL AND HUMAN CHARACTERISTICS OF PLACES**

. . . .

By the end of the eighth grade, the student knows and understands:

1. **How different physical processes shape places**

2. **How different human groups alter places in distinctive ways**

3. **The role of technology in shaping the characteristics of places**

Therefore, the student is able to:

A. **Analyze the physical characteristics of places, as exemplified by being able to**

Use field observations, maps, and other tools to identify and compare the physical characteristics of places (e.g., soils, landforms, vegetation, wildlife, climate, natural hazards)

Develop and test hypotheses regarding ways in which the locations, building styles, and other characteristics of places are shaped by natural hazards such as earthquakes, floods, and hurricanes (e.g., building design and land use in Tokyo, Los Angeles, Manila)

Use maps, graphs, satellite-produced images, or tables to make inferences about the causes and effects of changes over time in physical landscapes (e.g., forest cover, water distribution, temperature fluctuations)

B. **Analyze the human characteristics of places, as exemplified by being able to**

Use field observation, maps, and other tools to identify and compare the human characteristics of places (e.g., cultural characteristics such as religion, language, politics, and the use of technology; population characteristics; land uses; levels of development)

Use photographs to develop and test hypotheses about similarities and differences in cultural landscapes (e.g., street scenes in Miami versus street scenes in Latin American cities)

Use maps, aerial photographs, and satellite-produced images to make inferences

Forest in Belize. Airborne sensors register data remotely, but researchers matching features on the ground with the radar image are essential. They supply facts against which the instruments are calibrated and by which the images are interpreted. By correlating ground data with digital data from such sensors, scientists work toward the creation of computer programs to interpret future images.

KENNETH GARRETT

about the causes and effects of change in a place over time (e.g., urban growth, the clearing of forests, development of transportation systems)

c. Identify and analyze how technology shapes the physical and human characteristics of places, as exemplified by being able to

Analyze the effects of different types of technology on places (e.g., the impact of railroads in the nineteenth century and satellite communications in the twentieth century on the northeastern corridor of the United States)

Assess how variations in technology and perspectives affect human modification of landscapes over time and from place to place (e.g., tree clearing in rain forests, damming of rivers and destruction of wildlife habitats, replacement of farmlands with wetlands)

Explain how isolated communities have been changed by technology (e.g., changes resulting from new highways or the introduction of satellite dishes and computers)

Places and Regions

▶ **THAT PEOPLE CREATE REGIONS TO
INTERPRET EARTH'S COMPLEXITY**

. . . .

By the end of the eighth grade, the student knows and understands:

1. **The elements and types of regions**

2. **How and why regions change**

3. **The connections among regions**

4. **The influences and effects of regional labels and images**

Therefore, the student is able to:

A. **Identify the criteria used to define a region, as exemplified by being able to**

Give examples of regions at different spatial scales (e.g., hemispheres; regions within continents, countries, and cities)

Suggest criteria that identify the central focus of a region (e.g., a town as the headquarters of a sales region, Atlanta as a trade center in the Southeast, Amsterdam as a transportation center)

Describe the relationships between the physical and human characteristics of a region (e.g., the Sunbelt's warm climate and popularity with retired people)

B. **Identify types of regions, as exemplified by being able to**

Suggest criteria for and examples of formal regions (e.g., school districts, circuit-court districts, states of the United States)

Suggest criteria for and examples of functional regions (e.g., the marketing area of the *Los Angeles Times* in southern California, the "fanshed" of a professional sports team)

Suggest criteria for and examples of perceptual regions (e.g., the Bible Belt in the United States, the Riviera in southern France, the Great American Desert)

C. **Explain how regions change over space and time, as exemplified by being able to**

Use maps and other graphics to show regional change from decade to decade and how such changes affect the characteristics of places (e.g., Pittsburgh in 1920 versus today and the Aral Sea region in Kazakhstan in the 1930s versus today)

Assess the impact of regional transportation changes on the daily lives of people (e.g., the building of new highways, the abandonment of railroad lines, the construction of a new airport)

Explain the factors that contribute to changing regional characteristics (e.g., economic development, accessibility, migration, media image)

D. Explain how regions are connected, as exemplified by being able to

Use maps to show the physical and human connections between regions (e.g., links between watersheds and river systems and regional connections through patterns of world trade)

Use cultural clues such as food preferences, language use, and customs to explain how migration creates cultural ties between regions (e.g., Spanish-language newspapers in major U. S. cities, specialized ethnic-food stores in cities)

Explain the importance of trade and other connections between regions in the United States and the world, using maps, tables, and graphs

E. Evaluate the influences and effects of regional labels and images, as exemplified by being able to

Explain the significance of a region being known as a developing region rather than a less developed region

Evaluate the meaning and impact of regional labels (e.g., Twin Peaks in San Francisco, Capitol Hill in Washington, D.C., the South, the rust belt)

Evaluate regional events that contribute to that region's image (e.g., crime in Miami, natural disasters in California, the destruction of the Berlin Wall)

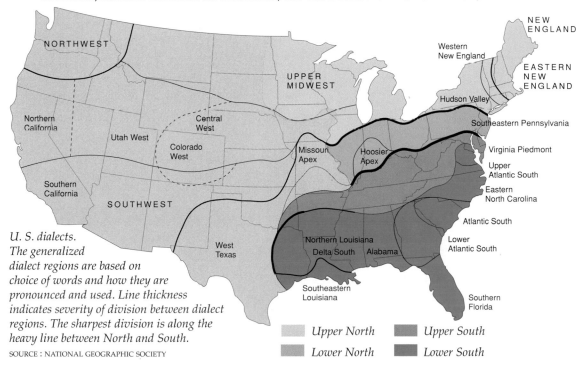

U. S. dialects. The generalized dialect regions are based on choice of words and how they are pronounced and used. Line thickness indicates severity of division between dialect regions. The sharpest division is along the heavy line between North and South.

SOURCE : NATIONAL GEOGRAPHIC SOCIETY

Places and Regions

▶ HOW CULTURE AND EXPERIENCE INFLUENCE
PEOPLE'S PERCEPTION OF PLACES AND REGIONS

. . . .

By the end of the eighth grade, the student knows and understands:

1. **How personal characteristics affect our perception of places and regions**

2. **How culture and technology affect perception of places and regions**

3. **How places and regions serve as cultural symbols**

Therefore, the student is able to:

A. **Evaluate the characteristics of places and regions from a variety of points of view, as exemplified by being able to**

Obtain information reflecting different points of view about the proposed use of a plot of land in the student's local community, and then analyze those views on the basis of what could be best for the community

Assess a place or region from the points of view of various types of people—a homeless person, a business person, a taxi driver, a police officer, or a tourist

Compare ways in which people of different cultural origins define, build, and name places and regions (e.g., street names in new subdivisions and names given to places or regions to symbolize an event or principle or to honor a person or cause)

B. **Explain how technology affects the ways in which culture groups perceive and use places and regions, as exemplified by being able to**

Explain the impact of technology (e.g., air-conditioning and irrigation) on the human use of arid lands

Trace the role of technology in changing culture groups' perceptions of their physical environments (e.g., the snowmobile's impact on the lives of Inuit people and the swamp buggy's impact on tourist travel in the Everglades)

Identify examples of advertising designed to influence cultural attitudes toward regions and places (e.g., the use of urban settings in music videos, use of mountain landscapes in automobile commercials)

C. **Identify ways culture influences people's perceptions of places and regions, as exemplified by being able to**

Irrigation (shown here, young banana trees in Cuba) is a technology that has enabled people to plant large quantities of income-producing crops and in the process to transform their environment. JOSÉ AZEL

Give examples of how, in different regions of the world, religion and other belief systems influence traditional attitudes toward land use (e.g., the effects of Islamic and Jewish dietary practices on land use in the Middle East)

Read stories about young people in other cultures to determine what they perceive as beautiful or valuable in their country's landscapes

Explain the enduring interest of immigrants in the United States in holding onto the customs of their home countries

D. Illustrate and explain how places and regions serve as cultural symbols, as exemplified by being able to

Compile a series of photographs from magazine advertisements or other sources that show buildings, structures, or statues that have come to represent or symbolize a city (e.g., Golden Gate Bridge in San Francisco; the Opera House in Sydney, Australia; the Gateway Arch in St. Louis; Tower Bridge in London)

Develop a map of the student's local community including local landmarks with a cultural identity, then extend that same process to the capital city of the state and to major cities in the region

List songs associated with specific regions and identify the kinds of images such songs suggest (e.g., "Waltzing Matilda" and Australia; "The Volga Boat Song" and Russia)

Physical Systems

▶ THE PHYSICAL PROCESSES THAT SHAPE THE
PATTERNS OF EARTH'S SURFACE

. . . .

By the end of the eighth grade, the student knows and understands:

1. **How physical processes shape patterns in the physical environment**

2. **How Earth–Sun relationships affect physical processes and patterns on Earth**

3. **How physical processes influence the formation and distribution of resources**

4. **How to predict the consequences of physical processes on Earth's surface**

Therefore, the student is able to:

A. **Use physical processes to explain patterns in the physical environment, as exemplified by being able to**

Explain how erosional agents such as water and ice produce distinctive landforms (e.g., water and badlands, ice and glacial valleys, waves and sea cliffs)

Account for the patterns of features associated with the margins of tectonic plates such as earthquake zones and volcanic activity (e.g., the Ring of Fire around the Pacific Ocean, the San Andreas Fault in coastal California)

Describe the ocean circulation system and the way it affects climate (e.g., North Atlantic Drift and the mild climate of Western Europe)

B. **Analyze physical patterns in terms of the processes that created them, as exemplified by being able to**

Construct and analyze climate graphs for selected places and suggest reasons for similarities and differences in climates

Compare regions of the world with similar physical features (e.g., desert regions in Nevada and western China, subarctic regions in Russia and Canada)

Use appropriate maps to generalize about the relationships between physical processes (e.g., the relationships between ocean currents, prevailing winds, and atmospheric pressure cells)

C. **Explain how Earth–Sun relationships affect Earth's physical processes and create physical patterns, as exemplified by being able to**

Setting off a chain of atmospheric and plate tectonic effects, Mount Pinatubo erupts, June 12, 1991. SHAWN HENRY

Use diagrams and maps to describe ways in which the Sun's position with respect to Earth affects the horizontal and vertical distribution of energy on Earth

Attribute occurrences of weather phenomena to annual changes in Earth–Sun relationships (e.g., hurricanes in the fall in subtropical areas, and tornadoes and floods in the spring and summer in mid-latitudes)

Explain the patterns of monsoon rainfall in terms of changing Earth–Sun relationships

D. Describe the processes that produce renewable and nonrenewable resources, as exemplified by being able to

Describe the processes that produce fossil fuels and relate the processes to specific locations (e.g., coal in the Appalachian Mountains and in Great Britain formed in tropical latitudes, and was later transported by plate tectonic movement to colder latitudes where coal does not form at present)

Predict the hydroelectric power potential of different regions given topographic maps and climate data (e.g., the hydroelectric potential of Sweden and Denmark; Washington State and Kansas)

Relate the patterns of world agriculture to the distribution of fertile soils and the physical processes that produce them (e.g., the cultivation of cotton on the rich alluvial soils of the Mississippi Delta)

E. Predict the consequences of a specific physical process operating on Earth's surface, as exemplified by being able to

Predict the effects of an extreme weather phenomenon on the physical environment (e.g., a hurricane's impact on a coastal ecosystem)

Infer the effect of heavy rainfall on hillslopes (e.g., after a forest fire, or after goats have overgrazed an area)

Predict the potential outcome of the continued movement of Earth's tectonic plates (e.g., continental drift, earthquakes, volcanic activity)

Physical Systems

▶ THE CHARACTERISTICS AND SPATIAL
DISTRIBUTION OF ECOSYSTEMS
ON EARTH'S SURFACE

· ·

By the end of the eighth grade, the student knows and understands:

1. **The local and global patterns of ecosystems**

2. **How ecosystems work**

3. **How physical processes produce changes in ecosystems**

4. **How human activities influence changes in ecosystems**

Therefore, the student is able to:

A. **Explain the distribution of ecosystems from local to global scales, as exemplified by being able to**

Describe ecosystems and the differences between them, using photographs and other media as illustrations (e.g., create collages showing flora and fauna, participate in making student videos of local ecosystems)

Explain how and why ecosystems differ from place to place as a consequence of differences in soils, climates, and human and natural disturbances

Identify changes in the local ecosystem resulting from human intervention (e.g., river wetlands being replaced by expanded farming activity on a floodplain)

B. **Explain the functions and dynamics of ecosystems, as exemplified by being able to**

Identify the flora and fauna of an ecosystem and tell how they are linked and interdependent

Explain the flow of energy and the cycling of matter through an ecosystem (e.g., the food chain or the hydrologic cycle)

Explain the feeding levels and location of elements in the food chain (e.g., carnivores eating herbivores)

C. **Explain how physical processes influence ecosystems, as exemplified by being able to**

Adapted to the harsh conditions of this Arctic ecosystem—poor soil, low temperatures, permafrost, and continuous sunlight—these low-growing flowers burst upon the tundra for as briefly as a six-week period during the Arctic summer. ENTHEOS

Explain how specific populations within ecosystems respond to environmental stress

Describe and explain the life cycle of a lake ecosystem, including the process of eutrophication

Explain ecosystems in terms of their characteristics and ability to withstand stress caused by physical events (e.g., a river system adjusting to the arrival of introduced plant species such as hydrilla; regrowth of a forest—with a modified set of flora and fauna—after a forest fire)

D. **Explain how human processes contribute to changes in ecosystems, as exemplified by being able to**

Identify changes over time in the ecosystem in or near the student's own community resulting from human intervention (e.g., natural wetlands on a floodplain being replaced by farms, farmlands on a floodplain being replaced by housing developments)

Predict the potential impact of human activities within a given ecosystem on the carbon, nitrogen, and oxygen cycles (e.g., the role of air pollution in atmospheric warming or the growing of peas and other legumes, which supply their own nitrogen and do not deplete the soil)

Explain ways that humans interact differently with ecosystems in different regions of the world (e.g., reasons for and characteristics of varied patterns of shifting cultivation in parts of Latin America, Africa, Southeast Asia)

Human Systems

▶ THE CHARACTERISTICS, DISTRIBUTION, AND MIGRATION OF HUMAN POPULATIONS ON EARTH'S SURFACE

. . . .

By the end of the eighth grade, the student knows and understands:

1. **The demographic structure of a population**

2. **The reasons for spatial variations in population distribution**

3. **The types and historical patterns of human migration**

4. **The effects of migration on the characteristics of places**

Therefore, the student is able to:

A. **Describe the structure of different populations through the use of key demographic concepts, as exemplified by being able to**

Describe differences in the rate of population growth in developing and developed countries, using such concepts as rates of natural increase, crude birth- and death rates, and infant mortality

Explain changes that occur in the structure (age and gender) of a population as it moves through the different stages of the demographic transition

Use population pyramids to depict the population structure of different societies (e.g., the youthful populations in Kenya and Mexico, the older populations in Germany and Sweden)

B. **Analyze the population characteristics of places to explain population patterns, as exemplified by being able to**

Create population pyramids for different countries and organize them into groups based on similarities of age characteristics

Demonstrate an understanding of demographic concepts (e.g., birthrate, death rate, population growth rate, doubling time, life expectancy, average family size) and explain how population characteristics differ from country to country

Use population statistics to create choropleth maps of different countries or regions and suggest reasons for the population patterns evident on the maps (e.g., population density in Madagascar, population growth rates in South Africa)

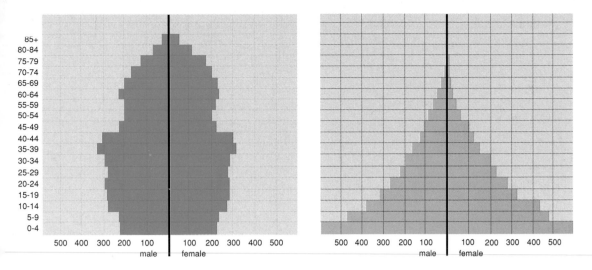

Population pyramids show the number of males and females (in thousands) in each age group. The graph on the left shows a slowly growing population; the graph on the right shows a rapidly growing population.

SOURCE: NATIONAL GEOGRAPHIC SOCIETY

c. **Explain migration streams over time, as exemplified by being able to**

Identify the causes and effects of migration streams (e.g., the movement of the Mongols across Asia and into Europe in the thirteenth century, Chinese workers to western North America in the second half of the nineteenth century)

Identify and explain how physical and other barriers can impede the flow of people and cite examples of ways in which people have overcome such barriers (e.g., the Berlin Wall, the Appalachian and Rocky Mountains, the closed border between North and South Korea)

Explain past and current patterns of rural–urban migration in the United States

D. **Describe ways in which human migration influences the character of a place, as exemplified by being able to**

Use maps and pictures from different periods to illustrate changes in a place due to migration (e.g., New Delhi before and after the partition of the Indian subcontinent in the 1940s and the massive realignment of the Hindu and Muslim populations; Boston before and after the large-scale influx of Irish immigrants in the mid-nineteenth century)

Explain how the movement of people can alter the character of a place (e.g., the impact of Indians settling in South Africa, Algerians settling in France, Vietnamese settling in the United States)

Identify the ways in which human migration patterns are currently evident in urban service industries in the United States (e.g., the prevalence of immigrants among the ranks of taxi drivers, tailors, music teachers, restaurant workers)

Human Systems

▶ THE CHARACTERISTICS, DISTRIBUTION, AND
COMPLEXITY OF EARTH'S CULTURAL MOSAICS

· ·

By the end of the eighth grade, the student knows and understands:

1. **The spatial distribution of culture at different scales (local to global)**

2. **How to read elements of the landscape as a mirror of culture**

3. **The processes of cultural diffusion**

Therefore, the student is able to:

A. **Identify ways in which communities reflect the cultural background of their inhabitants, as exemplified by being able to**

Describe visible cultural elements in the student's own local community or in another community (e.g., distinctive building styles, billboards in Spanish, foreign-language advertisements in newspapers)

Explain the presence of ethnic enclaves in cities resulting from voluntary or forced migration (e.g., Philippine workers in Kuwait, Portuguese in Boston, Sikhs in Vancouver)

Find evidence in the student's own community or another community of immigration from different regions of the world (e.g., use telephone directories to find lists of surnames, ethnic restaurants, stores, social clubs)

B. **Identify and describe the distinctive cultural landscapes associated with migrant populations, as exemplified by being able to**

Describe the landscape features and cultural patterns of Chinatowns in the Western world

Describe the landscape features and cultural patterns of the European enclaves in Japan and China in the nineteenth century

Explain the elements of landscape and culture that have been evident in the Little Italy sections of American cities from the beginning of the nineteenth century to the present

C. **Describe and explain the significance of patterns of cultural diffusion in the creation of Earth's varied cultural mosaics, as exemplified by being able to**

Belem, Brazil—known as "the gateway to the Amazon" because of its strategic location—brings fish, fruit, nuts, and other Amazon commodities to its people. After the morning arrival of fishing boats, shoppers converge on the Ver-o-Peso, Belem's most famous market. STEPHANIE MAZE

Research and make a presentation on the worldwide use of the automobile in the twentieth century, and suggest the cultural significance of this technology

Create a collage of pictures from at least four countries that illustrates a pattern of cultural diffusion (e.g., the use of terraced rice fields in China, Japan, Indonesia, and the Philippines; the use of satellite television dishes in the United States, England, Canada, and Saudi Arabia)

Create a series of maps of the global use of the English language in the sixteenth, the eighteenth, and the twentieth centuries and relate this diffusion to political and economic changes in the same time periods

Human Systems

▶ **THE PATTERNS AND NETWORKS OF ECONOMIC INTERDEPENDENCE ON EARTH'S SURFACE**

· ·

By the end of the eighth grade, the student knows and understands:

1. **Ways to classify economic activity**

2. **The basis for global interdependence**

3. **Reasons for the spatial patterns of economic activities**

4. **How changes in technology, transportation, and communication affect the location of economic activities**

Therefore, the student is able to:

A. **List and define the major terms used to describe economic activity in a geographic context, as exemplified by being able to**

Define and map three primary economic activities on a worldwide basis (e.g., coal mining, wheat growing, salmon fishing)

Define and map three secondary economic activities (e.g., the manufacture of steel and the worldwide resource movements vital to such production, the manufacture of shoes and the associated worldwide trade in raw materials)

Define tertiary economic activity and explain the ways it plays an essential role in settlements of almost every size (e.g., restaurants, theaters, and hotels; drugstores, hospitals, and doctors' offices)

B. **Explain the spatial aspects of systems designed to deliver goods and services, as exemplified by being able to**

Diagram the movement of a product (e.g., a pencil, automobile, or computer) from manufacture to use

Use data to list major United States imports and exports in a given year, map the locations of countries trading with the United States in those goods to identify trading patterns, and suggest reasons for those patterns

Given different interruptions in world trade (e.g., war, crop failures owing to weather and other factors, labor strikes), estimate the impact of such interruptions on people in various parts of the world

1962–1969

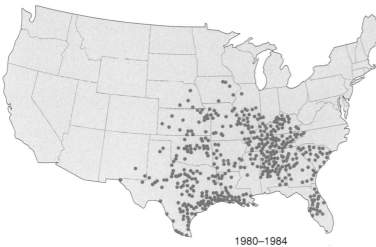

1980–1984

In thirty years Wal-Mart Stores, Inc. has become the largest retailer in the United States in terms of sales volume. Here, the stores opened in 1962–1969 are contrasted with those opened in 1980–1984. The spatial diffusion exemplifies a contagious pattern.

SOURCE: *THE PROFESSIONAL GEOGRAPHER* 46(1); 1994

C. Analyze and evaluate issues related to the spatial distribution of economic activities, as exemplified by being able to

Identify the locations of economic activities in the student's own community or another community and evaluate their impacts on surrounding areas

Describe the effects of the gradual disappearance of small-scale retail facilities (e.g., corner general stores, gas stations)

Analyze the economic and social impacts on a community when a large factory or other economic activity leaves and moves to another place (e.g., relocation of automobile manufacturing out of Michigan, textiles out of North Carolina, computer manufacturing into the Austin area in Texas)

D. Identify and explain the primary geographic causes for world trade, as exemplified by being able to

Apply the theory of comparative advantage to explain why and how countries trade (e.g., trade advantages associated with Hong Kong-made consumer goods, Chinese textiles, Jamaican sugar)

Identify and map international trade flows (e.g., coffee from Ethiopia and Colombia, bananas from Guatemala, automobiles from South Korea moving to Europe and North America)

Suggest reasons and consequences for countries that export mostly raw materials and import mostly fuels and manufactured goods

E. **Analyze historical and contemporary economic trade networks, as exemplified by being able to**

Map the triangular trade routes of the sixteenth and seventeenth centuries that linked North America, Africa, and Europe and explain how the trade influenced the history of those continents

Trace national and global patterns of migrant workers (e.g., the use of slaves, guest workers, seasonal migrant labor in the United States)

Use data to analyze economic relationships under imperialism (e.g., American colonies and England in the eighteenth and nineteenth centuries, Belgium and the Congo in the twentieth century)

F. **Identify and explain the factors influencing industrial location in the United States, as exemplified by being able to**

Map and explain the historical rise and persistence of the manufacturing belt in the United States

Discuss major industries in the United States from the perspective of how geography and the factors of production helped determine the locations of manufacturing plants (e.g., those producing steel, aircraft, automobiles, meat products, other food products)

Describe the changing spatial pattern of a major industry (e.g., steel production, furniture production)

G. **Compare and evaluate the roles of historical and contemporary systems of transportation and communication in the development of economic activities, as exemplified by being able to**

Compare the transportation and communications systems of the present to those of the past in terms of factors such as quality, efficiency, and speed

Make some general conclusions about how transportation and communications innovations affect patterns of economic interaction (e.g., the effect of refrigerated railroad cars, air-freight services, pipelines, telephone services, facsimile [fax] transmission services, satellite-based communications systems)

Compare the types of cargo handled by major world ports over time, and suggest reasons for the changes

GEOGRAPHY STANDARD **12** GRADES 5–8

Human Systems

▶ THE PROCESSES, PATTERNS, AND FUNCTIONS OF
HUMAN SETTLEMENT

. . . .

By the end of the eighth grade, the student knows and understands:

1. **The spatial patterns of settlement in different regions of the world**

2. **What human events led to the development of cities**

3. **The causes and consequences of urbanization**

4. **The internal spatial structure of urban settlements**

Therefore, the student is able to:

A. **Identify and describe settlement patterns, as exemplified by being able to**

List, define, and map major agricultural settlement types (e.g., plantation, subsistence farming, truck-farming communities)

List, define, and map major urban settlement types (e.g., port city, governmental center, planned city, single-industry city)

Conduct a survey of the student's class and get several student planning teams to design a city settlement pattern that incorporates most of the students' wishes for a new city

B. **Identify the factors involved in the development of cities, as exemplified by being able to**

Describe the kinds of settlements that existed before cities emerged (e.g., stopping places on the routes of hunters and gatherers, isolated farmsteads, villages)

Explain the geographic reasons for the location of the world's first cities (e.g., the effects of population density, transportation, food supply)

List and explain the reasons why people would choose to change from a dispersed rural to a concentrated urban form of settlement (e.g., the need for a marketplace, religious needs, or military protection)

C. **Analyze the ways in which both the landscape and society would change as a consequence of shifting from a dispersed to a concentrated settlement form, as exemplified by being able to**

Naples, Italy. This Senegalese laborer is one of the one million foreigners living in Italy, and one of 22 million in Western Europe. JOANNA B. PINNEO

Describe and explain the structural landscape changes that would occur if a village were to grow into a city (e.g., larger marketplace, city walls, grain-storage areas)

Explain the changes that would have to occur in farming patterns if a village were to grow into a city (e.g., the need for an agricultural surplus to provide for the urban population, the loss of some rural workers as people decided to move into the city)

Describe the development of early transport systems linking the city with the surrounding rural areas

D. Explain the causes and consequences of urbanization, as exemplified by being able to

Explain the links between industrial development and rural–urban migration (e.g., the movements of people into the mill towns of New England)

Describe the cultural activities (e.g., entertainment, religious facilities, higher education) that attract people to urban centers

Describe why people find urban centers to be economically attractive (e.g., business and entrepreneurial opportunities, access to information and other resources)

E. Identify and define the internal spatial structures of cities, as exemplified by being able to

Using the concentric zone model of a city, explain how a nearby city reflects that model (e.g., central city has the highest buildings, general decrease in density away from the center)

Using the sector model of a city, explain how a nearby city reflects that model (e.g., manufacturing areas in a sector, financial and professional services in a sector, and residential zones located away from those two sectors have distinctive neighborhoods)

Describe the impact of different transportation systems on the spatial arrangement of business, industry, and residences in a city

Human Systems

▶ **HOW THE FORCES OF COOPERATION AND CONFLICT AMONG PEOPLE INFLUENCE THE DIVISION AND CONTROL OF EARTH'S SURFACE**

· ·

By the end of the eighth grade, the student knows and understands:

1. **The multiple territorial divisions of the student's own world**

2. **How cooperation and conflict among people contribute to political divisions of Earth's surface**

3. **How cooperation and conflict among people contribute to economic and social divisions of Earth's surface**

Therefore, the student is able to:

A. **Identify and explain reasons for the different spatial divisions in which the student lives, as exemplified by being able to**

Identify different service, political, social, and economic divisions of the world in which the student functions (e.g., voting ward, township, county, state)

Explain the student's functional relationship to different spatial divisions (e.g., postal zone, school district, telephone area code)

Explain the need for multiple and overlapping spatial divisions in society

B. **Explain why people cooperate but also engage in conflict to control Earth's surface, as exemplified by being able to**

Explain the reasons for conflict over the use of land and propose strategies to shape a cooperative solution (e.g., try to resolve the controversies surrounding proposals to convert farmland to residential use, build entertainment facilities on national parkland, or set up a recycling center in a wealthy neighborhood)

Identify and explain the factors that contribute to conflict within and between countries (e.g., economic competition for scarce resources, boundary disputes, cultural differences, control of strategic locations)

Draw conclusions about how regional differences—or similarities—in religion, resources, language, political beliefs, or other factors may lead to cooperation or conflict

Michigan Meridian Survey

Toledo

FIRELANDS
1791

Cleveland

ELLIOT'S LINE

Twelve Mile
Reserve

North and East of
First Principal Meridian

CONNECTICUT WESTERN
RESERVE
1786 – 1800

FIRST PRINCIPAL MERIDIAN

Point of beginn
of the rectangu
system of surve
1785

South and East of
First Principal Meridian

Muskingham River Base

Ohio River Base

Geographer's Line

Robert's Line

Greenville Treaty Line 1795

Steubenville

Ludlow Line

U. S. MILITARY DISTRICT
1796

SEVEN
RANGES

Wheeling

Miami
River
Base

Between
the
Miamis

Zanesville

Columbus

Scioto
River
Base

Chillicothe

Marietta

DONATION
TRACT

Cincinnati

VIRGINIA
MILITARY
DISTRICT
1781

Scioto
River
Base

EAST
OF
THE
SCIOTO

OHIO
COMPANY
PURCHASE
1787

SYMMES
PURCHASE
1788

Portsmouth

Gallipolis

Congressional Land
Act of May, 1796

FRENCH
GRANTS

In Ohio, the first public domain state, a quarter of the land was reserved for Revolutionary War veterans; 5 percent went to land companies. Citizens of Connecticut cities razed during the Revolution settled the Firelands district. In much of Ohio, surveyors marked off five- and six-mile-square townships. Legislation based on land-division experiments in Ohio led to codification of the township-and-range system used today.

SOURCE: NATIONAL GEOGRAPHIC SOCIETY

C. **Describe the factors that affect the cohesiveness and integration of countries, as exemplified by being able to**

Given the shapes of different countries (e.g., Italy and Chile as elongated, Japan and Indonesia as a string of islands, and Egypt and Spain as roughly square), explain how that shape may affect political cohesiveness

Explain the symbolic importance of capital cities (e.g., Canberra, a planned city, as the capital of Australia, or The Hague as both a national capital of the Netherlands and a center for such global agencies as the World Court)

Explain factors that contribute to political conflict in specific countries (e.g., language and religion in Belgium, the religious differences between Hindus and Moslems in India, the ethnic differences in some African countries that have been independent for only a few decades)

D. **Analyze divisions on Earth's surface at different scales (local to global), as exemplified by being able to**

Compare different areas to identify examples of similar uses of political space at local, state, national, and international levels (e.g., counties and provinces in Canada and counties and states in the United States)

Compare organizations that transcend national boundaries to determine their social, political, and economic impact (e.g., transnational corporations, political alliances, economic groupings, world religions)

Using a particular continent, explain the role of various factors in the development of nation-states (e.g., competition for territory and resources, desire for self-rule, nationalism, history of domination by powerful countries)

Environment and Society

▶ HOW HUMAN ACTIONS MODIFY
THE PHYSICAL ENVIRONMENT

· ·

By the end of the eighth grade, the student knows and understands:

1. **The consequences of human modification of the physical environment**

2. **How human modifications of the physical environment in one place often lead to changes in other places**

3. **The role of technology in the human modification of the physical environment**

Therefore, the student is able to:

A. **Analyze the environmental consequences of humans changing the physical environment, as exemplified by being able to**

List and describe the environmental effects of human actions on the four basic components of Earth's physical systems: the atmosphere (e.g., effects of ozone depletion, climate change, changes in urban microclimates), the biosphere (e.g., the effects of deforestation, expansion of the savanna, reduction in biodiversity), the lithosphere (e.g., the effects of land degradation, soil salinization and acidification, gully erosion, weathering by polluted air and water), and the hydrosphere (e.g., the effects of ocean pollution, groundwater-quality decline)

Speculate on the environmental consequences of a major long-lasting energy crisis

Assess the environmental impact of plans to use natural wetlands for recreational and housing development in coastal areas (e.g., the Florida Everglades, South Padre Island of Texas, the low country of South Carolina)

B. **Identify and explain the ways in which human-induced changes in the physical environment in one place can cause changes in other places, as exemplified by being able to**

Explain how environmental changes made in one place affect other places (e.g., the effect of a factory's airborne emissions on air quality in communities located downwind and, because of acid rain, on ecosystems located downwind; effect of pesticides washed into river systems on water quality in communities located downstream)

Explain how the construction of dams and levees on river systems in one region affects places downstream (e.g., such construction limits the availability of water

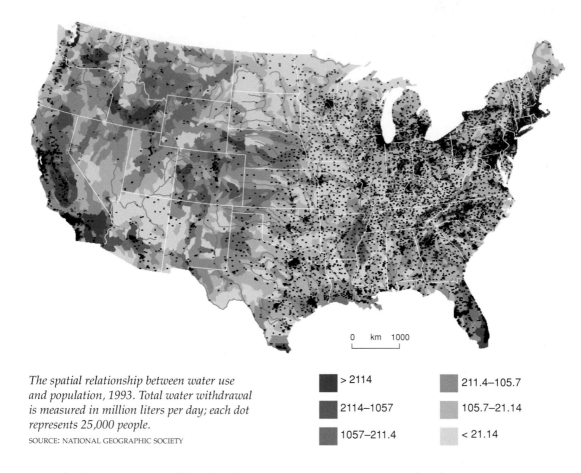

The spatial relationship between water use and population, 1993. Total water withdrawal is measured in million liters per day; each dot represents 25,000 people.
SOURCE: NATIONAL GEOGRAPHIC SOCIETY

■ > 2114	■ 211.4–105.7
■ 2114–1057	■ 105.7–21.14
■ 1057–211.4	■ < 21.14

for human use, enables electricity to be generated, controls flooding, improves river transportation, and leads to changes in ecosystems)

Develop maps, tables, or graphs to illustrate how environmental change in one part of the world can affect places in other parts of the world (e.g., industrial activity and acid rain in North America, the Chernobyl nuclear power plant accident and radioactive fallout in Europe and Asia)

C. **Evaluate the ways in which technology influences human capacity to modify the physical environment, as exemplified by being able to**

Analyze the environmental consequences of both the unintended and intended outcomes of major technological changes in human history (e.g., the effects of automobiles using fossil fuels, nuclear power plants creating the problem of nuclear-waste storage, and the use of steel-tipped plows or the expansion of the amount of land brought into agriculture)

Describe the role of technology in changing the physical environment of agricultural activities and list the environmental consequences of such actions (e.g., the effects of using chemical fertilizers and pesticides, using modern tilling equipment and techniques, and the hybridization of crops on biodiversity)

Identify, list, and evaluate the significance of major technological innovations that have been used to modify the physical environment, both in the past and in the present (e.g., the effects of the introduction of fire, steam power, diesel machinery, electricity, work animals, explosives)

Environment and Society

▶ HOW PHYSICAL SYSTEMS AFFECT HUMAN SYSTEMS

By the end of the eighth grade, the student knows and understands:

1. **Human responses to variations in physical systems**

2. **How the characteristics of different physical environments provide opportunities for or place constraints on human activities**

3. **How natural hazards affect human activities**

Therefore, the student is able to:

A. **Analyze ways in which human systems develop in response to conditions in the physical environment, as exemplified by being able to**

Collect visual and statistical data on patterns of land use, economic livelihoods, architectural styles of buildings, building materials, flows of traffic, recreational activities or other aspects of culture from the student's own community and from communities in other regions of the country to determine how the patterns reflect conditions of the physical environment

Compare agricultural production systems in different kinds of environmental regions (e.g., agricultural land use in areas with fertile soil and flat land in comparison to areas with less fertile soil and rough terrain)

Speculate on the effects of an undesirable change in the physical environment on human activities, and suggest how people might mitigate the problem in different cases (e.g., if the available supply of freshwater was cut in half by persistent drought, if an urban area was subjected to weeks of flooding, or if a heavily populated area was hit by a protracted series of earthquakes)

B. **Explain how the characteristics of different physical environments affect human activities, as exemplified by being able to**

Collect information on ways in which people adapt to living in different physical environments, and then write vignettes summarizing how the physical environment affects life in each region (e.g., how people in Siberia, Alaska, and other high-latitude places deal with the characteristics of tundra environments, such as frost heaves, spring snowmelt floods, freezing of public utilities, very short growing seasons, infertile soils, bogs that impede transportation)

Like ancient tombstones, pillars of limestone populate this barren desert known as the Pinnacles in Nambung National Park, Western Australia. Desert covers 29.6 percent of the Australian continent and is predominately uninhabited. OLIVER STREWE, WILDLIGHT PHOTO AGENCY

Give examples of ways people take aspects of the environment into account when deciding on locations for human activities (e.g., early American industrial development along streams and rivers at the fall line to take advantage of water-generated power)

Compare population distribution maps with environmental quality maps (resource distribution, rainfall, temperature, soil fertility, landform relief, and carrying capacity) and describe the associations between population density and environmental quality

c. **Describe the effects of natural hazards on human systems, as exemplified by being able to**

Despite the approximately 2.9 million square miles comprising Australia, most of the estimated 17.7 million inhabitants opt for the more fertile coast east of the Great Dividing Range. GEORGE HALL, WELDON TRANNIES

Describe the relationship between humans and natural hazards in different regions of the United States and the world (e.g., how the level of economic development and technology influences the effect of drought on populations in Ethiopia compared with populations in Australia or the southern part of the United States)

Rank natural hazards based on their severity of impact on humans (e.g., by length of event, total loss of life, total economic impact, social effects, long-term impacts, incidence of associated hazards)

Explain the ways humans prepare for natural hazards (e.g., earthquake preparedness, constructing houses on stilts in flood-prone areas, designation of hurricane shelters and evacuation routes in hurricane-prone areas)

GEOGRAPHY STANDARD 16 GRADES 5–8

Environment and Society

▶ **THE CHANGES THAT OCCUR IN THE MEANING, USE, DISTRIBUTION, AND IMPORTANCE OF RESOURCES**

. . . .

By the end of the eighth grade, the student knows and understands:

1. **The worldwide distribution and use of resources**

2. **Why people have different viewpoints regarding resource use**

3. **How technology affects the definitions of, access to, and use of resources**

4. **The fundamental role of energy resources in society**

Therefore, the student is able to:

A. **Describe and analyze world patterns of resource distribution and utilization, as exemplified by being able to**

Map and discuss the world patterns of such resources as petroleum, coal, copper, iron ore in terms of the locations of major deposits

Map and discuss the world patterns of such resources as diamonds, silver, gold, tungsten, and molybdenum in terms of the locations of major deposits

Develop a presentation, based on the use of research materials, on three major resource distribution patterns as they were in 1900 and in 1990 and explain the reasons for the differences between the two patterns

B. **Describe the consequences of the use of resources in the contemporary world, as exemplified by being able to**

Map the major present-day sources of key resources such as petroleum, anthracite and bituminous coal, diamonds, and copper and then trace the routes that link them to consuming countries (e.g., the movement of petroleum from the Persian Gulf to Japan and the Republic of Korea or of diamonds from South Africa to processing centers in Belgium, Israel, and New York City)

Discuss the relationship between a country's standard of living and its accessibility to resources (e.g., easy access to such resources as plentiful supplies of energy, foodstuffs, and materials from which consumer goods are manufactured usually means a higher standard of living and the opposite usually means a lower standard of living)

A San Diego family shows what the average American family of four now recycles in a year: 1,100 pounds of aluminum cans, glass containers, plastic bottles, steel cans, newspapers, and cardboard (left). The same average family also discards 5,300 pounds of trash (right). JOSÉ AZEL

Relate competition for resources to conflicts between regions and countries (e.g., the Japanese occupation of Manchuria in the 1930s, Iraqi invasion of Kuwait in 1991)

C. **Evaluate different viewpoints regarding resource use, as exemplified by being able to**

Assess the differing attitudes of people regarding the use and misuse of resources (e.g., attitudes toward electric cars, water-rationing, urban public transportation, use of fossil fuels)

Based on Environmental Protection Agency or other relevant standards, develop a list of examples of the misuse of resources and make recommendations for future use that are consistent with the standards (e.g., excessive timber-cutting in old-growth forests, buffalo in the western United States, soil conservation in semiarid areas)

Evaluate methods of extracting and using resources in terms of the impact on the environment (e.g., practicing sustainable forestry and agriculture, obtaining freshwater from icebergs, recycling urban waste)

D. **Identify the role of technology in resource acquisition and use, as exemplified by being able to**

Associate higher levels of resource extraction with advanced technology (e.g., the use of giant earth-moving machinery in strip-mining, and of advanced exploration techniques in the search for petroleum, bauxite)

Associate rates of resource consumption with levels of technological development (e.g., the high per capita use of energy in the developed societies of Europe and North America and the lower per capita use of energy in the developing countries of Africa and Latin America)

Explain the economic importance of satellite imagery technology in the search for petroleum (e.g., the ability to survey very large and inaccessible areas with preliminary exploration done in a laboratory)

E. **Identify and develop plans for the management and use of renewable, nonrenewable, and flow resources, as exemplified by being able to**

Create plans for the management of energy resources such as coal, petroleum, and natural gas

Speculate as to how long the world's known supply of fossil fuels might last, given varying rates of consumption and various estimates of the amounts of such resources left, and devise a plan for switching to alternative sources of energy when today's fossil fuels run out

Develop and implement a personal plan to conserve water and recycle materials and speculate as to how and why that plan might change within the next ten years

F. **Explain the critical importance of energy resources to the development of human societies, as exemplified by being able to**

Explain the importance of energy sources such as wood, charcoal, wind, and water to people settling new lands (e.g., settlers moving westward in the United States, eastward into Siberia)

Identify the ways in which coal, petroleum, natural gas, and nuclear power contribute to the functioning of societies (e.g., through providing power for transportation, manufacturing, the heating and cooling of buildings)

Explain how the development and widespread use of alternative energy sources, such as solar and thermal energy, might have an impact on societies (e.g., the impacts on air and water quality, on existing energy industries, on current manufacturing practices)

The Uses of Geography

▶ HOW TO APPLY GEOGRAPHY TO
INTERPRET THE PAST

· ·

By the end of the eighth grade, the student knows and understands:

1. **How the spatial organization of a society changes over time**

2. **How people's differing perceptions of places, peoples, and resources have affected events and conditions in the past**

3. **How geographic contexts have influenced events and conditions in the past**

Therefore, the student is able to:

A. **Describe the ways in which the spatial organization of society changes over time, as exemplified by being able to**

Trace the process of urban growth in the United States by mapping the locations of cities over time and noting differences in their site characteristics, situations, and functions

Trace changes in the internal structure, form, and function of urban areas in different regions of the world at different times

Describe and compare population settlement patterns during different periods and in different regions (e.g., medieval Europe versus modern Europe, the colonial South versus colonial North, southeast Australia versus southeastern China)

B. **Assess the roles that spatial and environmental perceptions played in past events, as exemplified by being able to**

Explain how the attitudes of people in the past affected settlement patterns in the United States (e.g., people's perceptions of Florida and continuing reappraisal of Alaska as a place to settle)

Use passages from literature and other texts (e.g., letters and newspapers) about nineteenth century America to understand the role of advertisements and promotional literature in the development of perceptions of the western United States

Explain how differing perceptions of local, regional, national, and global resources have stimulated competition for natural resources (e.g., the conflicts between Native Americans and colonists, between the Inuit and migrants to Alaska since 1950)

Green River, Wyoming. Union Pacific workers dress timbers shipped from the East. The Transcontinental Railroad was completed on May 10, 1869. OAKLAND MUSEUM

C. Analyze the effects of physical and human geographic factors on major historic events, as exemplified by being able to

Relate levels of technology and physical geographic features to the course and outcome of battles and wars (e.g., weather conditions at Valley Forge and the outcome of the American Revolution)

Trace the human and physical conditions that led to the enslavement and forced transport of Africans to North and South America (e.g., the need for cheap labor, the profitability of the triangle trade, the locations of prevailing wind and ocean currents)

Use maps to identify different land-survey systems used in the United States and assess the role they have played in establishing contemporary landscape patterns (e.g., compare the history and landscape of a metes and bounds state such as Georgia with a rectangular land-survey system state such as Iowa)

D. List and describe significant physical features that have influenced historical events, as exemplified by being able to

List, map, and discuss the locations of several mountain passes that have been significant in military campaigns in world history (e.g., the Khyber Pass, Burma Pass, Brenner Pass)

List, map, and discuss major water crossings that have been significant in U. S. history (e.g., the Delaware River near Trenton, New Jersey; the Tacoma Strait in Washington)

List, map, and discuss major water gaps, springs, and other hydrologic features that have been significant in settlement of the United States (e.g., the Delaware water gap, Cumberland Gap, Ogallala Aquifer, the artesian wells of the Great Plains)

The Uses of Geography

▶ HOW TO APPLY GEOGRAPHY TO INTERPRET
THE PRESENT AND PLAN FOR THE FUTURE

. . . .

By the end of the eighth grade, the student knows and understands:

1. **How the interaction of physical and human systems may shape present and future conditions on Earth**

2. **How varying points of view on geographic context influence plans for change**

3. **How to apply the geographic point of view to solve social and environmental problems by making geographically informed decisions**

Therefore, the student is able to:

A. **Analyze the interaction between physical and human systems to understand possible causes and effects of current conditions on Earth and to speculate on future conditions, as exemplified by being able to**

Compare life in a variety of cities in the developing world to assess the relationships involved in economic, political, social, and environmental changes

Prepare a series of graphs and maps on such factors as levels of infant mortality and rural poverty and the availability of hospitals and medical facilities and then describe differences in rural and urban access to health-care, water, and sanitation facilities

Evaluate the geographic impact of using petroleum, coal, nuclear power, and solar power as major energy sources in the twenty-first century

B. **Integrate multiple points of view to analyze and evaluate contemporary geographic issues, as exemplified by being able to**

Write a skit, play, or dialogue for two people with different points of view on the same geographic issue (e.g., a forester and a conservationist debating the use of a national forest or a man and a woman discussing gender-based divisions of labor in a developing nation)

Role play immigrants to describe how it feels to be in that situation, perceptions of the new nation, and how to adjust to life in an alien environment in order to appreciate the significance of people's beliefs, attitudes, and values in environmental adaptation

Do research on both the student's own point of view and other people's perceptions of a controversial social, economic, political, or environmental issue that has a geographic dimension (e.g., what to do about crime and juvenile delinquency, poverty, air pollution) and then write a report on that subject, which includes an informed judgment as to what solution should be implemented

c. **Demonstrate an understanding of the spatial organization of human activities and physical systems and be able to make informed decisions, as exemplified by being able to**

Describe what the future spatial organization of Earth might be: if present conditions and patterns of consumption, production, and population growth continue; if humans continue their present consumption patterns but engage in extensive recycling and research on new mining technologies; if the student's own preferences or predictions could be implemented

Analyze a geographic issue (e.g., building a dam and reservoir, construction to revitalize a downtown area, or development of light-rail mass transit) and then develop sound arguments in favor of recommendations for specific actions on the issue

Develop innovative plans, including specific recommendations illustrated by maps, to improve the quality of environments in large cities (e.g., greenways, transportation corridors, pedestrian walkways, bicycle lanes)

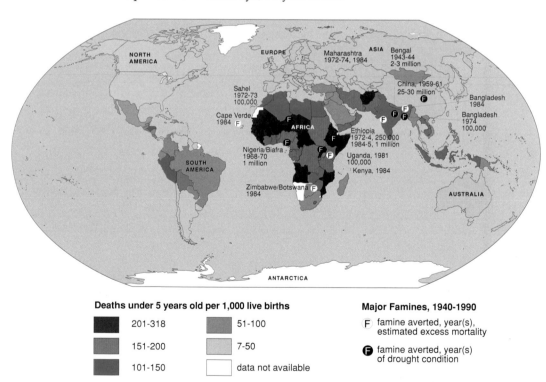

Deaths under 5 years old per 1,000 live births

■	201-318	■	51-100
■	151-200	■	7-50
■	101-150	□	data not available

Major Famines, 1940-1990

Ⓕ famine averted, year(s), estimated excess mortality

Ⓕ famine averted, year(s) of drought condition

Famine and child mortality, 1940–1990. Mortality alone is only part of the picture; many more people are chronically undernourished. The effects of frequent drought, aggravated by war, price controls that sap farmers' incentive, and inadequate means of transporting goods to market combine to give Africa the highest per capita incidence of hungry people. Asia contains the largest number. SOURCE: NATIONAL GEOGRAPHIC SOCIETY

NATIONAL GEOGRAPHY STANDARDS : 1994

CHAPTER 7

National Geography Standards

Grades 9–12

The World in Spatial Terms

▶ **HOW TO USE MAPS AND OTHER GEOGRAPHIC REPRESENTATIONS, TOOLS, AND TECHNOLOGIES TO ACQUIRE, PROCESS, AND REPORT INFORMATION FROM A SPATIAL PERSPECTIVE**

. . . .

By the end of the twelfth grade, the student knows and understands:

1. **How to use maps and other graphic representations to depict geographic problems**

2. **How to use technologies to represent and interpret Earth's physical and human systems**

3. **How to use geographic representations and tools to analyze, explain, and solve geographic problems**

Therefore, the student is able to:

A. **Produce and interpret maps and other graphic representations to solve geographic problems, as exemplified by being able to**

Develop maps to illustrate how population density varies in relation to resources and types of land use (e.g., variations in population density in cattle-raising areas versus truck-farming areas, residential areas versus inner cities, unused desert areas versus year-round vacation resorts)

Compile information from various media and then transform the primary data into maps, graphs, and charts (e.g., bar graphs showing wheat production in Argentina over a five-year period, charts developed from recent census data ranking selected information on such topics as high-school dropout rates per state, or literacy rates for the countries of Southwest Asia, cartograms depicting the relative sizes of Latin American countries based on their urban populations)

Develop maps and graphs to show the spatial relationships within and between regions (e.g., transportation networks illustrating rail, air, and highway connections between northern and southern Europe, or time-to-travel distance ratios within the Northeast megalopolis in the United States)

B. Use maps and other geographic representations to analyze world events and suggest solutions to world problems, as exemplified by being able to

Develop maps, tables, graphs, charts, and diagrams to depict the geographic implications of current world events (e.g., maps showing changing political boundaries and tables showing the distribution of refugees from areas affected by natural disasters)

Modify selected characteristics of a region (e.g., population, environment, politics, economics, culture) to suggest long-range planning goals

Use several different maps to account for selected consequences of human/environment interactions (e.g., the impact of a tropical storm on a coral island, the draining of wetlands on bird and marine life, desertification on human settlement)

C. Evaluate the applications of geographic tools and supporting technologies to serve particular purposes, as exemplified by being able to

Provide evidence regarding the central role of maps to study and explore Earth throughout history (e.g., maps made by early navigators and by such polar explorers as Robert F. Scott, Robert E. Peary, and Matthew Henson)

Collect, compare, and explain the significance of maps from different sources and different points of view to illustrate the same phenomena (e.g., maps developed by the media, business, industry, and military to show how a recently closed military installation can be utilized for civilian purposes)

Choose and give reasons to use specific technologies to analyze selected geographic problems (e.g., aerial photographs, satellite-produced imagery, and geographic information systems [GIS] to determine the extent of water pollution in a harbor complex in South Africa or the range of deforestation in Madagascar)

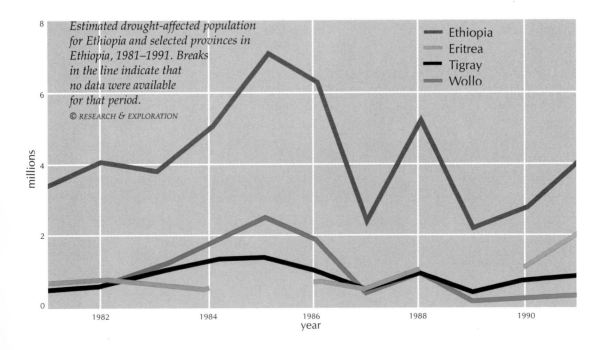

Estimated drought-affected population for Ethiopia and selected provinces in Ethiopia, 1981–1991. Breaks in the line indicate that no data were available for that period.

© RESEARCH & EXPLORATION

The World in Spatial Terms

▶ HOW TO USE MENTAL MAPS TO ORGANIZE INFORMATION ABOUT PEOPLE, PLACES, AND ENVIRONMENTS IN A SPATIAL CONTEXT

. . . .

By the end of the twelfth grade, the student knows and understands:

1. **How to use mental maps of physical and human features of the world to answer complex geographic questions**

2. **How mental maps reflect the human perception of places**

3. **How mental maps influence spatial and environmental decision-making**

Therefore, the student is able to:

A. **Use maps drawn from memory to answer geographic questions, as exemplified by being able to**

Prepare sketch maps indicating the approximate locations of different political cultures in the United States to predict voting patterns (e.g., changes in votes cast in presidential elections since 1960 related to voter migration to the Sunbelt states)

Prepare a sketch map to illustrate the spatial dynamics of contemporary and historical events (e.g., the spread of radiation from the Chernobyl nuclear accident or of the bubonic plague in fourteenth-century Europe, how physical features have deterred migrations and invasions)

Analyze world patterns of the diffusion of contagious diseases (e.g., AIDS, cholera, measles) to draw conclusions about spatial interactions (trade and transportation) in the present-day world

B. **Identify the ways in which mental maps influence human decisions about location, settlement, and public policy, as exemplified by being able to**

Collect information to understand decision-makers' mental maps (e.g., conduct interviews with community leaders regarding their perceptions of the location of different community activities)

Identify the ways in which values, attitudes, and perceptions are reflected in past and present decisions concerning location (e.g., locating houses in areas with scenic views, selecting a building site in a dramatic physical setting for a house of worship in a new suburban community)

Draw conclusions about the roles that different sources of information play in people's decisions to migrate to other countries (e.g., letters from relatives and friends, newspaper and magazine advertisements, television programs and movies)

c. Compare the mental maps of individuals to identify common factors that affect the development of spatial understanding and preferences, as exemplified by being able to

Speculate about the differences in people's mental maps based on differences in their life experiences (e.g., the influence of age and sex on how people view housing preferences or public transportation in a city)

Analyze factors that influence people's preferences about where to live (e.g., surveys of fellow students identifying choice residential areas within the community or within the country)

Compare maps of the world using different projections and perceptions of space (e.g., a map centered on the Pacific Ocean or a world map with Australia at the top) to draw conclusions about factors that influence mental maps

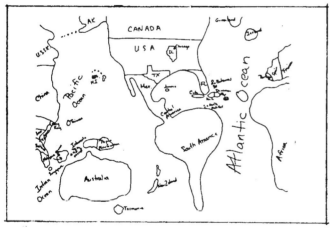

When asked to sketch a map of the world and label the countries, students tended to draw maps from a focus that is Eurocentric (not shown), Americentric (the upper map by an American student), or Sinocentric (the lower map by a Japanese student).

© *NATIONAL GEOGRAPHIC RESEARCH*

The World in Spatial Terms

▶ HOW TO ANALYZE THE SPATIAL
ORGANIZATION OF PEOPLE, PLACES, AND
ENVIRONMENTS ON EARTH'S SURFACE

· ·

By the end of the twelfth grade, the student knows and understands:

1. **The generalizations that describe and explain spatial interaction**

2. **The models that describe patterns of spatial organization**

3. **The spatial behavior of people**

4. **How to apply concepts and models of spatial organization to make decisions**

Therefore, the student is able to:

A. **Apply concepts of spatial interaction (e.g., complementarity, intervening opportunity, distance decay, connections) to account for patterns of movement in space, as exemplified by being able to**

Explain how places that are close together usually interact more than places that are far apart because the effort to overcome the friction of distance imposes costs in money and in time

Predict the effects of changing community transportation routes on the current structure and pattern of retail-trade areas, parks, and school-bus routes, given that such changes may create a new network of connections between locations and new intervening opportunities for shopping or services

Analyze the patterns of trade between the United States and Japan to explain the concept of complementarity (e.g., lumber from the United States to Japan and consumer electronics goods from Japan to the United States)

B. **Use models of spatial organization to analyze relationships in and between places, as exemplified by being able to**

Examine the differences in threshold population or demand needed to support different retail activities in a place and estimate how many people are needed to support a neighborhood convenience store, supermarket, regional shopping mall, and regional cancer-treatment center

Use Christaller's central place theory to explain why there are many small central places and few very large central places (i.e., small communities serve small areas because they offer less expensive and less specialized goods and services, whereas very large cities such as London, New York, Moscow, and Tokyo serve large areas because they offer many expensive and specialized goods and services)

Conduct a community survey to test the law of retail gravitation (i.e., the number of visits a resident makes to competing shopping centers is inversely proportional to the distances between residence and center and proportional to center size)

c. **Explain how people perceive and use space, as exemplified by being able to**

Describe activity spaces of people according to such characteristics as age, sex, employment, and income level (e.g., school-age children traveling to and from school, employed people commuting by public transit, high-income people traveling long distances for vacations)

Explain why people have different preferences for residential locations and use different means to search for satisfactory residences (e.g., some people prefer to live in suburbs or edge cities and may search for a residence by working closely with a realtor, whereas others may explore many suburbs on their own before making a decision)

Evaluate reasons why people decide to migrate (e.g., people being influenced by pull factors of the potential destination or by push factors of the home area, people selecting different types of locations if they are seeking employment rather than a place for retirement)

d. **Apply concepts and models of spatial organization to make decisions, as exemplified by being able to**

Explain why optimum plant-location decisions in a commercial economy take into consideration labor costs, transportation costs, and market locations (e.g., the least-cost decision as to where to locate a furniture factory requires knowing wage levels for skilled workers, the cost of transporting raw wood and finished furniture, and the location of competing firms and wholesale and retail furniture outlets)

Explain why some specialized agricultural products are grown far from the point of consumption (e.g., cut flowers are grown in Venezuela, Colombia, and Israel because of transportation costs, labor costs, and climate)

Explain why there are advantages for retailers to locate in malls rather than in dispersed locations (e.g., malls bring many large and small stores together in close proximity and take advantage of sharing costs for parking lots, lighting, and other utilities while providing convenience and time efficiency for customers)

Places and Regions

▶ THE PHYSICAL AND HUMAN
CHARACTERISTICS OF PLACES

. . . .

By the end of the twelfth grade, the student knows and understands:

1. **The meaning and significance of place**

2. **The changing physical and human characteristics of places**

3. **How relationships between humans and the physical environment lead to the formation of places and to a sense of personal and community identity**

Therefore, the student is able to:

A. **Explain place from a variety of points of view, as exemplified by being able to**

Describe the same place at different times in its history (e.g., London as a Roman outpost in Britain, as a medieval trading center, and as the seat of a global empire in the nineteenth century or Tokyo in the three decades immediately before and after the Meiji Restoration)

Explain why places have specific physical and human characteristics in different parts of the world (e.g., the effects of climatic and tectonic processes, settlement and migration patterns, site and situation components)

Develop a definition of place appropriate for inclusion in a glossary of geographic terms

B. **Describe and interpret physical processes that shape places, as exemplified by being able to**

Describe how forces from within Earth (e.g., tectonic processes such as volcanic activity and earthquakes) influence the character of place

Analyze the role of climate (e.g., the effects of temperature, precipitation, wind) in shaping places

Describe and interpret the importance of erosional processes in shaping places (e.g., the cliffs of Malibu or the sand dunes of Cape Cod)

Borana woman drawing water from a cistern in southern Ethiopia—evidence of modern influences on traditional lifeways in this semiarid region. SHEWANGIZAW BEKELE

C. **Explain how social, cultural, and economic processes shape the features of places, as exemplified by being able to**

Describe how culture (e.g., toponyms, food preferences, gender roles, resource use, belief systems, modes of transportation and communication) affects the characteristics of place

Identify how places have been altered by major technological changes (e.g., advances brought about by the agricultural and industrial revolutions, the invention of the automobile, the development of machinery for large-scale agriculture, the invention of the computer)

Analyze the ways in which the character of a place relates to its economic, political, and population characteristics (e.g., how a large state university influences the small town in which it is located or how the location of a regional medical center attracts senior citizens as residents)

D. **Evaluate how humans interact with physical environments to form places, as exemplified by being able to**

Identify the locational advantages and disadvantages of using places for different activities based on their physical characteristics (e.g., floodplain, forest, tundra, earthquake zone, river crossing, or coastal flood zone)

Explain how places are made distinctive and meaningful by human activities that alter physical features (e.g., the construction of the interstate highway system in the United States, the terracing of hillsides to grow rice in Thailand)

Evaluate the effects of population growth and urbanization on places (e.g., air pollution in Mexico City, Los Angeles, and Milan; the loss of farmlands to rapidly growing urban areas)

Places and Regions

▶ THAT PEOPLE CREATE REGIONS TO
INTERPRET EARTH'S COMPLEXITY

. . . .

By the end of the twelfth grade, the student knows and understands:

1. **How multiple criteria can be used to define a region**

2. **The structure of regional systems**

3. **The ways in which physical and human regional systems are interconnected**

4. **How to use regions to analyze geographic issues**

Therefore, the student is able to:

A. **List and explain the changing criteria that can be used to define a region, as exemplified by being able to**

Identify the physical or human factors that constitute a region (e.g., soils, climate, and vegetation have created the fertile triangle in Russia; common language, religion, and history have established Portugal as a region)

Explain how changing conditions can result in a region taking on a new structure (e.g., the reshaping of Miami and south Florida resulting from the influx of people and capital from some areas of the Caribbean Basin, or the reshaping of southern Africa resulting from the economic and political realignments that followed the end of European colonialism)

Explain why regions once characterized by one set of criteria may be defined by a different set of criteria today (e.g., the Caribbean Basin's transition from a major sugarcane and hemp producer to a center for tourism, New England's gradual conversion from a region of small textile mills and shoe factories in the nineteenth and early twentieth centuries to one of high-technology industries in the 1980s and 1990s)

B. **Describe the types and organization of regional systems, as exemplified by being able to**

Identify the differences among formal, functional, and perceptual regions (e.g., a formal region with some homogeneous characteristic in common, such as a desert climate; a functional region marked by its interdependent parts, such as the structure

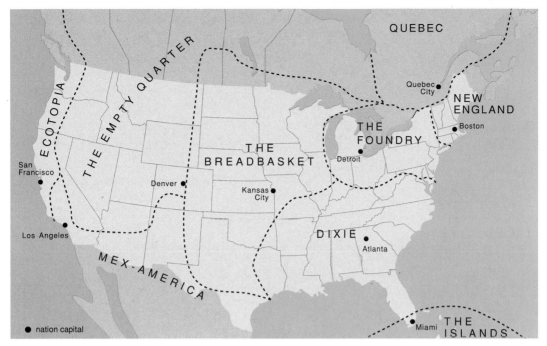

The emerging nine nations of North America is a regionalization scheme. Its thesis is that this culture realm is reorganizing into nations based on separate loyalties, interests, and plans for the future. SOURCE: JOEL GARREAU, *THE NINE NATIONS OF NORTH AMERICA*

of the Federal Reserve banking system in the United States; or a perceptual region as a commonly understood conceptual construct such as Dixie or the rust belt)

Explain how functional regions are held together (e.g., by nodal centers such as a neighborhood coffee shop, city hall, or suburban shopping mall)

Identify the ways in which the concept of a region can be used to simplify the complexity of Earth's space (e.g., by arranging an area into sections to help understand a particular topic or problem)

c. **Identify human and physical changes in regions and explain the factors that contribute to those changes, as exemplified by being able to**

Use maps to illustrate how regional boundaries change (e.g., changes resulting from shifts in population, environmental degradation, or shifts in production and market patterns)

Identify some of the reasons for changes in the world's political boundaries (e.g., the frequently changing political boundaries of Poland over the centuries owing to Poland being partitioned by stronger neighbors, the creation of landlocked states such as Bolivia as a result of wars, or territorial issues resulting from disputes about access to resources)

Explain factors that contribute to the dynamic nature of regions (e.g., human influences such as migration, technology, and capital investment; physical influences such as long-term climate shifts and seismic activity)

D. **Explain the different ways in which regional systems are structured, as exemplified by being able to**

Describe how cities are organized into regional systems (e.g., small cities linked to larger cities by flows of goods, services, ideas, and people)

Examine political structures and governments as regional systems (e.g., the hierarchy of political units such as village, town, city, county, state, and country; the hierarchy of political party structures—precinct, ward, county, state, and national levels)

Describe the different ways in which governments and businesses establish regional systems (e.g., hub-and-spoke airline operations, postal-service zip codes, assignment of Social Security numbers by region)

E. **Interpret the connections within and among the parts of a regional system, as exemplified by being able to**

Describe some of the relationships existing between and within regions (e.g., the links involving neighborhoods within a city, municipalities within a metropolitan area, or power blocs within a defense or economic alliance)

Explain the ways in which regional systems are interconnected (e.g., similarities in physical and cultural characteristics used in selecting "sister cities")

Explain how physical and human environments form webs of interacting systems within and among regions (e.g., the use of dams and levees to create the Tennessee Valley Authority)

F. **Use regions to analyze geographic issues and answer geographic questions, as exemplified by being able to**

Identify and explain the criteria that gave regions their identities in different periods of U. S. and world history (e.g., the cotton South prior to the Civil War, the Nile Valley in the age of the pharaohs, India in the age of the moguls, the Pacific rim in the late twentieth century)

Identify places participating in past and present regional alliances (e.g., the central powers in World War I, and the European Union in the 1990s) and evaluate the advantages and disadvantages of these alliances from the perspective of their member states

Examine the historic reasons for conflicts within specific world regions (e.g., Southeast Asia, the Horn of Africa, the states in the Balkans)

Places and Regions

▶ HOW CULTURE AND EXPERIENCE INFLUENCE
PEOPLE'S PERCEPTIONS OF PLACES AND REGIONS

. . . .

By the end of the twelfth grade, the student knows and understands:

1. **Why places and regions serve as symbols for individuals and society**

2. **Why different groups of people within a society view places and regions differently**

3. **How changing perceptions of places and regions reflect cultural change**

Therefore, the student is able to:

A. **Explain why places and regions are important to individual human identity and as symbols for unifying or fragmenting society, as exemplified by being able to**

Interpret how people express attachment to places and regions (e.g., by reference to essays, novels, poems, and short stories, feature films, or such traditional musical compositions as "God Bless America" and "America the Beautiful")

Explain how point of view influences a person's perception of a place (e.g., how various ethnic groups have a point of view about what constitutes an ideal residential landscape, how an environmentalist and real estate developer would be likely to differ on the best use for a barrier island)

Identify how places take on symbolic meaning (e.g., Jerusalem as a holy city for Muslims, Christians, and Jews; Arlington National Cemetery and the Tomb of the Unknown Soldier as places to honor the war dead of the United States)

B. **Explain how individuals view places and regions on the basis of their stage of life, sex, social class, ethnicity, values, and belief systems, as exemplified by being able to**

Make inferences about differences in the personal geographies of men and women (e.g., perceptions of distance, impressions about what makes a place secure, or how space can be organized)

Wilshire Boulevard, Los Angeles: 1922 (left), when it was surrounded by barley fields; 1965 (right), long after it had become a chic retail district. Wilshire stores were the first to turn their main entrances to the parking lot rather than the sidewalk. UNIVERSITY OF CALIFORNIA, LOS ANGELES

Speculate on how the socioeconomic backgrounds of people influence their points of view about a place or a region (e.g., their views of public housing, wealthy urban neighborhoods, or busy commercial strips along an arterial street)

Explain how places and regions are stereotyped (e.g., how the West became "wild" or how all of Appalachia is associated with poverty)

C. **Analyze the ways in which people's changing views of places and regions reflect cultural change, as exemplified by being able to**

Explain how shifts from a predominantly rural to a predominantly urban society influences the ways in which people perceive an environment (e.g., rural settings becoming attractive as recreation areas to people living in densely populated cities, old mining ghost towns becoming tourist and gambling centers)

Explain how increases in income, longer life expectancy, and attitudes toward aging influence where people choose to live (e.g., retirement communities in Florida and Arizona)

Examine the sequential occupance of a specific habitat (e.g., the impact of settlement on an Arctic archipelago by: indigenous peoples; a group of nineteenth century shipborne explorers; subsequent settlers from abroad who came to hunt, fish, and trade; seasonal whalers and fishermen; and geologists searching for petroleum reserves in the area)

Physical Systems

▶ THE PHYSICAL PROCESSES THAT SHAPE THE
PATTERNS OF EARTH'S SURFACE

. . . .

By the end of the twelfth grade, the student knows and understands:

1. **The dynamics of the four basic components of Earth's physical systems: the atmosphere, biosphere, lithosphere, and hydrosphere**

2. **The interaction of Earth's physical systems**

3. **The spatial variation in the consequences of physical processes across Earth's surface**

Therefore, the student is able to:

A. **Describe how physical processes affect different regions of the United States and the world, as exemplified by being able to**

Explain how extreme physical events affect human settlements in different regions (e.g., the destructive effects of hurricanes in the Caribbean Basin and the eastern United States or of earthquakes in Turkey, Japan, and Nicaragua)

Use maps to illustrate how such natural disasters as floods and hurricanes can alter landscapes (e.g., the impact of the Mississippi River floods of the summer of 1993 on the structure of the river valley in Illinois, Iowa, and Missouri or the changes along the Florida coast caused by Hurricane Andrew in 1992)

Describe the physical processes that occur in dry environments (e.g., desertification and soil degradation, flash floods, dust storms, sand movement, soil erosion, salt accumulation)

B. **Explain Earth's physical processes, patterns, and cycles using concepts of physical geography, as exemplified by being able to**

Explain the distribution of different types of climate (e.g., marine climate or continental climate) that is produced by such processes as air-mass circulation, temperature, and moisture

Describe the physical processes (e.g., erosion, folding and faulting, volcanism) that produce distinctive landforms (e.g., specific types of mountains, such as buttes and mesas, block mountains or horsts, ridge-and-valley systems)

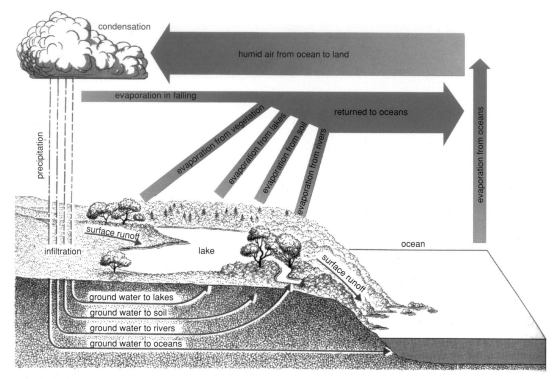

The hydrologic cycle. Evaporation from the soil returns moisture to the atmosphere, where it is released as precipitation. At the same time, the roots of plants absorb soil moisture and transfer it through trunks and branches to the leaves where it is lost to the atmosphere through leaf pores during transpiration.
SOURCE: *THE EARTH*, JOHN WILEY & SONS

Explain the effects of different physical cycles (e.g., world atmospheric circulation, ocean circulation) on the physical environment of Earth

C. Explain the various interactions resulting from Earth–Sun relationships, as exemplified by being able to

Describe the effects of the tilt of the Earth's axis on the cycle of the seasons in the Northern and Southern Hemispheres

Explain the difference between solstices and equinoxes and the reasons why they occur

Speculate on various possible scenarios of future world climates should there be an increase in the greenhouse effect

D. Describe the ways in which Earth's physical processes are dynamic and interactive, as exemplified by being able to

Explain why the features of the ocean floor are evidence of the dynamic forces that shape continents and ocean basins

Explain the relationships between changes in landforms and the effects of climate (e.g., the erosion of hill slopes by precipitation, deposition of sediments by floods, shaping of land surfaces by wind)

Identify the conditions that cause changes in climate and the consequent effects on ocean levels, agricultural productivity, and population distribution

Physical Systems

▶ **THE CHARACTERISTICS AND SPATIAL DISTRIBUTION OF ECOSYSTEMS ON EARTH'S SURFACE**

· ·

By the end of the twelfth grade, the student knows and understands:

1. **The distribution and characteristics of ecosystems**

2. **The biodiversity and productivity of ecosystems**

3. **The importance of ecosystems in people's understanding of environmental issues**

Therefore, the student is able to:

A. **Analyze the distribution of ecosystems by interpreting relationships between soil, climate, and plant and animal life, as exemplified by being able to**

Analyze the nature of plant communities in an area in terms of solar energy and water supply

Describe how physical characteristics such as climate and soil affect the number, kinds, and distribution of plants and animals in an ecosystem

Describe the factors and processes involved in the formation of soils in different ecosystems (e.g., climate type, parent-rock materials, slope of land, effects of human activities)

B. **Evaluate ecosystems in terms of their biodiversity and productivity, as exemplified by being able to**

Use knowledge of the variable productivity of different ecosystems to develop a set of general statements about the nature of such systems

Characterize ecosystems by their level of biodiversity and productivity (e.g., the low productivity of deserts and the high productivity of mid-latitude forests and

Arizona copper-mine tailings impoundment with toxic sulfide-tinged rainwater pooling on the surface. If such mining residue is not effectively contained, chemicals may leach into soil and groundwater. JOEL SARTORE

tropical forests) and describe their potential value to all living things (e.g., as a source of oxygen for life forms, as a source of food for indigenous peoples, as a source of raw materials for international trade)

Evaluate the carrying capacity of different ecosystems in relation to land-use policies (e.g., the optimal number of cattle per square mile in a grassland)

c. Apply the concept of ecosystems to understand and solve problems regarding environmental issues, as exemplified by being able to

Describe the effects of biological magnification on ecosystems (e.g., the increase in contaminants in succeeding levels of the food chain and the consequences for different life-forms)

Describe the effects of both physical and human changes on ecosystems (e.g., the disruption of energy flows and chemical cycles and the reduction of species diversity)

Evaluate the long-term effects of the human modification of ecosystems (e.g., how acid rain resulting from air pollution affects water bodies and forests and how depletion of the atmosphere's ozone layer through the use of chemicals may affect the health of humans)

GEOGRAPHY STANDARD 9 GRADES 9–12

Human Systems

▶ THE CHARACTERISTICS, DISTRIBUTION, AND MIGRATION OF HUMAN POPULATIONS ON EARTH'S SURFACE

· ·

By the end of the twelfth grade, the student knows and understands:

1. **Trends in world population numbers and patterns**

2. **The impact of human migration on physical and human systems**

Therefore, the student is able to:

A. **Predict trends in the spatial distribution of population on Earth, as exemplified by being able to**

Develop and defend hypotheses on how the spatial distribution of population may change in response to environmental changes (e.g., global warming, desertification, changes in sea level, tectonic activity)

Develop and defend hypotheses on how the spatial distribution of population may change in response to sociocultural changes (e.g., technological advances, political conflict, the growth of ethnic enclaves)

Develop and defend hypotheses on how changes in the spatial distribution of population may result in changes in social and economic conditions (e.g., availability of water and space for housing, transportation facilities, educational and employment opportunities)

B. **Analyze population issues and propose policies to address such issues, as exemplified by being able to**

Evaluate past and present government policies designed to change a country's population characteristics (e.g., the ongoing policies to limit population growth, the policy in the former Soviet Union to encourage ethnic Russians to have large families)

Explain how government population policies are linked to economic and cultural considerations (e.g., the belief systems of the people, the food traditions of the people, the country's need for more or fewer workers)

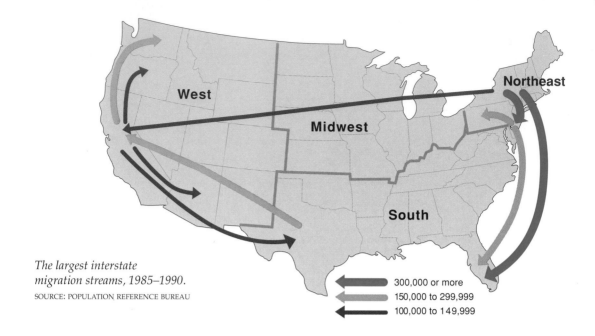

The largest interstate
migration streams, 1985–1990.
SOURCE: POPULATION REFERENCE BUREAU

West

Midwest

Northeast

South

300,000 or more

150,000 to 299,999

100,000 to 149,999

Describe the reasons why a government's population policy may be opposed by the people (e.g., the policy may be in conflict with the people's cultural values and attitudes toward family size, cultural traditions, and belief systems)

c. Explain the economic, political, and social factors that contribute to human migration, as exemplified by being able to

Explain how human mobility and city/region interdependence can be increased and regional integration can be facilitated by improved transportation systems (e.g., the national interstate-highway system in the United States, the network of global air routes)

Explain how international migrations are shaped by push and pull factors (e.g., political conditions, economic incentives, religious values, family ties)

Explain why countries develop emigration and immigration policies (e.g., to control population size and density or encourage immigration to meet demands for either skilled or unskilled workers)

d. Evaluate the impact of human migration on physical and human systems, as exemplified by being able to

Describe how mass migrations have affected ecosystems (e.g., the impact of European settlers on the High Plains of North America in the nineteenth century)

Describe how large-scale rural-to-urban migration affects cities (e.g., suburban development, lack of adequate housing, stress on infrastructure, difficulty in providing such city services as police and fire protection)

Describe the socioeconomic changes that occur in regions that gain population and in regions that lose population (e.g., the expansion of population and jobs in the southeastern United States and the concurrent decline in parts of the northeastern United States during the 1970s and 1980s)

Human Systems

► THE CHARACTERISTICS, DISTRIBUTION, AND
COMPLEXITY OF EARTH'S CULTURAL MOSAICS

. . . .

By the end of the twelfth grade, the student knows and understands:

1. **The impact of culture on ways of life in different regions**

2. **How cultures shape the character of a region**

3. **The spatial characteristics of the processes of cultural convergence and divergence**

Therefore, the student is able to:

A. **Compare the role that culture plays in incidents of cooperation and conflict in the present-day world, as exemplified by being able to**

Identify the cultural factors that have promoted political conflict (e.g., the national, ethnic, and religious differences that led to conflict in sub-Saharan Africa in the 1960s, central Europe in the 1980s and 1990s, countries within the former Soviet Union in the 1990s)

Identify the cultural characteristics that link regions (e.g., the religious and linguistic ties between Spain and parts of Latin America; the linguistic ties between Great Britain and Australia; the ethnic ties among the Kurds living in Iran, Iraq, and Turkey)

Explain how members of the U. S. Peace Corps have to adjust to living and working in countries with cultural traditions that differ significantly from their own (e.g., how they learn and are taught to adapt themselves to non-American dietary habits, social customs, lifestyles, and family and community values)

B. **Analyze how cultures influence the characteristics of regions, as exemplified by being able to**

Analyze demographic data (e.g., birthrates, literacy rates, infant mortality) to describe a region's cultural characteristics (e.g., level of technological achievement, cultural traditions, social institutions)

Compare the economic opportunities for women in selected regions of the world using culture to explain the differences (e.g., the lives of Bedouin women within the Islamic tradition versus those of women in Scandinavian countries)

In Hanoi, Vietnam, a woman welds bicycle frames for a nation that is now encouraging independent production of consumer goods. DAVID ALAN HARVEY

Describe the relationship between patterns of in-migration and cultural change in large urban and manufacturing centers, especially those near international borders (e.g., how the presence of large numbers of guest workers or undocumented aliens results in modification of an urban center's cultural characteristics)

c. **Explain how cultural features often define regions, as exemplified by being able to**

Identify the human characteristics that make specific regions of the world distinctive (e.g., the effects of early Spanish settlement in the southwestern United States, the influence of mercantilism and capitalism as developed in post-Renaissance Europe on the economies of North and South America)

Explain the importance of religion in identifying a culture region (e.g., the impact of Buddhism in shaping social attitudes in Southeast Asia, the role of Christianity in structuring the educational and social-welfare systems of Western Europe)

Explain why great differences can exist among culture regions within a single country (e.g., the specific qualities of Canada's culture regions resulting from the patterns of migration and settlement over four centuries)

d. **Investigate how transregional alliances and multinational organizations can alter cultural solidarity, as exemplified by being able to**

Explain the adaptation of non-governmental organizations (NGOs) to different cultural contexts (e.g., the Red Cross versus the Red Crescent distinction)

NATIONAL GEOGRAPHY STANDARDS : 1994

In Rajasthan, India, a woman shapes cow dung into disks to dry in the sun before being burned as fuel. Although this technology provides fuel where wood is scarce, it deprives the soil of fertilizer. ROLAND MICHAUD

Identify and map changes in the nature of selected international partnerships and alliances (e.g., NATO and the former Warsaw Pact nations since the collapse of the Soviet Union, the additions to OPEC since its creation in 1960)

Predict how evolving political and economic alliances affect the traditional cohesiveness of world culture regions (e.g., post-reunification Germany and its economic effect on the European Union, NAFTA's effect on trade relations among the United States, Canada, and Mexico)

E. Explain the spatial processes of cultural convergence and divergence, as exemplified by being able to

Describe how communications and transportation technologies contribute to cultural convergence (e.g., how electronic media, computers, and jet aircraft connect distant places in a close network of contact through cross-cultural adaptation)

Analyze how the communications and transportation technologies that contribute to cultural convergence may also stimulate cultural divergence (e.g., how culture groups use such technologies to reinforce nationalistic or ethnic elitism or cultural separateness and independence)

Evaluate examples of the spread of culture traits that contribute to cultural convergence (e.g., U. S.-based fast-food franchises in Russia and Eastern Europe, the English language as a major medium of communication for scientists and business people in many regions of the world, the popularization of Chinese foods in many countries)

Human Systems

▶ THE PATTERNS AND NETWORKS OF ECONOMIC INTERDEPENDENCE ON EARTH'S SURFACE

· ·

By the end of the twelfth grade, the student knows and understands:

1. **The classification, characteristics, and spatial distribution of economic systems**

2. **How places of various size function as centers of economic activity**

3. **The increasing economic interdependence of the world's countries**

Therefore, the student is able to:

A. **Classify and describe the spatial distribution of major economic systems and evaluate their relative merits in terms of productivity and the social welfare of workers, as exemplified by being able to**

Describe the characteristics of traditional, command, and market economic systems and describe how such systems operate in specific countries (e.g., describe North Korea as a command economy, Burkina Faso as a traditional economy in the hinterlands beyond its cities, Singapore as a market economy)

Use multiple points of view to evaluate the advantages and disadvantages of different economic systems (e.g., unemployment as viewed by an economist in China versus unemployment as viewed by an economist in Japan)

Identify geographic problems in the transition period as a country shifts from one economic system to another (e.g., from a command economy to a market economy in the republics of the former Soviet Union)

B. **Identify and evaluate the spatial aspects of economic systems, as exemplified by being able to**

Identify market areas around major business establishments (e.g., supermarkets, shopping malls, banks, discount centers, theme parks) in the student's own community on the basis of surveying consumer travel behavior

Explain how market areas are examples of functional regions (e.g., newspaper-circulation areas, television-viewing areas, radio-listening areas)

Explain why some places have locational advantages as assembly and/or parts distribution centers (e.g., furniture manufacture and assembly in North Carolina; electronics assembly in northern Mexico; a wholesale auto parts distribution company near a regional trucking facility)

C. **Analyze the relationships between various settlement patterns, their associated economic activities, and the relative land values, as exemplified by being able to**

Analyze the spatial relationships between land values and prominent urban features (e.g., central business districts, open spaces near public parks, prominent natural features [e.g., waterfronts, land elevation, prevailing wind direction])

Explain the spatial relationships between the zoned uses of land and the value of that land (e.g., an industrial park for light industry in a planned community versus a discount mall in an unincorporated ex-urban area)

Relate economic factors to the location of particular types of industries and businesses (e.g., least-cost location in terms of land values, transportation, agglomeration, utilities)

D. **Identify and analyze the historical movement patterns of people and goods and their relationships to economic activity, as exemplified by being able to**

Analyze the spatial patterns of early trade routes in the era of sailing ships (e.g., explorers probing along the coasts of continents and making use of prevailing winds and ocean currents)

Discuss the land-use patterns that resulted in a system of monoculture (e.g., European colonial initiatives resulting in sugar plantations in the Caribbean, tobacco plantations in Virginia, tea plantations in Sri Lanka)

Compare global trade routes before and after the development of major canals (e.g., shipping routes between Western Europe and Asia before and after the opening of the Suez Canal) and develop hypotheses to explain the changes that occurred in world trade

E. **Analyze and evaluate international economic issues from a spatial point of view, as exemplified by being able to**

Explain how land values in an area may change owing to the investment of foreign capital (e.g., increases in land values in British Columbia in the 1990s as people from other parts of Canada and from Hong Kong sought new places to reside and conduct business, increases in land values in resort areas in the Dominican Republic as a result of Canadian and German investment)

Formulate reasoned arguments regarding the causes and geographic consequences of an international debt crisis (e.g., the events associated with a loss of foreign capital and a failure to complete infrastructure development)

Evaluate the advantages and disadvantages of allowing foreign-owned businesses to purchase land, open factories, or conduct other kinds of business in a country (e.g., the flow of capital out of the host country possibly resulting in a budget deficit or loss of investment opportunities, but a resultant increase in trade opportunities for the investing country)

GEOGRAPHY STANDARD **12** GRADES 9–12

Human Systems

▶ THE PROCESSES, PATTERNS, AND FUNCTIONS OF
   HUMAN SETTLEMENT

. . . .

By the end of the twelfth grade, the student knows and understands:

1. **The functions, sizes, and spatial arrangements of urban areas**
2. **The differing characteristics of settlement in developing and developed countries**
3. **The processes that change the internal structure of urban areas**
4. **The evolving forms of present-day urban areas**

Therefore, the student is able to:

A. **Analyze the functions of cities, as exemplified by being able to**

Analyze the site and situation of selected cities in different regions of the world (e.g., Sydney's harbor location, Denver as the Mile High City, Montreal as an island city)

Explain how the functions of cities differ from those of towns and villages (e.g., they offer more specialized economic and social activities, greater concentration of services, greater availability of the same services)

Explain how the functions of present-day cities differ from those of cities in earlier times (e.g., single- versus multiple-function cities, simple versus complex functions)

B. **Analyze the internal structure and shape of cities, as exemplified by being able to**

Use aerial photographs, topographic maps, and census data to learn about land uses in the student's own city or in another city in the same region and then speculate about the city's primary function within its region (e.g., commercial center, university community, transportation hub)

Analyze and compare the shapes of cities to identify factors that influence urban morphology (e.g., transportation routes, physical barriers, zoning regulations)

Identify those ways in which a city has remained the same for many years, as well as those ways it has changed (e.g., on the basis of histories, old newspapers, public records, maps, aerial photographs, census data)

NATIONAL GEOGRAPHY STANDARDS : 1994

C. **Classify the characteristics of settlements in developing or developed countries, as exemplified by being able to**

Identify the characteristics of cities in developing countries and compare them to those of cities in developed countries in terms of physical features, site, situation, function, internal structure, and other geographic factors

Compare residential as well as transportation patterns in the urban settlements of developing and developed countries (e.g., the bus system of New York City versus the jitney system in Kingston, Jamaica or the freeway systems in United States cities versus the narrow streets in such cities as Cairo and Addis Ababa)

Compare the efficiency of alternative urban structures in providing basic services in developing and developed countries (e.g., the travel distance to schools, shopping areas, health-care facilities)

D. **Describe the nature, causes, and geographic impact of change in urban areas, as exemplified by being able to**

Predict the impacts of population growth or decline on an urban area in terms of such factors as the stress on infrastructure, problems of providing efficient and effective public safety and fire protection, availability of jobs, demands placed on the tax base

Trace changes in the locations of ethnic neighborhoods in a city to draw general conclusions about the settlement patterns of immigrant groups in terms of such factors as proximity to the central business district, location in marginal housing areas, and lack of access to areas with job opportunities

Predict the likely effect on an urban area's internal structure of the arrival or departure of a major industry or business (e.g., the closing of an automobile assembly plant, or the relocation and downsizing of a national, full-service insurance company)

E. **Evaluate the physical and human impacts of emerging urban forms in the present-day world, as exemplified by being able to**

Identify urban forms that characterize recent changes in urban structure (e.g., the rise of megalopoli, edge cities, metropolitan corridors)

Explain the relationships between changing transport technologies and changing urban forms (e.g., improved light-rail systems within cities providing ease of access to ex-urban areas, interurban rapid-transit systems, airplane shuttles connecting cities conveniently and cost effectively)

Describe the cultural imprints of increasing urbanization (e.g., the increasing numbers of ethnic enclaves in urban areas, the development of legislation to protect the rights of ethnic and racial minorities)

Human Systems

▶ **HOW THE FORCES OF COOPERATION AND CONFLICT AMONG PEOPLE INFLUENCE THE DIVISION AND CONTROL OF EARTH'S SURFACE**

· ·

By the end of the twelfth grade, the student knows and understands:

1. **Why and how cooperation and conflict are involved in shaping the distribution of social, political, and economic spaces on Earth at different scales**

2. **The impact of multiple spatial divisions on people's daily lives**

3. **How differing points of view and self-interests play a role in conflict over territory and resources**

Therefore, the student is able to:

A. **Analyze how cooperation and conflict influence the development and control of social, political, and economic entities on Earth, as exemplified by being able to**

Explain how cooperation and/or conflict can lead to the allocation of control of Earth's surface (e.g., the formation and delineation of regional planning districts, regional school districts, countries, free-trade zones)

Identify the causes of boundary conflicts and internal disputes between culture groups (e.g., the conflict between North Korea and South Korea, friction between the Spanish majority and Basque minority in Spain, the civil war between the Hutus and the Tutsis in Rwanda)

Explain why the boundaries of congressional districts change in the United States (e.g., the effects of statutory requirements, population shifts, ethnic and racial considerations, shifts in political power)

B. **Explain the changes that occur in the extent and organization of social, political, and economic entities on Earth's surface, as exemplified by being able to**

Interpret the spatial extent and organizational structure of an imperial power (e.g., the Roman Empire, Han Dynasty, Carolingian Empire, British Empire)

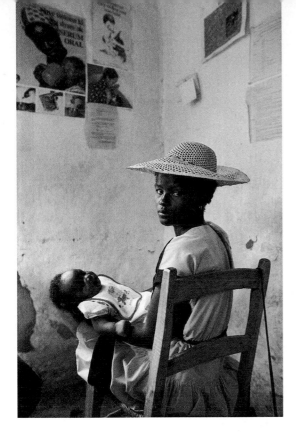

Political and economic stability are intertwined with every aspect of an inhabitant's quality of life. Here, a mother in Haiti cradles her sick child while awaiting medical treatment at a clinic.
JAMES P. BLAIR

Explain why some countries are landlocked (e.g., as a consequence of war between rival countries, isolation owing to the size of landmasses, or racial and cultural divisions)

Describe the functions of the United Nations and its specialized agencies in dealing with various global issues (e.g., peacekeeping, emergency aid, disease prevention)

c. **Explain how external forces can conflict economically and politically with internal interests in a region, as exemplified by being able to**

Describe how new technologies, new markets, and revised perceptions of resources act as agents of change in a region (e.g., how the Pampas in Argentina underwent a significant socioeconomic transformation in the nineteenth and early twentieth centuries as a consequence of European demands for grain and beef)

Explain how a country's ambition to obtain markets and resources can cause fractures and disruptions in areas of the world that are targets of its ambition (e.g., the consequences of French colonization of Indochina in the nineteenth century to procure tin, tungsten, and rubber; Italian designs on the Libyan coast for farmlands to accommodate its burgeoning population in the 1930s)

Illustrate how religious conflict or expansion can cause political and cultural changes in a region (e.g., the friction between Hindus and Moslems in the Indian subcontinent in the 1940s led to the formation of India and Pakistan; the impact of the Crusades on the cultures of Western Europe and Southwest Asia in the eleventh and twelfth centuries)

GEOGRAPHY STANDARD **14** GRADES 9–12

Environment and Society

▶ HOW HUMAN ACTIONS MODIFY
THE PHYSICAL ENVIRONMENT

· ·

By the end of the twelfth grade, the student knows and understands:

1. **The role of technology in the capacity of the physical environment to accommodate human modification**

2. **The significance of the global impacts of human modification of the physical environment**

3. **How to apply appropriate models and information to understand environmental problems**

Therefore, the student is able to:

A. **Evaluate the ways in which technology has expanded the human capability to modify the physical environment, as exemplified by being able to**

Evaluate the limitations of the physical environment's capacity to absorb the impacts of human activity (e.g., use the concepts of synergy, feedback loops, carrying capacity, thresholds to examine the effects of such activities as levee construction on a floodplain, logging in an old-growth forest, construction of golf courses in arid areas)

Analyze the role of people in decreasing the diversity of flora and fauna in a region (e.g., the impact of acid rain on rivers and forests in southern Ontario, the effects of toxic dumping on ocean ecosystems, the effects of overfishing along the coast of northeastern North America or the Philippine archipelago)

Compare the ways in which the student's local community modified the local physical environment (e.g., rivers, soils, vegetation, animals, climate) a hundred years ago with the community's current impact on the same environment, and project future trends based on these local experiences

B. **Explain the global impacts of human changes in the physical environment, as exemplified by being able to**

Describe the spatial consequences, deliberate and inadvertent, of human activities that have global implications (e.g., the dispersal of animal and plant species worldwide, increases in runoff and sediment, tropical soil degradation, habitat destruction, air pollution, alterations in the hydrologic cycle)

Days after the Exxon Valdez oil spill, fishermen find foot-thick oily residue clogging a bay on Eleanor Island some 35 miles from the wrecked tanker. Vast stocks of fish, tens of thousands of birds, at least a thousand sea otters, and untold numbers of plants died as a result of being coated with oil. NATALIE FOBES

Identify and debate the positive and negative aspects of landscape changes in the student's local community and region that relate to people's changing attitudes toward the environment (e.g., pressure to replace farmlands with wetlands in floodplain areas, interest in preserving wilderness areas, support of the concept of historic preservation)

Examine the characteristics of major global environmental changes and assess whether the changes are a result of human action, natural causes, or a combination of both factors (e.g., increases in world temperatures attributable to major global environmental change, results of the greenhouse effect attributable to human action, the link between changes in solar emissions and amounts of volcanic dust in the atmosphere attributable to natural causes)

c. **Develop possible solutions to scenarios of environmental change induced by human modification of the physical environment, as exemplified by being able to**

Identify possible responses to the changes that take place in a river system as adjacent farmland is fertilized more intensively and as settlement expands into the floodplain

Choose examples of human modification of the landscape in the nineteenth and twentieth centuries and compare the ways in which the physical environment's ability to accommodate such modification has changed (e.g., urban development in the United States, especially in the High Plains, the Southwest, and Northeast; suburban and residential expansion into farmland areas)

Develop a list of the potential global effects to the environment of human changes currently in progress and devise strategies that could lessen the impacts in each case (e.g., the effects of groundwater reduction caused by overpumping of center-pivot irrigation systems could be lessened by implementing changes in crops and farming techniques; desiccation of the Aral Sea and associated dust storms caused by the diversion of water to irrigation projects in Central Asia could be lessened by ending the diversion and finding alternative water sources)

Environment and Society

▶ HOW PHYSICAL SYSTEMS AFFECT HUMAN SYSTEMS

· ·

By the end of the twelfth grade, the student knows and understands:

1. **How changes in the physical environment can diminish its capacity to support human activity**

2. **Strategies to respond to constraints placed on human systems by the physical environment**

3. **How humans perceive and react to natural hazards**

Therefore, the student is able to:

A. **Analyze examples of changes in the physical environment that have reduced the capacity of the environment to support human activity, as exemplified by being able to**

Describe and evaluate the carrying capacity of selected regions to predict the likely consequences of exceeding their environmental limits (e.g., the impact of the economic exploitation of Siberia's resources on a fragile sub-Arctic environment)

Develop contemporary and historical case studies to serve as examples of the limited ability of physical systems to withstand human pressure or of situations in which the environment's quality and ability to support human populations has diminished because of excessive use (e.g., the drought-plagued Sahel, the depleted rain forests of central Africa, the Great Plains Dust Bowl)

Develop a model using concepts of synergy, feedback loops, carrying capacity, and thresholds to describe the limits of physical systems in different environments to absorb the impacts of human activities

B. **Apply the concept of "limits to growth" to suggest ways to adapt to or overcome the limits imposed on human systems by physical systems, as exemplified by being able to**

Describe the limits to growth found in physical environments and describe ways in which technology and human adaptation enable people to expand the capacity of such environments

Describe the conditions and locations of soil types (e.g., soils with limited nutrients, high salt content, shallow depth) that place limits on plant growth and therefore on

Firewood gatherers, such as the ones here in Tukl Baab, Sudan, must go farther and farther from home to find wood for fuel because they have already harvested nearer sources. JAMES NACHTWEY

the expansion of human settlement and suggest alternative uses for areas of those soil types

Identify physical environments in which limits to growth are significant (e.g., extremely cold, arid, or humid tropical climates and mountainous and coastal environments), describe the conditions that may threaten humans in these environments (e.g., rises in population that place pressure on marginal areas), and then develop plans to alleviate such stresses

c. Explain the ways in which individuals and societies hold varying perceptions of natural hazards in different environments and have different ways of reacting to them, as exemplified by being able to

Collect personal and group responses to different natural hazards before, during, and after the event, and summarize the varying perceptions of natural hazards in different regions of the world

Conduct interviews to assess people's attitudes, perceptions, and responses toward natural hazards in the local community and explain patterns that may emerge (e.g., the effects of religious beliefs, socioeconomic status, previous experience, and other factors on perception and response toward hazards)

Evaluate the effectiveness of human attempts to limit damage from natural hazards and explain how people who live in naturally hazardous regions adapt to their environments (e.g., the use of sea walls to protect coastal areas subject to severe storms, the use of earthquake-resistant construction techniques in different regions within the Ring of Fire)

Environment and Society

▶ THE CHANGES THAT OCCUR IN THE MEANING, USE, DISTRIBUTION, AND IMPORTANCE OF RESOURCES

. . . .

By the end of the twelfth grade, the student knows and understands:

1. **How the spatial distribution of resources affects patterns of human settlement**

2. **How resource development and use change over time**

3. **The geographic results of policies and programs for resource use and management**

Therefore, the student is able to:

A. **Analyze the relationships between the spatial distribution of settlement and resources, as exemplified by being able to**

Describe how patterns of settlement are associated with the location of resources (e.g., the organization of farming activities around agglomerated settlements in Southeast Asia; the spatial arrangement of villages, towns, and cities in the North American corn belt)

Explain how the discovery and development of resources in a region attract settlement (e.g., the development of cities in Siberia resulting from the discovery of coal, nickel, and iron ore; the increasing occupance of the Laurentian Shield in northern Ontario and Quebec as a consequence of the area's mining and hydroelectric-power potential)

Describe how settlement patterns are altered as a result of the depletion of a resource (e.g., the creation of ghost towns in the mining areas of Colorado; the depopulation of fishing communities in Canada's Maritime Provinces)

B. **Explain the relationship between resources and the exploration, colonization, and settlement of different regions of the world, as exemplified by being able to**

Explain the geographic consequences of the development of mercantilism and imperialism (e.g., the settlement of Latin America by the Spanish and Portuguese in the sixteenth and seventeenth centuries, the development of spheres of influence by the Dutch and the British in Asia in the nineteenth century)

Deadwood, South Dakota, 1876. Mule-drawn wagons skirt a gold mine dug into the middle of shop-lined Main Street during the Black Hills gold boom.
NEBRASKA STATE HISTORICAL SOCIETY

Identify and discuss historic examples of exploration and colonization of the world in a quest for resources (e.g., the voyages of Columbus undertaken to find a passage to India and China for easy access to spices and precious metals; Russian settlement of Siberia, Alaska, and California as sources of fur, fish, timber, and gold)

Identify and discuss examples of resources that have been highly valued in one period but less valued in another (e.g., the use of salt and spices for the preservation of food before the advent of refrigeration, the dismissal of petroleum as a nuisance product known as "ground oil" before the invention of the internal combustion engine)

c. **Evaluate policy decisions regarding the use of resources in different regions of the world, as exemplified by being able to**

Discuss how and why some countries use greater than average amounts of resources (e.g., German iron-ore imports, and petroleum consumption in the United States and Japan)

Explain the geographic consequences of the development and use of various forms of energy (e.g., renewable, nonrenewable, and flow resources)

Evaluate the short- and long-term economic prospects of countries that rely on exporting nonrenewable resources (e.g., the long-term impact on the economy of Nauru when its phosphate reserves are exhausted; the economic and social problems attendant to the overcutting of pine forests in Nova Scotia)

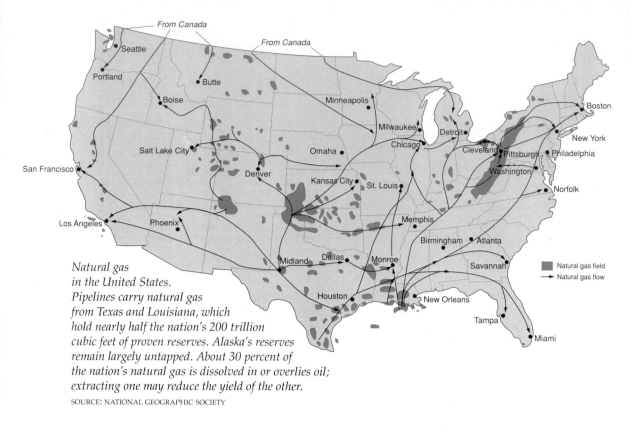

Natural gas
in the United States.
Pipelines carry natural gas
from Texas and Louisiana, which
hold nearly half the nation's 200 trillion
cubic feet of proven reserves. Alaska's reserves
remain largely untapped. About 30 percent of
the nation's natural gas is dissolved in or overlies oil;
extracting one may reduce the yield of the other.

SOURCE: NATIONAL GEOGRAPHIC SOCIETY

D. **Identify the ways in which resources can be reused and recycled, as exemplified by being able to**

Explain the changing relocation strategies of industries seeking access to recyclable material (e.g., paper factories, container and can companies, glass, plastic, and bottle manufacturers)

Discuss the geographic issues involved in dealing with toxic and hazardous waste at local and global levels (e.g., the movement, handling, processing, and storing of materials)

Compare recycling laws in states of the United States and other countries to explain people's attitudes toward resource management (e.g., attitudes on comprehensive versus haphazard, stringent versus permissive, fully enforced versus consistently neglected approaches to resource management)

E. **Evaluate policies and programs related to the use of resources on different spatial scales, as exemplified by being able to**

Evaluate the geographic impacts of policy decisions related to the use of resources (e.g., community regulations for water usage during drought periods; local recycling programs for glass, metal, plastic, and paper products)

Develop objective evaluations regarding the performance of the last four presidential administrations in the United States in terms of resource management policies

Evaluate resource degradation and depletion in less developed countries from multiple points of view (e.g., different points of view regarding uses of the Malaysian rain forests expressed by a Japanese industrialist and a conservationist with the United Nation's Food and Agricultural Organization)

GEOGRAPHY STANDARD **17** GRADES 9–12

The Uses of Geography

▶ HOW TO APPLY GEOGRAPHY TO
INTERPRET THE PAST

. . . .

By the end of the twelfth grade, the student knows and understands:

1. **How processes of spatial change affect events and conditions**

2. **How changing perceptions of places and environments affect the spatial behavior of people**

3. **The fundamental role that geographical context has played in affecting events in history**

Therefore, the student is able to:

A. **Explain how the processes of spatial change have affected history, as exemplified by being able to**

Trace the spatial diffusion of a phenomenon and the effects it has had on regions of contact (e.g., the spread of bubonic plague in the world; the diffusion of tobacco smoking from North America to Europe, Africa, and Asia)

Use maps and other data to describe the development of the national transportation systems that led to regional integration in the United States (e.g., the construction of a canal system in the early nineteenth century, the transcontinental railroad in the 1860s, the national interstate highway system in the mid-twentieth century)

Trace the geographic effects of migration streams and counterstreams of rural African Americans from the South to urban centers in the North and West throughout the twentieth century

B. **Assess how people's changing perceptions of geographic features have led to changes in human societies, as exemplified by being able to**

Compare the attitudes of different religions toward the environment and resource use and how religions have affected world economic development patterns and caused cultural conflict or encouraged social integration

Research and develop a case study to illustrate how technology has enabled people to increase their control over nature and how that has changed land-use patterns (e.g., large-scale agriculture in Ukraine and northern China, strip-mining in Russia, center-pivot irrigation in the southwestern United States)

Immigrants on the deck of S. S. Amerika arrive in New York, 1905. KEYSTONE/MAST COLLECTION, UNIVERSITY OF CALIFORNIA, RIVERSIDE

Prepare a series of maps to illustrate the Russian perception of encirclement by enemies and how this perception influenced the development of Russian (and Soviet) foreign policy

c. Analyze the ways in which physical and human features have influenced the evolution of significant historic events and movements, as exemplified by being able to

Assess the role and general effects of imperialism, colonization, and decolonization on the economic and political developments of the nineteenth and twentieth centuries (e.g., European disregard for existing African political boundaries in the organization of colonies and subsequent independent nations; the exploitation of indigenous peoples in the European colonization of the Americas)

Examine the historical and geographical forces responsible for the industrial revolution in England in the late eighteenth and early nineteenth centuries (e.g., the availability of resources, capital, labor, markets, technology)

Evaluate the physical and human factors that have led to famines and large-scale refugee movements (e.g., the plight of the Irish in the wake of the potato famine in 1845 to 1850, the cyclical famines in China, the droughts and famines in the Sahel in the 1970s and 1980s)

The Uses of Geography

▶ HOW TO APPLY GEOGRAPHY TO INTERPRET
·THE PRESENT AND PLAN FOR THE FUTURE

· ·

By the end of the twelfth grade, the student knows and understands:

1. **How different points of view influence the development of policies designed to use and manage Earth's resources**

2. **Contemporary issues in the context of spatial and environmental perspectives**

3. **How to use geographic knowledge, skills, and perspectives to analyze problems and make decisions**

Therefore, the student is able to:

A. **Develop policies that are designed to guide the use and management of Earth's resources and that reflect multiple points of view, as exemplified by being able to**

Prepare a panel simulation with participants who represent different points of view on sustainable development to explain the effects of such a concept in a variety of situations (e.g., toward cutting the rain forests in Indonesia in response to a demand for lumber in foreign markets, or mining rutile sands along the coast in eastern Australia near the Great Barrier Reef)

Explain the extent and geographic impact of changes in the global economy on the lives of affluent and poor people (e.g., in African, Asian, and South American cities) to demonstrate the inequities of urban life, resource use, and access to political and economic power in developing countries

Use a variety of resources, including maps, graphs, and news clippings, to describe the impact of a natural disaster on a developed country versus a developing country, to understand the private and public reaction to the disaster, and to evaluate the policies that have been formulated to cope with a recurrence of the disaster (e.g., compare the 1991 eruption of Mount Unzen in western Japan with the 1991 eruption of Mount Pinatubo in central Luzon, the Philippines; the 1993 floods in the Mississippi Valley with the 1993 floods in the Rhine River Valley; Hurricane Andrew in 1992 and the 1992 monsoon-caused floods in Bangladesh)

B. **Develop plans to solve local and regional problems that have spatial dimensions, as exemplified by being able to**

Develop plans to safeguard people and property in the event of a major natural disaster (e.g., use maps to prepare an evacuation plan for low-lying islands threatened by hurricanes)

Use a series of maps or a geographic information system (GIS) to obtain information on soil, hydrology and drainage, sources of water, and other factors and then use the information to choose the best site for a sanitary landfill in an urban region

Design a mass-transit system to move large groups of people from the site of a new sports arena in a city, taking into account such factors as where people live, present transportation facilities, and carrying capacities

C. **Analyze a variety of contemporary issues in terms of Earth's physical and human systems, as exemplified by being able to**

Explain the processes of land degradation and desertification as the interaction of physical systems (e.g., dry lands, drought, and desiccation) and human systems (e.g., exceeding the ability of vulnerable land to support settlement)

List the consequences of population growth or decline in a developed economy for both human and physical systems (e.g., dependency problems, exceeding available resources, contracting economic markets)

Write a scenario predicting the likely consequences of a world temperature increase of 3° F on humans, other living things (including plants and phytoplankton), and physical systems

D. **Use geography knowledge and skills to analyze problems and make decisions within a spatial context, as exemplified by being able to**

Develop a strategy to substitute alternative sustainable activities for present economic activities in regions of significant resource depletion (e.g., propose alternatives to fishing in Atlantic Canada, where fish populations have been depleted; alternatives to irrigated farming in the area served by the Ogallala Aquifer, which has been used too intensively)

Prepare a mock State Department-style briefing on a specific world region (e.g., outline broad global and region-specific patterns in the locations, distribution, and relationships of countries, their borders, relief features, climatic patterns, ecosystems, and population distribution and density, as well as the urban arrangement and communication networks within them, and evaluate the future of the region based on appropriate sustainable approaches to economic, social, and political development)

Examine tourism in a developed or a developing country to identify conflicts over resource use, the relative advantages and disadvantages of tourism to local residents, and the costs and benefits of tourism from several points of view (e.g., those of the owner of a diving shop, a hotel maid, a tourist, and a local fisherman) to put together a position paper for or against developing tourism in a new location

CHAPTER 8

Student Achievement in Geography

Interpreting Student Achievement Using the National Geography Standards

The National Geography Standards will enable students to use their geographic knowledge in real-life situations and as a basis for lifelong learning. Each of the standards has practical applications that encourage students to know and understand geographic concepts, and to use the skills of geographic inquiry in decision-making throughout their lives. The study of geography is an interpretive endeavor that draws on the natural and social sciences and the humanities to help students develop an informed world view. As a core school subject, students will be expected to demonstrate their proficiency in a range of learning behaviors, including:

▶ Recalling relevant content from geographic subject matter

▶ Understanding the rich and diverse characteristics of people, places, and environments

▶ Interpreting maps, globes, and other geographic tools and technologies, such as charts, graphs, aerial photographs, and satellite-produced images

▶ Understanding that space and spatial relationships are fundamental components of human interdependence on the local, regional, or global scales

▶ Recognizing the spatial relationships between people and their environments

▶ Distinguishing fact from opinion and relevant from irrelevant information in resources and databases

▶ Accessing geographic information from a variety of print and electronic sources

▶ Solving problems systematically using geographic methods

These learning behaviors reflect the National Geography Standards which are built upon geography's five themes (location, place, human–environmental interaction, movement, and region) as presented in *Guidelines for Geographic Education*. The five themes function as an organizing structure for geography instruction across the grade levels. The geography standards are also based on the three learning outcomes (space and place, environment and society, and spatial dynamics and connections) that are the basis for the *National Assessment of Educational Progress* in Geography. Each outcome is addressed at every grade level and provides an assessment framework around which to construct multiple-choice questions as well as short- and extended-answer questions. What results is a unity of themes, outcomes, and standards that defines world-class proficiency in geography and demonstrates how geographic learning is cumulative and spiraling.

What follows are achievement-level narratives that describe what should be expected of students in terms of their proficiency in geography. The narratives, like the standards, are organized on the basis of three grade levels—the end of the fourth grade, eighth grade, and twelfth grade.

The extent to which students at the three levels are able to demonstrate proficiency in geography provides a frame of reference to help teachers identify specific degrees of student achievement—whether an individual does not meet, meets, or exceeds the standards. Teachers will be able to recognize those students who are aspiring to standard, performing at standard, and achieving beyond standard. In addition, they will be able to construct appropriate test instruments for assessing their students' knowledge of geography.

Achievement Level Narratives for Fourth Grade

FOURTH-GRADE STUDENTS ASPIRING TO STANDARD

Fourth graders who are aspiring to standard exhibit an inconsistent mastery of the information and concepts presented to them. They may be able to locate specific places on a map if given verbal prompts or describe key features associated with familiar places. However, they seldom exercise any learning initiative and tend to be teacher-dependent. Seldom do they go beyond providing an incomplete definition of a geographic term or anything more than a minimal description of such physical phenomena as basic landforms and simple weather patterns. They might, for example, be able to locate the world's continents on a map and name them, but they cannot describe the relative locations of continents.

These students often cannot go beyond the basic place-name curriculum. Much of their difficulty in determining relationships between discrete elements of information and explaining the significance of fundamental ideas in geography results from a limited proficiency in reading and writing skills. In addition, they

SUMMARY OF FOURTH GRADERS ASPIRING TO STANDARD:

▶ Tend to be easily distracted from the task at hand because of a short attention span

▶ Possess limited knowledge of the most basic geographic concepts

▶ Demonstrate incomplete understanding of the local community's interaction with services such as transportation systems and communications facilities

▶ Lack well-developed reading, writing, and vocabulary skills

▶ Demonstrate an imprecise sense of place and place location

▶ Tend to ethnocentricity because of an inability to understand or appreciate other cultures

▶ Show an inconsistent understanding of how humans adapt to their environment or how environment influences decision-making

▶ Possess a vague and imprecise sense of the connection of the local community to the rest of the world

▶ Know how to use an alphanumeric reference system to locate places on a local map, but are unable to apply the principles of latitude and longitude to locate places on maps

have a narrow vocabulary and, when responding to geographic questions, are restricted to providing the simplest explanations, which often are fragmented and incomplete.

Aspiring-to-standard fourth graders can use maps and globes showing physical features and political boundaries. They can point to large physical features such as the Rocky Mountains or the Indian Ocean, and they can locate the United States. Their sense of place, however, is often confused (e.g., they may perceive Canada and Mexico as being part of the United States). In addition, these students seldom have a clear understanding of the difference between a continent and a country or between a city and a state. Nor can they explain why certain physical features might influence the location of a place. For these students, the transfer of learning is a difficult process. For example, they may have discovered reasons why cities are frequently located on the floodplains of rivers, but when asked

to explain why a city they are familiar with became important they are hard pressed to provide an answer. These students can manage simple charts and tables, but they exercise only one-step translations of the data (e.g., they can determine the amount of annual precipitation in a particular country from a table that lists countries and their average annual precipitation in inches, but they are unable to deal with questions of comparative analysis). These fourth graders demonstrate minimal ability to analyze part–whole or relevant–irrelevant relationships. Thus they find it difficult to make any significant spatial associations using maps and globes.

Trial and error tends to characterize the problem-solving skills of these students. If an answer or a solution is not readily at hand, they abandon the project and turn to something else. When challenged with a question about a place or a locational problem requiring the use of a map, they respond in only the most basic and literal manner. To complete any task they require step-by-step assistance, including being guided through information from maps, textbooks, teacher's handouts, and standard reference works.

Whatever geographic skills these students have acquired, they tend to apply unsystematically in decision-making. They cannot judge a solution as appropriate or inappropriate, or determine and propose alternatives.

They are also unable to foresee the consequences of their choices, because they have not yet developed the ability to find relationships between various physical and human phenomena. Neither are they able to recognize the connections between causes and their effects that exist within physical and human environments. When asked to describe an environmental or cultural issue from more than a single perspective, they cannot.

FOURTH-GRADE STUDENTS AT STANDARD

Fourth graders who are performing at standard can recall significant data, define key terms, and explain basic geographic concepts with some measure of consistency. They can use maps and globes as the basic tools of geography to locate physical and human phenomena. Describing these features using relevant geographic vocabulary is also within their realm of competence. These students can access information from several sources with only minimal direction from the teacher. They also have a general understanding of geography's five organizing themes and can use them to describe their own school or community environment. They also understand how the themes apply in other areas of the curriculum.

Fourth graders at standard can provide reasons for the location of places from data gathered from maps, aerial photographs, and photographs. They can compare two places and recognize physical and human similarities and differences, and they can prepare simple maps of their own design and plot a route on the basis of written and oral directions. Map development includes being able to draw the continents in rough outline as well as sketch the boundaries that delineate the United States, Canada, and Mexico within North America. As part of their map imaging, these students know the various physical regions of the United States and understand the basic relationships between the features of these regions and the people who live and work in them (e.g., housing, recreational activities, resources, climate, and job opportunities). Such students can use latitude and longitude as well as alphanumeric grid systems to locate places on maps and globes.

Students performing at standard have developed a world sense and can demonstrate an understanding of their dependency on other places for clothing, foodstuffs, information, and raw materials. They can provide examples of how settlers adapt to a place as well as how they introduce technology and cultural values to that place. Because of their awareness of how people interact with their environment, such students can predict future trends in realistic and thoughtful ways. Thus they can describe convincingly how they are connected to parts of Earth beyond their immediate experience.

Group problem-solving is clearly an identifiable characteristic of fourth graders who perform at standard. They can apply a multiple-step process in defining and analyzing situations. They also have research skills adequate for acquiring information from library sources, atlases, and textbooks. When presented with a geographic issue relating to a natural hazard

SUMMARY OF FOURTH GRADERS AT STANDARD:

► Use the five themes in geography as an organizational framework

► Possess a solid command of geographic vocabulary and concepts

► Use maps and globes to locate places and gather data for locational decisions

► Apply the skills of place location using latitude and longitude as well as alphanumeric grid systems

► Present an environmental or cultural issue from more than a single point of view

► Possess a global sense and have an awareness of economic and political interdependence

► Make simple comparisons showing the similarities and differences between places

► Demonstrate how people have adapted to and been influenced by their physical environment

► Acquire geographic information from a variety of sources

► Develop alternative solutions to geographic issues

► Participate effectively in collaborative learning situations

common to the area where they live (violent summer storms, blizzards, hurricanes) and the natural disasters that often result, they can evaluate such situations from personal research and observation. Group discussion is a common vehicle for such evaluation: These students can often present alternative solutions to problems and establish criteria for weighing the importance and value of those alternatives in joint decision-making activities.

FOURTH-GRADE STUDENTS BEYOND STANDARD

Fourth graders who are performing beyond standard demonstrate significantly greater consistency in the recall of specific geographic information than students functioning at standard. Their geographic vocabulary ranges beyond what has been introduced in the classroom. They can interpret and analyze data acquired from maps, charts, tables, and other graphics, and can produce simple maps and graphs of their own design. Acquiring information from a variety of sources is also a skill that these students possess. They often use such reference materials when working in other school subjects, and can place much of what they learn across the curriculum in a spatial framework. Their knowledge is integrated and not bound by disciplinary definitions. In addition, in their written and oral work, they can present a balanced perspective.

Beyond-standard students are independent learners. They show great curiosity about spa-

SUMMARY OF FOURTH GRADERS BEYOND STANDARD:

▶ Function as independent learners in all school subjects

▶ Use themes and ideas from many subject areas

▶ Exhibit consistency and depth in dealing with complex geographic concepts

▶ Incorporate the vocabulary of geography in both oral and written expression

▶ Address and solve problems on several levels

▶ Identify options and suggest alternatives when resolving geographic issues

▶ Compare different physical regions to determine their advantages and disadvantages for human activity

tial connections and can give examples of how humans have adapted to their environments in different parts of the world at different times. For example, they can explain how, in their own communities in an earlier era, weather patterns affected industry, transportation, communication, and the ways people made their living and then contrast the changes that have taken place as a result of technology.

These fourth graders have well-developed mental maps of the world. They can draw and label all the continents and oceans and can include key physical features (e.g., mountains, deserts, and the Great Lakes). On outline maps they can label the countries of North America as well as one or two countries of South America, Europe, Africa, and Asia. They also have an accurate knowledge of some of the basic political geography of the United States and can locate and label their own state and bordering states. In addition, they can identify their state's capital city. Beyond that, they have a generally well-for-

mulated knowledge of the country's major physical regions (e.g., Great Plains, Rocky Mountains, and Atlantic Coastal Plain). They also know how such regions interact and how they depend upon one another economically and culturally.

Because these fourth-grade students are able to integrate the information and skills they have learned in their various school subjects, they tend to be effective problem solvers. Using their broad knowledge base as well as their ability to make connections and see relationships, they can examine many sides of an issue in geography, identify and weigh options, and then reach a decision and draw a conclusion (e.g., when asked why the price of orange juice might increase abruptly in U. S. supermarkets, they can relate it to a recent freeze in the Florida citrus groves). Making connections about places and events and using multi-step procedures to acquire and evaluate information characterizes how these children think and how they manage learning.

Achievement Level Narratives for Eighth Grade

Eighth graders who are aspiring to standard have limited mastery of the skills, facts, and concepts required in geography of middle school or junior high school students. Their knowledge base is both imprecise and incomplete. Although they can define and use some of the terminology standard to physical and human geography, they cannot develop ideas or connect them to other geographic elements. For example, these students may be able to define such terms as "site" and "situation," but they cannot apply the meaning of either to a specific place. Nor can they distinguish between the two with any clarity when challenged to do a simple locational analysis of familiar places within their community.

The thinking skills of these students are largely undeveloped as is their ability to use such basic geographic tools as maps, globes, standard reference works (e.g., almanacs, geographic dictionaries, and encyclopedias), and databases. Their understanding of geography does not go beyond being able to locate places on a map using latitude and longitude or recognizing basic physical and human features in a landscape. They have only a limited ability to describe significant geographic issues relating to such topics as reforestation, the use of natural resources, or factors influencing changes in political boundaries. Geography's five themes are isolated ideas for these students, who are seldom able to connect or apply them to any aspect of their own experience. Further, they do not recognize the interaction between natural and cultural environments, or how the needs and events at one place have any impact on the needs and events at other places.

Eighth graders at this level have only a limited awareness of the subject matter of geography and are unable to differentiate in any meaningful way between various classifica-

SUMMARY OF EIGHTH GRADERS ASPIRING TO STANDARD:

▶ **Possess limited mastery of geographic information (e.g., vocabulary, facts, concepts, map and globe skills)**

▶ **Develop spatially related ideas in a limited way because of poorly developed reading, writing, and oral skills**

▶ **Recognize and describe basic physical and human features in a landscape**

▶ **May be able to identify and define the five themes of geography, but can only apply them inconsistently**

▶ **Relate to ideas in geography primarily on the basis of their own life experiences (e.g., watching films or television, and taking trips)**

▶ **Manage problem-solving challenges on the simplest level**

tions (physical systems and landscapes, human systems and landscapes, or spatial systems and connections). Instead they tend to relate to events with which they have had direct personal experience (e.g., they are likely to identify the Rocky Mountains not as a physical feature but as a high, angular rock formation they have seen on television, in a film, or on a recent summer vacation). They need considerable guidance from their teachers to make connections. They see places largely as separate and isolated entities. As a result, the test model they best respond to expects only the recall of specific information through multiple choice, fill-in-the-blank, and true-or-false answers.

Aspiring-to-standard eighth graders can manage only one kind of problem-solving situation in geography: Responding to a well-defined, narrowly focused question with the necessary reference information at hand. Their reading, writing, and oral skills are still basic (e.g., their out-of-class reports and in-class presentations are likely to be reproduced from yearbooks and encyclopedias). As a result, these students often have difficulty participating effectively in group learning situations.

EIGHTH-GRADE STUDENTS AT STANDARD

Eighth graders who are performing at standard exhibit the benefits of systematic instruction in geography. Their knowledge base is broad. They can use the vocabulary of geography comfortably and effectively to describe locations as well as physical and human landscape features. They are familiar with major geographic concepts and can use them to analyze spatial relationships on a local to global scale (e.g., they can explain why there are generally arid conditions on the lee-ward side of high mountain ranges and relate such rain shadows to the hydrologic cycle).

These students draw upon all of the subject matter of geography. They understand the ideas of space and place, environment and society, and spatial dynamics and connections, and can place them within the context of geography's five themes. As a result, these eighth graders can identify relationships and connections affecting the physical environment, human settlement patterns, and other distributions. They can general-

SUMMARY OF EIGHTH GRADERS AT STANDARD:

▶ Have a well-formed base in the vocabulary and concepts of geography
▶ Know basic geographic subject matter relating to space and place, environment and society, and spatial dynamics and connections
▶ Recognize the role of the five themes of geography
▶ Relate geography to life experiences
▶ Understand the patterns, systems, and processes of physical and human geography
▶ Possess well-developed skills in the use of maps, globes, and standard reference sources
▶ Recognize the spatial context of historical and contemporary issues
▶ Apply the principles of geography to solving social and environmental problems

ize about such broad concepts as change, diversity, systems, and culture. Although their response to questions on geographic issues may be incomplete and sometimes imprecise, they demonstrate mastery of essentials.

In the skills area, these students are able to use maps and globes not only to locate places but also at more sophisticated levels involving locational analysis and the description of relative location. They can interpret simple databases, graphs, and charts; collect and classify information from several reference sources; and assess problems and analyze issues effectively enough to suggest multiple solutions. Their skill base includes being able to use a number of research tools. They can extrapolate information effectively and present it in a coherent manner.

These eighth graders in order to recognize trends, themes, and key ideas draw on both their own life experience and current events. They use their knowledge of content, their skill base, and their understanding of geography's multiple points of view in ways that show they have an awareness of the complexity of Earth. Further, these students are beginning to recognize how the planet is an integrated expression of physical and human systems and patterns. At the same time, they have their own perspective of the natural and human-modified environment and understand how, as global citizens, they relate to the rest of world.

EIGHT-GRADE STUDENTS BEYOND STANDARD

Eighth graders who are performing beyond standard differ only by degree from at-standard students. They display a greater consistency in the recall of information and in the application of skills. They can interpret and analyze data rooted in each of geography's five themes, and consistently recall specific geographic information, including essential vocabulary, basic concepts, and key ideas. In addition, they are capable of thinking innovatively about geographic issues (e.g., when asked to speculate on how the United States might be regionalized beyond the typical textbook treatment of New England, the Midwest, the Pacific Northwest, etc., they are able to develop different sets of criteria and suggest arrangements that might include the rust belt, the Sunbelt, and the Northwest Cornucopia).

The information these students have acquired accrues from a variety of sources, including atlases, text materials, standard reference works, and computer databases (when that technology is available). In all that they do, these students demonstrate that their geographic knowledge is both broad and deep.

As a result, in any problem-solving situation, they can pursue a multi-level approach using subject matter, skills, and perspectives, and they are able to develop and test hypotheses and identify alternative solutions.

These eighth graders can use the themes and subject matter of geography in a variety of contexts. They recognize that historic time interacts with geographic space and that events always occur within the context of place (e.g., Napoleon's invasion of Russia in 1812 becomes meaningful when placed against the harsh reality of the bitter winters common in that part of Europe). Further, they can make connections across time and space (e.g., they recognize the similarities between the centuries-long ethnic strife over territory in southeastern Europe and the turf wars among urban street gangs in modern-day New York, Chicago, and Los Angeles).

Their ability to identify relationships is not bound by the constraints of a single discipline. Rather, their learning is an integrative experience. For these eighth graders, the humanities and the social and physical sciences provide a context for understanding the world.

Achievement Level Narratives for Twelfth Grade

. . . .

TWELFTH-GRADE STUDENTS ASPIRING TO STANDARD

Twelfth-grade students who are aspiring to standard can be characterized as inconsistent learners who are most responsive to knowledge that is practical and immediately applicable. Because these students often have insufficiently developed reading, writing, and language skills, their information base is restricted. They may understand some of the subject matter of geography, but they lack the depth and breadth of understanding that will equip them to be fully functional and productive in a complex, information-based, technological society. Although their knowledge of absolute and relative location, the physical and human aspects of places, and human–environmental relationships has expanded since their middle and early high school years, twelfth graders at this achievement level are often unable to recognize the nature of spatial relationships or put the essentials of geography in any kind of spatial context. Their understanding of basic vocabulary is restricted, as is their ability to use it effectively.

Such students can identify key physical and human features on a world map. However, they find it difficult to explain and interpret the significance of such features or identify the relationships that exist among such features. These twelfth graders understand the fundamental geographic processes responsible for the physical and human characteristics of places, but they cannot identify or interpret the dynamics of such processes. Beyond that they are generally unable to account for changes in these environments. They also lack an informed sense of the fragility of Earth's ecosystems, and an understanding of strategies that people might develop to encourage the renewal of ecosystems or options they might pursue to accomplish such a renewal.

These students have a basic knowledge of location and such natural phenomena as weather and climate, landforms, and the hydrologic cycle. They understand such human phenomena as the general function of nation-states, the distribution of cities, and the distribution of population. They also comprehend the importance of maintaining connections between places in the world through an awareness of transportation and communication networks, migration patterns, and the distribution of goods and services. But their understanding of the fullness and complexity of geography is only partially formed. Students aspiring to standard at this level see the various components of geography as separate threads rather than the full fabric. As a result, they treat the elements of the discipline as independent and unrelated parts.

These twelfth-grade students at this level tend to be literal learners. Just as their knowledge base in geography has a narrow focus, so does their skill base. They have difficulty accessing information and evaluating data. Although they can use reference systems to locate places on maps and globes and can describe the general positions of places in relative terms, they find it difficult to establish relationships or to identify and define locational issues. They also are limited in their ability to ask incisive questions. They tend to seek simple and singular solutions to geographic problems, and they generally fail to speculate about the outcome of their decisions. Such students have only marginally mastered the survival skills that will make them functional citizens beyond the school community.

SUMMARY OF TWELFTH GRADERS ASPIRING TO STANDARD:

▶ **Possess a restricted information base**

▶ **Exercise thinking skills at the lower cognitive levels (e.g., recalling information)**

▶ **Are well grounded in only a few subject-matter areas**

▶ **Lack breadth of knowledge or understanding**

▶ **Recognize physical and human phenomena but cannot place them in context**

▶ **Fail to perceive connections among the components of geography**

▶ **Seek simple and singular solutions to issues**

▶ **Perceive geography primarily as place location**

TWELFTH-GRADE STUDENTS AT STANDARD

Twelfth-grade students who are performing at standard have mastered the essential content of both the physical and human aspects of geography. Beyond their knowledge of fundamental vocabulary and their competence in using the skills of acquiring, interpreting, and presenting geographic data, these students understand how the five themes of geography serve as subject matter organizers. They also recognize how the five themes can be used to present the complexity of geography in a straightforward manner. Such students understand that geography describes Earth in spatial terms and explains not only where places are located, but also the reasons for the distribution of physical and human phenomena across the planet's surface. Through their knowledge of space and place, these twelfth graders understand spatial patterns as well as the physical and human processes that shape such patterns.

In addition, they can explain multiple interactions between the environment and human society and illustrate these with examples from real-life situations. They can identify and interpret spatial variations between people, places, and environments. Their knowl-

SUMMARY OF TWELFTH-GRADERS AT STANDARD:

- ► Are conversant with geographic subject matter
- ► Recognize that geography is the study of space and spatial relationships
- ► Use geographic vocabulary appropriately, in oral, written, and graphic communication
- ► Utilize a range of skills to acquire and present information
- ► Apply the principles of geography to real-life situations
- ► Understand how the three components of geography are interrelated
- ► Accept that geography is fundamental to understanding change in the physical and human environments
- ► Interpret the interaction between physical and human environments
- ► Understand the concept of global interdependence
- ► Understand the concept of "region" as an organizing principle

edge of world geography reinforces their awareness of how the United States relates to other places and other cultures across space and time.

Twelfth graders performing at standard possess the skills necessary to identify, access, analyze, and present geographic information. They are able to define and use the vocabulary specific to geography; distinguish between factual evidence, speculation, and hypothesis; recognize the nature and importance of spatial relationships; and specify and evaluate alternatives to geographic issues based on available data. These students are able to analyze new situations by drawing on their geographic knowledge and skills to solve problems. They understand the complexity of the global community, and know that being able to interpret the variety of human experience represented by the world's

cultures will enable them to compete successfully in the twenty-first century's economy.

At-standard twelfth graders understand that people depend on products, information, and ideas from beyond their immediate environment and that such interdependency creates networks that are interactive and complex. These students understand the concept of "region" in both physical and human terms. They know why regions form and why and how they change. They also recognize that regions are human creations developed to simplify the study and understanding of specific areas of the world. These students use their knowledge to respond constructively to new questions and problems. They have a sufficiently well-developed repertoire of skills and a base in geography to effectively address the range of challenges that they will face in their adult lives.

Twelfth-grade students who are performing beyond standard demonstrate broad knowledge of skills in geography. Their grasp of subject matter is both extensive and thorough. Their comprehension and application of the foundations of the discipline go well beyond the norm. These students can identify and use spatial relationships at a variety of levels and incorporate them in analyzing other physical and social sciences and the humanities. Advanced students can and do go beyond the immediate issue or question. They integrate diverse sources and types of data in order to develop comprehensive answers to issues in geography that are both contemporary and historical, physical and human, local and global.

Students performing beyond standard are also skilled researchers. They know how to locate and acquire useful geographic information and organize it effectively to extend their knowledge of geography and create hypotheses of their own design. They have well-developed analytic, synthetic, and evaluative skills that they can apply in a variety of contexts. They can write clearly, develop an argument, and carry it through to a conclusion.

These twelfth-grade students recognize that geography is expressed in multiple forms as a biophysical science, a study in human ecology, an investigation of societal and environmental relationships, an inquiry about the nature of the landscape, an assessment of the purpose and structure of regions, and an analysis of the distribution of physical and human phenomena.

Students at the beyond-standard level can draw upon a broad range of knowledge. They understand that change is the constant that defines both the physical and human realms of Earth. Their ability to examine and seek a more complete understanding of any question sets them apart from other students. They tend to be independent thinkers who enjoy the challenge of structuring and managing their own learning. Finally, these students understand that geography is a part of the fabric of knowledge that is both seamless and enduring.

SUMMARY OF TWELFTH-GRADERS BEYOND STANDARD:

▶ **Identify and use relationships across subject areas**

▶ **Relate geographic concepts to concepts in other subject areas**

▶ **Apply thinking skills in a number of contexts**

▶ **Exhibit well-developed geographic skills**

▶ **Confront new situations about the realities of geography constructively and creatively**

▶ **Use a broad range of research skills and apply them to a number of resources**

▶ **Assume responsibility for their own learning**

This Landsat image shows the red flames of oil-well fires, lit by Iraqi forces just prior to the Allied ground campaign. An oil-soaked cormorant (inset) is illuminated by the light of such a fire.

....

Thinking Geographically

The National Geography Standards contain what is most important and enduring in geography. They help teachers to decide what to teach, at what grades to teach it, and what to expect of students as a result. They give students rigorous but realistic benchmarks for which to strive. Geography provides students with skills for the workplace and skills for civic decision-making. Events around the world affect jobs and business at home. A change in the price of Persian Gulf oil affects the number of jobs in Louisiana and Texas, and agricultural policies in Japan and the European Union affect agricultural markets throughout the United States. By learning geography thoroughly, students come to understand the connections and relationships among themselves and people, places, and environments across the world. This is vital knowledge in today's society.

The National Geography Standards reflect the belief that geography must be as rigorously taught in the United States as it is in other countries. All countries depend upon their citizen's knowledge of the world to compete in the global economy, to ensure the viability of Earth's environments, and to comprehend the cultures of the diverse peoples who share our planet. The standards are designed to inspire students to do better and to learn enough geography to enable them to lead fulfilling and responsible lives.

The Role of Parents in Geography Education

....

Parents play a very important role in the education of their children. They can reinforce the concepts and skills learned in school. Children's attitudes toward school and school subjects reflect their parents' attitudes. Research indicates the positive effect on language acquisition when parents read with their children. The same may be true for geography. Parental interest in what children are doing

Earth is our only suitable habitat. Geography's task is to discover and capture its horizons in order to understand how people live and work and utilize resources. This understanding is more urgently required than ever for all students because of new global realities—the interconnected, integrated, and interdependent character of our lives.

Earth as seen from the moon, Apollo 17. NASA

in the classroom sends a powerful message to both children and the community at large about the importance of schooling.

Geography for Life encourages you to become involved with your child's education and to support school programs that teach geography. These activities are practical applications of the subject matter, skills, and perspectives featured in the National Geography Standards. Some tasks call for you and your child to "do geography" together. Other tasks are designed for your child to complete on her or his own. All of these activities may be used as an indication of how well your child is learning geography, and may inspire your interest as well. They exemplify the power of geography as a way of understanding Earth, our home.

NATIONAL GEOGRAPHY STANDARDS : 1994

What Does Your Fourth-Grader Know?

▶ Give clear and precise verbal directions to you describing a route between home and school?

▶ Describe the purpose of latitude and longitude and, using a world map or a globe, identify the absolute location of some specific places (e.g., Chicago, Illinois, or the Cape of Good Hope)?

▶ Locate the seven continents and four oceans on a world map, and point to and identify several countries in South America, Europe, Africa, and Asia?

▶ Describe the relative location of your local community in terms of its situation in your state and region (e.g., My town is halfway between the state capital and largest city in the state. My state is in the south-central part of the United States.)?

▶ Measure the straight-line distance between two places on an interstate highway map using the bar scale?

▶ Locate specific physical features on a map of North America (e.g., the Ozark Plateau, the Central Valley of California, the Susquehanna River, and Lake Okeechobee)?

▶ Locate specific human features on a map of North America (e.g., the corn belt, New England, the capital of the United States, and where the Declaration of Independence was signed)?

▶ Cite specific examples from anywhere in the world to illustrate environmental issues (e.g., deforestation and air and water pollution)?

▶ Explain how the local physical environment has affected the way people live in your community (e.g., how it has influenced choices of building materials, housing styles, and types of flowers and vegetables grown)?

▶ Find an answer to a geographic question using an encyclopedia, world atlas, gazetteer, computer database, or other library resources (e.g., identify the five largest cities in your state or the U. S. state that has the most tornadoes per year)?

▶ Tell a story about what it is like to travel to or live in another region of the country or world?

▶ Take you for a walk in a familiar environment and describe some of the physical and human features of the landscape?

▶ Describe, in her or his own words, what geography is about?

What Does Your Eighth-Grader Know?

CAN YOUR CHILD

▶ Describe the location and some of the physical and human characteristics of places mentioned in one of the day's newscasts?

▶ Draw a map and give detailed instructions on how to get to your home from specific points in the community that could be used by people who wish to visit?

▶ From memory draw a map of the world on a single sheet of paper and outline and label the major physical features (e.g., continents, oceans, major mountain ranges, significant desert regions and river systems) and important human features (e.g., major cities of the world, imaginary lines such as the Prime Meridian and the Equator)?

▶ Write a letter to a peer in another part of the United States or world explaining the physical and human geographic characteristics of your community?

▶ Explain the causes and consequences of seasons to younger sisters, brothers, or children in the neighborhood?

▶ Use a road atlas and other sources of information, such as travel brochures and guidebooks, to plan a personal trip and identify points of interest along the route?

▶ Watch a television show or movie with you and discuss the geographic aspects of it?

▶ Explain why many of the fresh fruits and vegetables in the supermarket in January come from countries in the Southern Hemisphere?

▶ Describe the stages of historical development and cultural landscape of an ethnic community in your area or a nearby community?

▶ Discuss the descriptions of different places (their geography) from a book you have both read?

▶ Explain in a few sentences the meaning of a graph, chart, map, or diagram printed in a newspaper, news magazine, or textbook?

▶ Answer the kinds of questions that are asked in the National Geography Bee or the International Geography Olympiad?

▶ Use an almanac or other sources to answer questions concerning a geographic topic (e.g., population of the world; the lowest temperature ever recorded; gross domestic product [GDP] statistics for selected countries in Southeast Asia; the crime rates in world cities with populations in excess of three million people)?

▶ Write a set of instructions on what your family should do in case of a natural disaster (e.g., hurricane, earthquake, mud slide, fire, tornado, blizzard, flood)?

▶ Describe, in her or his own words, what geography is about?

What Does Your Twelfth-Grader Know?

CAN YOUR CHILD

▶ Locate on a world map some of the places mentioned on a television or radio news broadcast and describe the cultural, political, and economic characteristics of those places?

▶ Name three locations in your community or region that have been affected by pollution, identify the sources and types of pollution and explain how each type affects the people living there?

▶ Draw from memory a map of the world, outline significant nations, and use the map to explain patterns of the standard of living in today's world?

▶ Plan a tour of your community for a visiting foreign exchange student or sister city group that highlights the community's most important physical and human geographic characteristics?

▶ Use a bus schedule, subway map, or city map to plan a trip from home to a sports arena, theater, or other point of interest using public transportation?

▶ Exchange points of view with a senior citizen about changes in your community over the past several decades and likely changes in the future?

▶ Hold a conversation with you on the geographic differences between developing and developed regions of the world and discuss the consequences of these differences?

▶ Use a topographic map to lay out a five-mile hike through the countryside or local community, noting such items as elevation, slope, distance, direction, and geographic features along the route?

▶ Explain the geographic reasons for the natural hazards in the Pacific rim region (e.g., plate tectonics and subduction causing earthquakes and volcanic eruptions and cyclonic wind patterns causing typhoons)?

▶ Use such regional alliance identifiers as OPEC (Organization of Petroleum Exporting Countries), NATO (North Atlantic Treaty Organization), and OAS (Organization of American States) comfortably in a conversation about the changing geopolitical realities of the post-Cold War world?

▶ Talk about college or job options after high school in terms of such geographic features as climate, accessibility, proximity to major metropolitan areas, or distance from home?

▶ Describe the economic conditions in the area where you live and explain the area's linkages to other parts of the world?

▶ Explain how job opportunities in different parts of the United States are related to trade with other countries?

▶ Describe, in her or his own words, what geography is about?

A

Genesis of the National Geography Standards

In Title I of the Educate America Act, Congress declared what the National Education Goals include and what their objectives would be (see the first 1994 entry below). Title II of the Act established the National Education Standards and Improvement Council (see the second 1993 entry below) to work with appropriate organizations and to determine the criteria for certifying voluntary standards. The council had three objectives in mind:

▶ to ensure that the standards are internationally competitive

▶ to ensure that they reflect the best knowledge about teaching and learning

▶ to ensure that they have been developed through a broad-based, open consensus process

The geography community responded as follows:

1984 *Guidelines in Geographic Education, K–12* published (the five themes of geography)

1985 Geography Education National Implementation Project (GENIP) founded (members: American Geographical Society, Association of American Geographers, National Council for Geographic Education, and National Geographic Society)

1985 Geography Education Program of the National Geographic Society (NGS) founded

1986 National Geographic Society Alliance network started with eight states

1987 *K–6 Guidelines* published by GENIP

1988 *Geography: International Gallup Survey* published

1988 *Strengthening Geography in the Social Studies* published (Bulletin 81, the National Council for the Social Studies)

1989 *7–12 Guidelines* published by GENIP

1989 The nation's governors and President George Bush determined at the Education Summit in Charlottesville, Virginia, that teaching and learning in kindergarten through grade 12 should focus on five subjects: geography, science, mathematics, English, and history

The enormity of the volcanic plume in this satellite photograph, taken ninety minutes after the 1980 eruption of Mount St. Helens, is only apparent when one recognizes the outline of the West Coast below it and the green of the Great Plains to its right. NOAA IMAGE BY IBM PALO ALTO SCIENTIFIC CENTER

1989 Goals 2000: Educate America Act drafted

1989 Annual National Geography Bee founded (National Geography Bee)

1989 Annual American Express Geography Competition founded (Association of American Geographers)

1990 National Education Goals (established at the Education Summit) adopted:

By the year 2000, every adult American will be literate and will possess the knowledge and skills necessary to compete in a global economy and exercise the rights and responsibilities of citizenship....

By the year 2000, American students will leave grades 4, 8, and 12 having demonstrated literacy in challenging subject matter including English, mathematics, science, history, and geography; and every school in America will ensure that all students learn to use their minds well, so they may be prepared for responsible citizenship, further learning, and productive employment in our modern economy.

1991 America 2000 plan includes geography as one of five core subjects (Department of Education)

1991 National Council on Education Standards and Testing (NCEST) established

1991–
1992 National Assessment of Educational Progress (NAEP) in geography developed

1992 NCEST concluded, "It is feasible as well as desirable to create national education standards."

1992–
1994 National Geography Standards developed

1993 National Geographic Society Alliance network reaches fifty states, Puerto Rico, the District of Columbia, and Ontario, Canada

1993 *Promises to Keep: Creating High Standards for American Students* published (National Education Goals Panel)

1994 Goals 2000: Educate America Act states:
[Section 102] Student Achievement and Citizenship

(A) By the year 2000, all students will leave grades 4, 8, and 12 having demonstrated competency over challenging subject matter including English, mathematics, science, foreign languages, civics and government, economics, arts, history, and geography; and every school in America will ensure that all students learn to use their minds well, so they may be prepared for responsible citizenship, further learning, and productive employment in our Nation's modern economy.... [The objectives for this goal include the following:]

(ii) the percentage of all students who demonstrate the ability to reason, solve problems, apply knowledge, and write and communicate effectively will increase substantially;

(iii) all students will be involved in activities that promote and demonstrate good citizenship, good health, community service, and personal responsibility;...

(vi) all students will be knowledgeable about the diverse cultural heritage of this Nation and about the world community.

1994 *Prisoners of Time* published (National Education Commission on Time and Learning)

1994 NAEP assessment in geography, grades 4, 8, and 12

1994 *Geography for Life: National Geography Standards 1994* published

The Consensus Process

Members of the Geography Education Standards Project are indebted to all the individuals and organizations whose assistance made *Geography for Life: National Geography Standards 1994* possible. First we acknowledge the elected officials who adopted the National Education Goals, which were incorporated into Goals 2000: Educate America Act. The Goals 2000 legislation identifies geography as one of the core subjects for the schools of the United States. Without the support of public officials there would have been no national standards for geography.

We thank the U. S. Department of Education, the National Endowment for the Humanities, and the National Geographic Society for their financial support and interest in our work. We appreciate the wise counsel of our project officers, Jaymie L. Lewis of the U. S. Department of Education and Jeffrey D. Thomas of the National Endowment for the Humanities. They kept us focused on the task. To both, thanks, with freedom from responsibility for the result. Gratitude is also due to Gilbert M. Grosvenor, President and Chairman, National Geographic Society. In the last several years he has almost single-handedly put geography back on the map of American education. To do so he has teamed up academic and professional geographers with classroom teachers. In the process he has made all Americans more aware that geography is central to their lives and critical to their future. His campaign for geography inspired us throughout our work.

We cannot adequately acknowledge the contributions of all the people who took the time to testify at hearings or to write productive reviews of drafts. These people—parents, teachers, curriculum developers, and business and policy leaders—provided us with insights crucial to the success of our consensus project.

A major word of thanks must go to those people who assisted us in the late stages of the project. Tom Berry, Carl Miller, Salvatore Natoli, Sarah Pratt, Linda Reeves, Geraldeen Rude, Martha Sharma, and Patrice St. Peter read the manuscript and gave us much help. Sona K. Andrews, Daniel D. Arreola, and Michal L. LeVasseur also read the manuscript but with one question in mind: Are the National Geography Standards flexible, adaptable, and respectful of diversity? Stanley D. Brunn and John F. Watkins very ably edited the glossary.

Finally, we acknowledge the support staffs at the National Council for Geographic Education and the National Geographic Society. They worked on all the details from arranging meetings to fact checking. For them the word "acknowledge" is grossly inadequate.

Committees and the Consensus Model

The National Geography Education Standards Project's committees consisted of:

> • Management • Eight authors • Writing Committee of experienced K–12 teachers and geography educators • Content Development Committee of scholars and instructors • Content Advisory Committee of geographers • Environmental Education Committee of specialists • International Committee of geography educators • Committee of Advisers, distinguished geographers from academe, government, and industry • Oversight Committee of public policy makers, educators, parents, and business leaders

The committee structure incorporated a broad-based consensus process by involving both the consumers of education and the providers of education, including all of the major geography organizations in the United States. This consensus process was patterned after the model used in the development of the *Geography Assessment Framework for the 1994 National Assessment of Educational Progress* (NAEP). As drafts of the standards were developed, they were disseminated widely to readers who were invited to comment. Further input was received from nine public hearings, each held in a different city. In addition to the more than 2,000 persons who were asked to review the standards, project administrators sent drafts for critique to a hundred state social studies and science coordinators, 750 geography teachers, all National Geographic Society Alliance network coordinators, legislative aides to state education committees, governors' aides to education, and stakeholders whose names were provided by the National Parent–Teachers Association, the Association for Supervision and Curriculum Development, state and local boards of education, the Business Roundtable, the American Geographical Society's business members, and teachers' unions. Project members met directors of other standards-writing projects and shared drafts among all the writing groups. Furthermore, the authors maintained close contact with the history and science groups—the disciplines with the strongest curriculum ties to geography.

Along with the advice and counsel from these groups, the authors used materials from many national and international sources including *Guidelines for Geographic Education (Joint Committee on Geographic Education 1984)* and the *Geography Assessment Framework for the 1994 National Assessment of Educational Progress.*

In developing drafts, the standard writers followed the U. S. Department of Education's criteria for national standards projects and the National Council on Education Standards and Testing's recommendations. They also paid attention in the later stages of the project to *Promises to Keep: Creating High Standards for American Students,* a report on the Review of Education Standards from the Goals 3 and 4 Technical Planning Group to the National Education Goals Panel (November 1993).

Members of the Geography Education Standards Project

OFFICERS

ANTHONY R. DE SOUZA, Executive Director
National Geographic Society

RUTH I. SHIREY, Project Administrator
National Council for Geographic Education

NORMAN C. BETTIS, Project Co-Chair
Illinois State University

CHRISTOPHER L. SALTER, Project Co-Chair
University of Missouri

ROGER M. DOWNS, Writing Coordinator
The Pennsylvania State University

THE STAFF

CONSTANCE MCCARDLE, Administrative Assistant
National Council for Geographic Education

HEATHER C. SCHOFIELD, Administrative Assistant
National Geographic Society

DESIGN, PRODUCTION,
AND EDITORIAL SERVICES

ANTHONY R. DE SOUZA, Editor
National Geographic Society

ROGER M. DOWNS, Geography Consultant
The Pennsylvania State University

PAUL ELLIOTT, Editorial Consultant

JEANNE E. PETERS, Editorial Consultant
National Geographic Society

WINFIELD SWANSON, Editorial Consultant
National Geographic Society

MICHAELINE A. SWEENEY, Editorial Consultant
National Geographic Society

GERARD A. VALERIO, Design Director
Independent Consultant

BRIDGET L. SNYDER, Assistant Art Director
National Geographic Society

HYLAH L. HILL, Production Assistant
National Geographic Society

ALICE B. GOODMAN, Editorial Assistant
National Geographic Society

JULIAN WATERS, Calligrapher

CHRISTINE FELTER YGLESIAS, Graphic Consultant

THE AUTHORS

SARAH WITHAM BEDNARZ
Texas A&M University

NORMAN C. BETTIS
Illinois State University

RICHARD G. BOEHM
Southwest Texas State University

ANTHONY R. DE SOUZA
National Geographic Society

ROGER M. DOWNS
The Pennsylvania State University

JAMES F. MARRAN
New Trier High School

ROBERT W. MORRILL
Virginia Polytechnic Institute and State University

CHRISTOPHER L. SALTER
University of Missouri

COMMITTEE CHAIRS

SAUL B. COHEN, Advisers
Hunter College–CUNY

SUSAN W. HARDWICK, Content Development
California State University–Chico

A. DAVID HILL, International
University of Colorado–Boulder

LYDIA LEWIS, Writing
National Geographic Society

MICHAEL J. LIBBEE, Environmental Education
Central Michigan University

RAMSAY SELDEN, Oversight
Council of Chief State School Officers

THOMAS J. WILBANKS, Content Advisory
Oak Ridge National Laboratory

COMMITTEE MEMBERS

ADVISERS: Brian J. L. Berry, *University of Texas–Dallas*; Harm J. de Blij, *Georgetown University*; Robert Britton, *American Airlines*; Larry E. Carlson, *Dayton–Hudson Corporation*; Kimberly Crews, *Population Reference Bureau*; George J. Demko, *Dartmouth College*; Ronald I. Dorn, *Arizona State University*; Philip J. Gersmehl, *University of Minnesota*; Michael F. Goodchild, *University of California–Santa Barbara*; Sidney R. Jumper, *University of Tennessee*; Robert W. Kates, *independent scholar*; Victoria A. Lawson, *University of Washington*; James E. McConnell, *State University of New York–Buffalo*; Alice T. M. Rechlin, *National Geographic Society*; Jeanette L. Rice, *Holliday, Fenoglio, Dockerty & Gibson, Inc.*; Erica Schoenberger, *Johns Hopkins University*; Allen J. Scott, *University of California–Los Angeles*; Eric S. Sheppard, *University of Minnesota*; Frederick P. Stutz, *San Diego State University*; Yi-Fu Tuan, *University of Wisconsin–Madison*; Billie L. Turner II, *Clark University*; Donald E. Vermeer, *George Washington University*; Barney L. Warf, *Florida State University*; Gilbert F. White, *University of Colorado–Boulder*; Cort J. Willmott, *University of Delaware*; Julian Wolpert, *Princeton University*.

CONTENT ADVISORY: James P. Allen, *California State University–Northridge*; J. W. Harrington, *George Mason University*; Sally P. Horn, *University of Tennessee*; Peter J. Hugill, *Texas A&M University*; Diana M. Liverman, *The Pennsylvania State University*; Melvin G. Marcus, *Arizona State University*; John Mercer, *Syracuse University*; Joel L. Morrison, *U. S. Geological Survey*; William B. Wood, *U. S. Department of State*.

CONTENT DEVELOPMENT: James S. Fisher, *Florida Atlantic University*; Donald G. Janelle, *University of Western Ontario*; Tom L. McKnight, *University of California–Los Angeles*; Thomas R. Vale, *University of Wisconsin–Madison*.

ENVIRONMENTAL EDUCATION: Ken Bingman, *Shawnee Mission West High School*; J. Ronald Gardella, *Northern Kentucky University*; Orin G. Gelderloos, *University of Michigan–Dearborn*; Wayne E. Kiefer, *Central Michigan University*; Melvin G. Marcus, *Arizona State University*; Rosalyn McKeown-Ice, *University of Tennessee*; Charles Roth, *U. S. Environmental Protection Agency*; George Walker, *U. S. Environmental Protection Agency*.

INTERNATIONAL: Klaus M. Aerni, *Universität Bern, Bern, Switzerland*; Henk A. M. Ankoné, *National Institute on Curriculum Development, Enschede, Netherlands*; Hugo Bodini Cruz-Carrera, *Universidad de La Serena, La Serena, Chile*; Yee-Wang Fung, *Chinese University of Hong Kong, Hong Kong*; Rodney V. Gerber, *Queensland University of Technology, Brisbane, Australia*; R. H. Goddard, *education consultant, Mississauga, Ontario, Canada*; Ad Goedvolk, *National Institute on Curriculum Development, Enschede, Netherlands*; Agustin Hernando, *Universitat de Barcelona, Barcelona, Spain*; Manik Hwang, *Seoul National University, Seoul, Republic of Korea*; Alexander Kondakov, *Moscow State Pedagogical University, Moscow, Russia*; Chi Chung Lam, *Chinese University of Hong Kong, Hong Kong*; John Lidstone, *Queensland University of Technology, Brisbane, Queensland, Australia*; Vladimir Maksakosky, *Moscow State Pedagogical University, Moscow, Russia*; Lucile Marbeau, *independent teacher consultant, Paris, France*; Shuichi Nakayama, *Hiroshima University, Hiroshima, Japan*; Günter Niemz, *Johann Wolfgang Goethe-Universitat, Frankfurt, Germany*; Ken Purnell, *University of Central Queensland, Rockhampton, Australia*; Eleanor M. Rawling, *Oxford University, Oxford, England*; Hannele Rikkinen, *University of Helsinki, Helsinki, Finland*; Stuart Semple, *Dalhousie University, Halifax, Nova Scotia, Canada*; Frances Slater, *University of London, London, England*; Norman C. Tait, *University of the North, Pietersburg, South Africa*; Margit K. Werner, *Göteborg Universitet, Göteborg, Sweden*; Zhang Yanan, *National Education Commission, Beijing, People's Republic of China*.

OVERSIGHT: Richard Aieta, *National Council for the Social Studies*; Frank Betts, *Association for Supervision and Curriculum Development*; The Honorable Jeffrey Bingaman, *U.S. Senator, New Mexico*; The Honorable Carroll Campbell, *Governor, South Carolina*; Admiral Geoffrey Chesbrough, *U. S. Department of Defense*; Christopher Cross, *Business Roundtable*; Thomas Dunthorn, *Florida Department of Education*; Chester E. Finn, Jr., *Edison Project, Whittle Schools LP*; Gilbert M. Grosvenor,

National Geographic Society; A. David Hill, *University of Colorado–Boulder*; Steven C. Kussmann, *Alliance for Environmental Education*; Richard P. Mills, *Vermont Department of Education*; The Honorable Jere W. Schular, *Pennsylvania House of Representatives*; Harold P. Seamon, *National School Boards Association*; Walt Tremer, *National Education Association*; Manya S. Ungar, *National Parent Teachers Association*; Gary M. Walton, *Foundation for Teaching Economics*; Ruth Wattenberg, *American Federation of Teachers*; Brenda Lilienthal Welburn, *National Association of State Boards of Education*; Gwendolyn T. Wilson, *National Science Teachers Association.*

AND THE FOLLOWING EX OFFICIO MEMBERS:

Mary Lynne Bird, *American Geographical Society*; Osa Brand, *Association of American Geographers*; Robert E. Dulli, *National Geographic Society*; David H. Florio, *National Academy of Sciences*; Thomas Hatfield, *National Art Education Association*; Martharose Laffey, *National Council for the Social Studies*; Lydia Lewis, *National Geographic Society*; Michael J. Libbee, *Central Michigan University*; Barbara Moses, *School District of Philadelphia*; Salvatore J. Natoli, *National Council for the Social Studies*; John J. Patrick, *National History Standards Project*; Charles N. Quigley, *Center for Civic Education*; William R. Strong, *University of North Alabama*; Thomas J. Wilbanks, *Association of American Geographers.*

WRITING: Judith K. Bock, *Lake Villa Intermediate School, IL*; John Brierley, *Venice High School, CA*; Rita Duarte Herrera, *Alum Rock School District, CA*; Gail A. Hobbs, *Pierce College*; Joan Longmire, *Kimball Middle School, IL*; Marianne Kenney, *Colorado Department of Education*; Barbara Moses, *School District of Philadelphia*; Corrine O'Donnell, *Campbell Elementary School, CO*; Linda Reeves, *Pat Nixon Elementary School, CA*; Cathy Riggs-Salter, *educational consultant, MO*; Martha B. Sharma, *National Cathedral School, Washington, D.C.*; Joseph P. Stoltman, *Western Michigan University*; Fred Walk, *Normal Community High School, IL*; Barbara J. Winston, *Northeastern Illinois University.*

Witnesses at Public Hearings

. . . .

► SANTO DOMINGO, DOMINICAN REPUBLIC • September 23, 1992

Ronald F. Abler, *Association of American Geographers*; Robert S. Bednarz, *Texas A&M University*; David B. Cole, *University of Northern Colorado*; Dorothy W. Drummond, *Indiana State University*; Edward A. Fernald, *Florida State University*; Celeste J. Fraser, *geography textbook author, IL*; Carter B. Hart, Jr., *Department of Education, NH*; A. Priscilla Holland, *University of North Alabama*; Gail S. Ludwig, *University of Missouri–Columbia*; Constance M. Manter, *Department of Education, ME*; Laurie E. Molina, *Florida State University*; M. Duane Nellis, *Kansas State University*; Dixie A. Pemberton, *Center for Environmental and Estuarine Studies, MD*; Frederick Wilman, *Jefferson Junior High School, IL*; Nancy L. Winter, *education consultant.*

WRITTEN TESTIMONY

Henry A. DeVona, *George C. Calef Elementary School, RI*; Carole J. Mayrose, *Northville High School, IN*; Rosalyn R. McKeown-Ice, *University of Tennessee.*

► DETROIT, MICHIGAN • November 21, 1992

Philip Bacon, *University of Houston*; Connie Binsfeld, *Lt. Governor of Michigan*; Edward A. Bonne, *Greenwood Elementary, MI*; Emily S. Clott, *Encyclopedia Britannica Educational Corporation*; Charles F. Gritzner, *South Dakota State University*; James N. Hantula, *University of Northern Iowa*; Deborah S. Johnston, *Plymouth North High School, MA*; Terry Kuseske, *Patrick Hamilton Middle School, MI*; Margaret Legates, *Milford Middle School, DE*; Kenneth D. Mareski, *St. Clair Middle School, MI*; Alan Markowitz, *Board of Education, NJ*; Marianna McJimsey, *Colorado College*; John Metzke, *Northfield Middle School, MN*; Douglas A. Phillips, *National Council for Geographic Education*; Patrick V. Riley Jr., *Rand McNally*; Terry Robidoux, *Redford High School, MI*; Robert D. Swartz, *Wayne State University*;

Wayne State University; Karen Thompson, *Massachusetts Council for the Social Studies;* Virginia L. Wazny, *Dwight Rich Middle School, MI;* Brenda S. Woemmel, *Central Junior High School, MO.*

WRITTEN TESTIMONY
Amy Zorn, *Jackson Center High School, OH.*

▶ GAINESVILLE, FLORIDA • February 19, 1993

Nikki L. Born, *Harlee Middle School, FL;* Bruce C. Bradford, *Stetson University;* Edward A. Fernald, *Florida State University;* Deborah Hagenbuch-Reese, *Florida State University;* Marci D. Jacobs, *Tyrone Elementary School, FL;* John Langraf, *Langraf Marketing Services, FL;* Cynthia L. Malecki, *William S. Talbot Elementary School, FL;* Edward J. Malecki, *University of Florida;* Paul A. Ryder, *Galaxy Middle School, FL.*

▶ GREELEY, COLORADO • March 6, 1993

Lane R. Adams, *Broadwater Elementary School, CO;* Raymond E. Best, *Central High School, CO;* Kenneth R. Cinnanmon, *University of Northern Colorado;* Craig L. Cogswell, *Westminster High School, CO;* John L. Dietz, *University of Northern Colorado;* Jean M. Eichhorst, *Grand Forks Public Schools, ND;* Linda L. Goedeke, *Littleton Public Schools, CO;* James Timothy Heydt, *Thompson Elementary School, CO;* Dianne Hill, *Muskogee High School, OK;* Laural J. Hoppes, *Centennial Middle School, CO;* Nancy Hurianek, *St. Vrain School, CO;* Mark A. Jeffryes, *Jefferson County Schools, CO;* Ginny Jones, *Skyland High School, CO;* M. Kathleen Lomshek, *McCune Elementary, KS;* Mary Claire May, *Horizons Middle School, NE;* Harris C. Payne, *North High School, NE;* Janet Pommrehn, *Denver Public Schools, CO;* Robert H. Stoddard, *University of Nebraska;* Patrick Sullivan, *State Representative of Colorado.*

WRITTEN TESTIMONY
Susan M. Gay, *Grand Island Senior High School, NE.*

▶ ATLANTA, GEORGIA • April 7, 1993

Edward Bergman, *Lehman College;* Larry E. Ford, *San Diego State University;* Clarissa T. Kimber, *Texas A&M University;* Neal G. Lineback, *Appalachian State University;* Ted D. Springer, *Harrison Middle School, IN;* Howard A. Stafford, *University of Cincinnati;* Frederick P. Stutz, *San Diego State University.*

▶ NASHVILLE, TENNESSEE • November 20, 1993

Edward A. Bonne, *Greenwood Elementary School, MI;* James N. Hatula, *University of Northern Iowa;* John D. Hoge, *University of Georgia;* Catherine G. Kelly, *McMurray Middle School, TN;* Margaret Legates, *Milford Middle School, DE;* Jody S. Marcello, *Blatchley Middle School, AK;* Ester L. Martens, *National Computer Systems;* Dean W. Moore, *Ohio Office of Education;* Joan Pederson, *Nystrom Divison of Herff Jones, Inc.;* Ben A. Smith, *Kansas State University.*

▶ CHICAGO, ILLINOIS • March 21, 1994

Phyllis A. Arnold, *Arnold Publishing, Ltd.;* Robert Dick, *St. Louis Public Schools, MO;* Erica Speight, *UNICEF;* Louise Swiniarski, *Salem State College;* Margaret C. Trader, *Washington County Board of Education, MD;* Roycealee J. Wood, *North Chicago Community Unit, School District 187, IL.*

▶ SAN FRANCISCO, CALIFORNIA • March 30, 1994

Thomas J. Baerwald, *National Science Foundation;* Barbara P. Buttenfield, *National Center for Geographical Information and Analysis;* John W. Florin, *University of North Carolina–Chapel Hill;* Truman A. Hartshorn, *Georgia State University;* Donald G. Holtgrieve, *California State University–Chico;* Phil Klein, *University of Colorado–Boulder;* David A. Lanegran, *Macalester College;* Miriam K. Lo, *Mankato State University;* Salvatore J. Natoli, *independent scholar.*

Alice C. Andrews, *American Express*; Elizabeth S. Andrews, *Sato Travel Academy, VA*; Thomas J. Baerwald, *National Science Foundation*; Angela B. Bell, *Birney Elementary School, Washington, DC*; John R. Dixon, *U.S. Army*; James W. Fonseca, *Prince William Institute, VA*; Milton Goldberg, *National Education Commission on Time and Learning*; Laure Ann Hunter, *Janney Elementary School, Washington, DC*; Margie J. Legowski, *Peace Corps*; Amy J. Maglio, *Greenpeace, Inc.*; Robert W. Marx; *U.S. Bureau of the Census*; Sister Catherine T. McNamee, *National Catholic Education Association*; Charles E. McNoldy, *Prince William County Government, VA*; Susan M. Mockenhaupt, *Partners for Resource Education*; Raiford S. Pierce, *Executive Travel Associates*; Martha Z. Reinhart, *planning consultant*; Norton D. Strommen, *U.S. Department of Agriculture*; Ray Suarez, *National Public Radio*; Jack C. Williams, *USA Today*; William B. Wood, *U.S. Department of State*.

WRITTEN TESTIMONY

James Chan, *Asia Marketing & Mangagement*; Shelley Lucke–Jennings, *Oyster Bilingual Elementary School, Washington, DC*; Peter F. Mason, *Bechtel Power Corporation.*

Reviewers of Drafts

· ·

Dominick Aira	Barbara J. Braithwaite	Carolyn Fiori
James Akenson	Harvey Brandt	Roger Fisher
Danielle L. Alduino	Anne Buckton	Rosanne W. Fortner
Roberta Al-Saiihi	Judy Butler	Eric J. Fournier
Peggy Altoff	Susan Cahalan	Denise Frederick
Maria Andel	Gloria Chernay	Robert French
Carolyn P. Anderson	Carol M. Clarke	Virginia George
Lisa Rae Anderson	Regina Cocolin	Sandra Goldick
Patty Anderson	Sidney Cohen	Reginald G. Golledge
Mechelle Andrews	Tom Collins	David Greenland
Suzon Arsiga	Kathleen Falslev Cottle	Gloria Gregg
Rebecca Augustin	Debora J. Craig	Millie Griswold
C. Murray Austin	Gerald L. Crawford	Charles F. Gritzner
Carmelita Austinberry	Jerry Croft	George Gruenther
Shari Avianantos	Donald C. Dahmann	Peter Halvorson
Barry Bachenheimer	Phyllis Darling	Michael Hartoonian
Marjane L. Baker	Rita Dolan	Truman Hartshorn
Lois Barry	Jeanne Doremus	John Hassan
Tom Barry	Gary S. Elbow	David M. Helgren
Wayland P. Bauer	John Ellington	Caroline J. Helmkamp
Linda S. Beckham	Beth A. Elver	Bette Hendrix
Carol Berger	Paul Engle	James Henry
Peggy J. Blackwell	Sherrill Evans	Shirley Herrick
Marci Bonham	Robert Fardy	R. James Heyl
Jacqueline R. Boykin	Marvin Fenichel	Linda Hillestad

Ann F. Hines
Linda Hollenbaugh
Kathy Hughes
Linda Hunt
Mary Husman
Jamie Hutchinson
Lillian Hynes
Ann Ishikawa
Marci Jacobs
Sheldon M. Jaffie
Richard W. Janson
David Jenkins
Liana Jenkins
John G. Johnson
Marcia Johnson
Mark C. Jones
Ken Jordan
Sidney R. Jumper
Ann F. Justice
Sharon Kaohi
Kristi Karis
Nancy Katz
Linda Kay
John Keill
Trudi Kepner
Joyce Kerr
Barbara Kline
Larry Koebel
Terry Kopple
Charles F. Kovacik
Gail Krause
Ann Frissell Lackey
Jacci Lackey
Edward P. Lang
Daniel J. Langen
Peter W. Leddy
Anne Plummer Linn
Paula Long
Shirley Long
Dennis LuBeck
Ann Lynch
Sharon Lynn
Irene MacConnell-Davinroy
Douglas MacLeod
Mary Anne Mansell
Connie Manter
Betty Marker

Susan C. Markle
Jean Marr
Marty Mater
Nina McBride
Libby J. McElduff
E. Melahn
Marjorie J. Menzi
Howard M. Metz
Bert Milburn
Richard R. Miller, Jr.
Wang Min
Robert C. Mings
Peter A. Mongillo
Janice Monk
Jack C. Morgan
Judy Morgan
Jane B. Moriarty
Frank H. Moyer
Sharon Mucha
Karen K. Muir
Alexander B. Murphy
M. Duane Nellis
Jim Norwine
Pat Oden
Kate O'Neill
William Osborne
Lawrence Osen
Michael Ostapuk
Norma Page
Roger Palmer
Margaret B. Parrish
Linda Partridge
Willie Pattillo
Dale Petersen
Donald D. Peterson
Hazel Peterson
Paul E. Phillips
Robert Picker
Sister Michaelinda Plante
Janet Pommrehn
Janet Porterfield
Sandra Pritchard
Judy Purcell
Phyllis M. Quinn
Dagoberto Ramirez
Norma Jean Remington
Peter Rhoades

Sally Riemer
Barbara R. Ringwald
Terry Salinger
Kay Sandmeier
Theodore H. Schmudde
Mary Jane Schott
James W. Shepard
Patricia J. Shepard
Patricia G. Sidas
Jeanie Sisson
Donna Smith
Jan Smith
Ken Smith
William Solava
Warren Solomon
Linda Stajich
Margaret Steidley
Susan Stewart
Sandra F. Stokely
Glenda Sullivan
Kathy Sundstedt
John Syphard
Lou A. Taft
Katherine Takvorian
Janet Thomasser
Robert Thompson
Margaret C. Trader
JoAnn Trygestad
Marcia A. Turpyn
Regina J. Vaughn
Donna Victors
Linda Voyles
Suzanne Wagg
Margaret Walden
Michael Watt
Jane Weber
Richard Weil
Pat Welker
Mark M. Wilson
Melissa N. Wisehaupt
Lois Ellis Wolfe
M. Gordon Wolman
Lois Wood
Nancy Wood
Barbara Woolsey
Susan Yohe
Donald J. Zeigler

Setting of the National Geography Standards

Different national curricula and standards reflect the educational priorities of different countries. Therefore, while the National Geography Standards draw on the experience of many other countries, they are based on what the United States needs and wants from a systematic program of instruction in geography. The objective of these standards is to develop world-class levels of understanding of geography which will be useful in the context of workplace, voter's booth, and people's lives in the United States. World-class means being equivalent to and perhaps leading the world in a system of outcomes-based geography education. Standards from other countries have been taken into account in setting reference levels, but we are committed to the idea that the National Geography Standards must address what America needs and wants.

Four decisions shaped the National Geography Standards: (1) setting a single achievement level; (2) establishing the role of standards; (3) stressing the voluntary nature of standards; and (4) designing dynamic and flexible standards.

First, a single level of achievement offers a simple and manageable target, one that is clear to students, teachers, and parents. A standard serves as a line separating qualitatively different types of achievement, a line that can be approached, attained, and even exceeded. Second, the National Geography Standards act as a guide for the American education system. The National Geography Standards offer students something to strive for and therefore inspire students to push themselves. As a consequence students will derive personal satisfaction from meeting these standards. Taken together, these two shaping decisions mean that standards will give responsibility and accountability to students and teachers. The National Geography Standards offer a goal toward which students will strive and a benchmark against which teachers can measure performance. The third decision is crucial to the successful adoption and implementation of geography standards. Standards alone do not constitute a national curriculum because the particular examples of content emphasized, the sequence of presentation, and the assessment of performance must be tailored to the specific institutional and geographic context of each school. Thus the set of essays of principles and purposes for the eighteen National Geography Standards is neither syllabus nor curriculum nor textbook, but it is the essential starting point for all three of these ideas. Fourth, standards are designed to be dynamic and flexible. The study of geography must change as the world changes. The illustrative character of the examples allows for continuous updating of the information base contained in the standards.

Time in
the Classroom

The National Education Goals require that students demonstrate "competency over challenging subject matter" and that teachers "will have continuing opportunities to acquire additional knowledge and skills needed to teach challenging subject matter." Meeting both of these challenges requires time. Members of the community and educators must rethink the time allocated to geography. There must be adequate space for geography in the curriculum for a student to become geographically informed and for teachers to be able to foster student learning.

At a public hearing for the Geography Education Standards Project, Milton Goldberg, executive director, the National Education Commission on Time and Learning, testified that:

> *little attention is given to the time it will take to learn new things, and*
> *not only in terms of the amount of time necessary but the different kinds*
> *of time necessary to learn new things.*

Time must be considered in both quantitative and qualitative terms. In quantitative terms more quality time is often required. At present geography plays only a minor role in the curriculum. In qualitative terms different kinds of time are required. Geography depends upon fieldwork, extended problem solving, laboratory work, and real-life projects.

We must reconceptualize and reorganize the school day. Without rethinking the temporal context of education, it will be impossible to carry out the mandate of Goals 2000: Educate America Act.

This table is a statement of the minimum requirements for geography in the American classroom. The five-step process relates time requirements to educational purposes, setting both within a context of developing competency in geography.

ERIK LARS BAKKE

Geography in the Classroom

STEP	GRADES	REQUIREMENTS INFUSED	STAND-ALONE	PURPOSE	MECHANISMS
1	K–3	access to and use of geography-based materials throughout the curriculum	none	develop working familiarity with basic concepts, approaches, and tools of geography	incorporated throughout the curriculum
2	4–5		series of six, two-week units in grade 4 and, eight, two-week units in grade 5	build a basic understanding of geographic approaches	set within the traditional geography of the state and the United States
3	6–8		a year-long course in geography	extend understanding of geographic approaches	focus on topics from local to global
4	9–11		a year-long course in geography	deepen understanding of geographic approaches	world geography
5	12		an elective, semester-long course in geography	capstone experience for students wishing to enhance their understanding of geography	an advanced topical or regional geography course

Role of Geographic Information Systems

At its simplest, a geographic information system (GIS) does what geographers have always done: It collects data about places on Earth, stores it, and manipulates the information to answer questions and solve problems. The principal difference is that a GIS is computer-based. Therefore, a more technical definition is: An integrated system of hardware, software, and procedures designed to support the collection, management, manipulation, analysis, modeling, and display of spatially referenced data about Earth's surface in order to solve complex planning and management problems.

All of the geographic skills discussed in Chapter 3 can be performed by a GIS; most can be performed with far greater amounts of data more rapidly, accurately, and reliably.

Does this mean that geography will simply be done by a machine, a computer system? The answer is no because every machine requires an operator, someone who decides what is to be done and why, someone who can ask questions about answers. The power of a GIS is that it allows us to ask questions of data and to perform spatial operations on spatial databases. To do this requires competency in geography itself.

A GIS can answer five generic questions:

QUESTION:	TYPE OF TASK
1. What is at . . . ?	inventory and/or monitoring
2. Where is . . . ?	inventory and/or monitoring
3. What has changed since . . . ?	inventory and/or monitoring
4. What spatial pattern exists . . . ?	spatial analysis
5. What if . . . ?	modeling

Question 2, for example, asks where are certain conditions satisfied. To an investor in a fast-food franchise, this might mean: Find those locations in the suburbs where land—at least a half acre in size—at a busy intersection is available for purchase at less than $X

Computers programmed with a geographic information system aid this oil exploration in the North Sea. GEORGE STEINMETZ

per square foot or find those downtown locations where daily foot traffic is high and a corner store is available at a rent of less that $Y per square foot.

Establishing the conditions for the GIS requires someone with a reasonable level of competency in geography. Asking geographic questions is the first of five geographic skills in Chapter 3.

In the next ten years GISs will play two major roles in geography education. First, the use of GISs in business, industry, government, and educational institutions will continue to grow rapidly. GISs will play a major role in the global economy and we need to ensure that our high-school graduates can take advantage of the power of a GIS. Second, GISs are being adapted more gradually for use in schools. While this transition is in its early stages, we must ensure that the National Geography Standards are flexible enough to take advantage of the technology as it becomes available.

Therefore, the standards were written with geographic information systems in mind but not immediately in sight. The cost of GIS technology is still beyond the means of most school districts in this country and the technology itself is evolving rapidly. We have neither specified nor required the use of a GIS in the National Geography Standards. We have illustrated the possibility of its use in some of the examples of things that students and teachers might do.

Glossary

absolute location - the location of a point on Earth's surface which can be expressed by a grid reference (e.g., latitude and longitude).

accessibility - the relative ease with which a place can be reached from other places.

acculturation - the process of adopting the traits of a cultural group.

acid precipitation (rain or snow) - precipitation with a pH value of 5.6 or lower (7 is neutral, less than 7 increasing in acidity, and more than 7 increasing in alkalinity). Precipitation becomes excessively acidic when oxides of sulfur and nitrogen released by combustion of fossil fuels combine with moisture in the atmosphere to form acids.

aerial photograph - a photograph of part of Earth's surface usually taken from an airplane.

agribusiness - the strategy of applying business practices to the operation of specialized commercial farms in order to achieve efficiency of operation and increased profit margins.

alluvial fan - a semi-conical land form that occurs where a canyon exits a mountain range. It is composed of stream and debris flow materials which are deposited as flow spreads out and slows down once it exits the canyon.

Antarctic Circle - latitude 66.5° S encircling the continent of Antarctica. From this latitude to the South Pole daylight lasts for twenty-four hours on the winter solstice, usually December 22; whereas on the summer solstice, usually June 22, continuous darkness prevails.

aquifer - an underground permeable rock layer within which water is stored and can flow, and from which water can be extracted for use at the surface.

artifacts - the material manifestations of a culture such as tools, clothing, and foods.

assimilation - the acceptance, by one culture group or community, of cultural traits normally associated with another.

atmosphere - the envelope of gases, aerosols, and other materials that surrounds Earth and is held close by gravity. The gases are dominated by nitrogen (78.1 percent), oxygen (20.9 percent), argon (0.93 percent), and carbon dioxide (0.03 percent) and include much smaller percentages of helium, methane, and hydrogen. Water vapor, clouds, dust, meteor debris, salt crystals, and pollutants also contribute to the atmosphere's mass, which is concentrated within a layer that extends about twelve miles from Earth's surface.

atmospheric pressure cells - areas of the atmosphere with relatively high or low barometric pressure referred to simply as "highs" and "lows." Winds on Earth are caused by air movement from areas of high pressure to areas of low pressure. Large areas of permanent high and low pressure, existing in bands or belts around Earth, influence world climate patterns and ocean currents (e.g., the Siberian High and the Icelandic Low).

barrier island - a long, narrow off-shore island built by deposits from wave action and separated from a low lying coastal mainland by a body of water.

biomes - very large ecosystems made up of specific plant and animal communities interacting with the physical environment (climate and soil). They are usually identified with the climate and climax vegetation of large areas of Earth's surface (e.g., the Equatorial and Tropical Rain Forest Biome).

biosphere - the realm of Earth which includes all plant and animal life forms.

birthrate - see **crude birthrate**.

boundary - the limit or extent within which a system exists or functions, including a social group, a state, or physical feature.

capital - one of the factors of production of goods and services. Capital can be goods (e.g., factories and equipment, highways, information, communications systems, etc.) and/or funds (investment and working capital) used to increase production and wealth. Other factors are land, water, and labor.

cardinal directions - the four main points of the compass—north, east, south, and west.

carrying capacity - the maximum number of animals and/or people a given area can support at a given time under specified levels of consumption.

cartographer - a person who designs and creates maps and other geographic representations.

central place - a village, town or city which provides services to a surrounding region functionally tied to it.

central place theory - the conceptual framework that explains the size, spacing, and distribution of settlements and their economic relationships with their hinterlands.

choropleth map - shows differences between areas by using colors or shading to represent distinct categories of qualities (such as vegetation type) or quantities (such as the percentage graduating from high school, population density, or birthrate).

climate - long-term trends in weather elements and atmospheric conditions.

climate graph (climagraph) - a graph which combines average monthly temperature and precipitation data for a particular place.

cognitive map - see **mental map**.

commercial agriculture - a form of agriculture in which crops are cultivated for sale rather than for personal consumption or subsistence.

Common Market - see European Union (EU).

comparative advantage - the specialization by a given area in the production of one or a few commodities for which it has particular advantages, such as labor or production costs.

complementarity - the mutually satisfactory exchange of raw materials, manufactured products, or information between two regions to fill the needs and wants of each.

concentric growth - refers to the zonal model of urban social or economic growth, which states that a city grows outward from a central area in a series of concentric rings or zones that are occupied by distinctive social groups or land uses.

continental drift - see **plate tectonics**.

contour map - a representation of some part of Earth's surface using lines along which all points are of equal elevation above or below a fixed datum, usually sea level.

cost-distance - the amount of money necessary for people, objects or information to travel between two places.

country - unit of political space, often referred to as a state.

crude birthrate - the total number of live births in a year for every 1000 people in a population.

crude death rate - the total number of deaths in a year for every 1000 people in a population.

culture - learned behavior of people, which includes their belief systems and languages, their social relationships, their institutions and organizations, and their material goods—food, clothing, buildings, tools, and machines.

cultural diffusion - the spread of cultural elements from one culture to another.

culture hearth - the place of origin of a culture group or of a series of material and nonmaterial innovations.

cultural landscape - the human imprint on the physical environment; the humanized landscape as created or modified by people.

database - a compilation, structuring, and categorization of information (print or electronic) for analysis and interpretation.

deforestation - the destruction and removal of forest and its undergrowth by natural or human forces.

demographic change - change in population size, composition, rates of growth, density, fertility and mortality rates, and patterns of migration.

demographic transition - a model showing changes over time in a country's birth- and death rates. The early stages of the model illustrates the high birth- and death rates (slow population growth) of a predominately agricultural society; middle stages show declines in both rates (death rate initially and birthrate later, thus causing rapid population growth) as economies change from agriculture to industry; and advanced stages indicate low birth- and death rates (slow population growth) typical of industrialized urban societies.

demography - the study of population statistics, changes, and trends based on various measures of fertility (adding to a population), mortality (subtracting from a population), and migration (redistribution of a population).

density - the population or number of objects per unit area (e.g., per square kilometer or mile).

desertification - the spread of desert conditions in arid and semiarid regions resulting from a combination of climatic changes and increasing human pressures, such as overgrazing, removal of vegetation, and cultivation of marginal land.

developed country - an area of the world that is technologically advanced, highly urbanized and wealthy, and has generally evolved through both economic and demographic transitions.

developing country - an area of the world that is changing from uneven growth to more constant economic conditions and that is generally characterized by low rates of urbanization, relatively high rates of infant mortality and illiteracy, and relatively low rates of life expectancy and energy use.

diffusion - the spread of people, ideas, technology, and products among places.

distribution - the arrangement of items over a specified area.

doubling time - the number of years needed to double a population, given a constant rate of natural increase.

earthquake - vibrations and shock waves caused by the sudden movement of tectonic plates along fracture zones, called faults, in Earth's crust.

ecology - the study of the interactions of living organisms between themselves, their habitats, and the physical environment.

ecosystem (ecological system) - a system formed by the interaction of all living organisms (plants, animals, humans) with each other and with the physical and chemical factors of the environment in which they live.

elevation - height of a point or place above sea level (e.g., Mount Everest has an elevation of 29,028 feet above sea level).

environment - everything in and on Earth's surface and its atmosphere within which organisms, communities, or objects exist.

environmental determinism - the theory that the physical environment controls various aspects of human behavior and cultural development.

Equator - latitude 0°. An imaginary line running east and west around the globe and dividing it into two equal parts known as the Northern and Southern Hemispheres; that place on Earth which always has approximately twelve hours of daylight and twelve hours of darkness.

equilibrium - the point in the operation of a system when driving forces and resisting forces are in balance.

equinox - the two days during the calendar year (usually September 23 and March 21) when all latitudes have twelve hours of both daylight and darkness, and the sun is directly overhead at the Equator.

ethnic enclaves - areas or neighborhoods within cities that are homogeneous in their ethnic makeup and are usually surrounded by groups of a different ethnic character (e.g., Little Italy, Chinatown).

ethnocentrism - the belief in the inherent superiority of one's own group and culture; a tendency to view all other groups or cultures in terms of one's own.

European Union (EU) - an association of a number of European countries promoting free trade, cultural and political linkage, and relatively easy access among their nations. Formed in 1957, the European Union was formerly called the European Community.

eutrophication - the process of natural aging in lakes and water bodies, characterized by increased amounts of sediments, nutrients, and organic material.

fauna - the animal life of an area or region.

fertility rate - the average number of children a woman will have during her child-bearing years (15 to 49 years of age).

floodplain - a generally flat valley area bordering a stream or river that is subject to inundation; the most common land area for human settlement.

flora - the plant life of an area or region.

flowchart - a chart or diagram showing a series of interconnected events, actions, or items that indicate the progressive development of a theme, product, or other objective.

flow map - a map with arrows and lines showing how something diffuses (e.g., migration or raw materials to industrial sites).

flow pattern - the regular movement of materials, products, people and/or ideas along a consistent route or path.

flow resources - resources that are neither renewable nor nonrenewable, but must be used as, when, and where they occur or they are lost (e.g., running water, wind, sunlight).

force - the power or energy in a process, such as weather, which activates both movement and friction.

formal region - a region defined by the uniformity or homogeneity of certain characteristics, such as precipitation, landforms, subculture, or type of economic production.

fossil fuel - energy source formed in past geologic times from organic materials (e.g., coal, petroleum, natural gas).

friction of distance - the force that inhibits the interaction of people and places on Earth. The frequency of interaction between people and places depends on the cost of overcoming this force (e.g., moving commodities over land).

functional region - the functional unity of a region is often provided by a strong node or center of human population and activity. Regions that are defined by their ties to a central node are classified as nodal or functional regions (e.g., banking linkages between large nodal cities and smaller cities and towns).

gentrification - the process in urban areas of upper- or middle-class families moving back into a zone in transition, which often surrounds the central business district of a city.

geographic information system (GIS) - a geographic database that contains information about the distribution of physical and human characteristics of places or areas. In order to test hypotheses, maps of one characteristic or a combination can be produced from the database to analyze the data relationships (see also Appendix E).

geomorphology - the science of the processes that develop land forms, and the history of landform development.

global warming - the theory that Earth's atmosphere is gradually warming due to the buildup of certain gases, including carbon dioxide and methane, which are released by human activities. The increased levels of these gases cause added heat energy from Earth to be absorbed by the atmosphere instead of being lost to space.

globe - a scale model of Earth that correctly represents area, relative size and shape of physical features, distance between points, and true compass direction.

greenhouse effect - the ability of certain gases in the atmosphere to absorb heat energy released from Earth's surface.

grid - a pattern of lines on a chart or map, such as those representing latitude and longitude, which helps determine absolute location and assists in the analysis of distribution patterns.

Gross Domestic Product (GDP) - the total monetary value of goods and services produced in a country during one year.

Gross National Product (GNP) - Gross Domestic Product adjusted to include the value of goods and services from other countries subsequently used in producing goods and services in the home country.

groundwater - subsurface water that saturates the soil and bedrock; constitutes most of the world's freshwater.

hemisphere - half a sphere. Cartographers and geographers, by convention, divide Earth into the Northern and Southern Hemispheres at the Equator, and the eastern and western hemispheres at the prime meridian (longitude 0°) and 180° meridian.

hills - landform features that may have steep slopes but lower elevations and less local relief than mountains (e.g., the Black Hills of South Dakota)

hinterland - service area surrounding an urban center, which supplies the goods, services, and labor needed in that area.

human process - a course or method of operation that produces, maintains, and alters human systems on Earth, such as migration or diffusion.

hurricane - severe tropical storm or low pressure cell of limited area/extent in the Atlantic and eastern Pacific with accompanying torrential rains and high-velocity winds— usually in excess of 80 miles per hour. These storms are known as typhoons in the western Pacific and cyclones in southern Asia.

hydroelectric power - electrical energy generated by the force of falling water which rotates turbines housed in power plants in dams on rivers.

hydrologic cycle - the continuous circulation of water from the oceans, through the air, to the land, and back to the sea. Water evaporates from oceans, lakes, rivers, and the land surfaces and transpires from vegetation. It condenses into clouds in the atmosphere, which may result in precipitation returning water to the land. Water then seeps into the soil or flows out to sea, completing the cycle.

hydrosphere - the water realm of Earth, which includes water contained in the oceans, lakes, rivers, ground, glaciers, and water vapor in the atmosphere.

industrialization - the growth of machine production and the factory system. The process of introducing manufacturing into countries or regions where most of the people are engaged in primary economic activities.

infant mortality rate - the annual number of deaths among infants under one year of age for every 1,000 live births; it usually provides an indication of health care levels. The United States, for example, has a 1994 rate of 8.3 infant deaths per 1,000 live births, while Angola has a rate of 137 infant deaths per 1,000 births.

interdependence - people relying on each other in different places or in the same place for ideas, goods, and services.

intermediate directions - the points of the compass that fall between north and east, north and west, south and east, south and west (e.g., NE, NW, SE, SW).

International Date Line - an imaginary line that roughly follows the 180° meridian in the Pacific Ocean. West of this line the calendar date is one day ahead of the calendar date east of the line. People crossing the date line in a westward direction lose a calendar day, while those crossing eastward gain a calendar day.

intervening opportunity - the availability of an opportunity closer at hand that reduces the attractiveness of a similar opportunity at locations farther away, (e.g., shoppers may purchase bread at a local bakery rather than a large grocery store).

lake dessication - the reduction in water level (drying out) of an inland water body.

landform - the shape, form, or nature of a specific physical feature of Earth's surface (e.g., plain, hill, plateau, mountain).

landlocked country - a state that is completely surrounded by the territory of one or more other countries, thus denying direct access to the sea or ocean.

land degradation - the physical process that wears down and levels landforms and carries away the loosened debris. This term is also used to define human misuse of the land or the environment (e.g. farming on steep slopes increases erosion).

land use - the range of uses of Earth's surface made by humans. Uses are classified as urban, rural, agricultural, forested, etc.; with more specific subclassifications useful for specific purposes (e.g., low-density residential, light industrial, nursery crops).

latitude - assuming that the Earth is a sphere, the latitude of a point on the surface is the angle measured at the center of the Earth between a ray lying on the plane of the Equator and a line connecting the center with the point on the surface.

legend - an explanatory description or key to features on a map or chart.

life expectancy - the average number of remaining years a person can expect to live under current mortality levels in a society. Life expectancy at birth is the most common use of this measure.

linkage - contact and therefore flow of ideas, information, people, or products between places.

lithosphere - the uppermost portion of the solid Earth, including soil, land, and geologic formations.

lithospheric plates - see **tectonic plates**.

local relief - in landforms, the difference in elevation between the highest and lowest points in a specified area.

location - the position of a point on Earth's surface expressed by means of a grid (absolute) or in relation (relative) to the position of other places.

longitude - the position of a point on Earth's surface expressed as its angular distance, east or west, from the prime meridian to 180°.

map - a graphic representation of a portion of Earth that is usually drawn to scale on a flat surface.

map projection - a mathematical formula by which the lines of a global grid and the shapes of land and water bodies are transferred from a globe to a flat surface.

megalopolis - the coalescence of two or more large metropolitan areas into a continuous or almost continuous built-up urban complex, sometimes referred to as conurbation.

mental map - a map which represents the mental image a person has of an area, including knowledge of features and spatial relationships as well as the individual's perceptions and attitudes regarding the place; also known as a cognitive map.

meridian - a north-south line of longitude used to measure both time and distance east and west of the prime meridian or longitude 0° (see prime meridian).

Metropolitan Area - the Federal Office of Management and Budget's designation for the functional area surrounding and including a central city: has a minimum population of 50,000; is contained in the same county as the central city; and includes adjacent counties having at least 15 percent of their residents working in the central city's county.

microclimate - a small, localized climate area within a larger climate region, which has significantly different atmospheric elements. Microclimates can be caused by human intervention or by local landform configurations (e.g., "heat islands" in central city's areas of high skyscrapers or sheltered south-facing slopes of hills).

migration - the act or process of people moving from one place to another with the intent of staying at the destination permanently or for a relatively long period of time.

monoculture - the practice of growing one or more cash crops for export to one or more countries.

monsoon - a wind system that changes direction seasonally, producing distinct wet and dry seasons; used especially to describe the low-sun and high-sun seasonal wind systems of South, Southeast and East Asia.

moraine - ridge composed of an unsorted mixture of boulders, sand, silt, and clay that is deposited in contact with a glacier; moraines usually reflect a period when the glacier has remained stationary, as opposed to advancing or retreating.

mortality rate - see **crude death rate**.

mountains - high elevation landform features composed mostly of steep slopes and large amounts of local relief within a specified area (e.g., the Alps of Europe).

multiculturalism - a pluralistic society in which there are a number of subcultures.

multinational organizations - organizations of nations aligned around a common economic or political cause, such as the Organization of Petroleum Exporting Countries (OPEC) or the Organization of American States (OAS).

nation - a cultural concept for a group of people bound together by a strong sense of shared values and cultural characteristics, including language, religion, and common history.

natural hazard - an event in the physical environment, such as a hurricane or earthquake, that is destructive to human life and property.

natural population increase - the changes in population size, expressed as a percentage, attributable solely to fertility (addition by births) and mortality (subtraction by deaths). Migration is not considered in this measure.

natural vegetation - plants originally found together in an area. Little of the world's vegetation is entirely unmodified by human activities.

network - a pattern of links between points along which movement can take place (e.g., streams, roads, or communication modes).

nonrenewable resource - a finite resource that cannot be replaced once it is used (e.g., petroleum, minerals).

North Pole - the geographic point farthest north on Earth. The northern end of Earth's axis. On globes and most maps, that place in the Northern Hemisphere where meridians converge.

oblate spheroid - the shape of Earth, which is larger in circumference around the Equator than the poles.

ocean currents - the regular and consistent horizontal flow of water in the oceans, usually in response to persistent patterns of circulation in the atmosphere.

OPEC - the Organization of Petroleum Exporting Countries is an international cartel of thirteen nations designed to promote collective pricing of petroleum, unified marketing policies, and regulation of petroleum extraction.

overpopulation - a situation in which the existing population is too large to be adequately supported by available resources at current levels of consumption. This should not be confused with dense population.

ozone layer - a layer in the stratosphere at an altitude of twelve to twenty-one miles that has a high concentration of ozone (O_3) and protects the lower atmosphere and Earth's surface by absorbing much of the ultraviolet radiation that reaches Earth from the sun.

Pacific rim - countries bordering the Pacific Ocean.

parallel - an east-west line of latitude used to measure angular distance north and south of the Equator or latitude $0°$.

perceptual region - an area of Earth, such as the Middle West, identified by expressions of feelings, attitudes and images.

physical feature - an aspect of a place or area that derives from the physical environment.

physical process - a course or method of operation that produces, maintains, or alters Earth's physical systems, such as glacial processes eroding and depositing landforms.

physiography - the study of Earth's surface and its physical features, including relationships between air, land, and water.

physiological population density - the relationship between the total population of a country and the quantity of land classified as arable or permanent pasture.

places - locations having distinctive characteristics which give them meaning and character and distinguish them from other locations.

plains - landform features characterized by a maximum of gentle slopes and minimum local relief within a specified area (e.g., the pampas of Argentina).

plantation agriculture - a type of agriculture involving large landholdings that produce cash crops such as tea, rubber, coffee, sugarcane, or cocoa.

plateaus - landform features characterized by high elevation and gentle upland slopes (e.g., the Grand Canyon area of the United States).

plate tectonics - the theory that Earth's surface is composed of rigid slabs or plates (see tectonic plates). The divergence, convergence, and slipping side-by-side of the different plates is responsible for present-day configurations of continents, ocean basins, and major mountain ranges and valley systems.

pollution - the direct or indirect process resulting from human action by which any part of the environment is made potentially or actually unhealthy, unsafe, or hazardous to the welfare of the organisms which live in it.

population density - the number of individuals occupying an area derived from dividing the number of people by the area they occupy (e.g., 2,000 people divided by ten square miles = 200 people per square mile).

population pyramid - a bar graph showing the distribution by gender and age of a country's population.

population structure - the age and gender makeup of a population, usually depicted on population pyramids.

prevailing winds - the direction from which the wind usually blows at a particular location (e.g., the westerlies in the middle latitudes of North America).

primary economic activity - the production of naturally existing, or culturally improved resources, (e.g., agriculture, ranching, forestry, fishing, extraction of minerals and ores).

primate city - the most important city in a country which often has a population three or four times the size of the second-ranked city.

prime meridian (Greenwich meridian) - 0°; the standard meridian from which longitude is measured. The prime meridian crosses Greenwich in London, England, the site of the Royal Naval Observatory.

principal meridians - the prime meridian (Greenwich meridian) and the International Date Line.

principal parallels - the Equator, the Tropics of Cancer and Capricorn, and the Arctic and Antarctic Circles.

pull factors - in migration theory, the social, political, economic, and environmental attractions of new areas that draw people away from their previous location.

push factors - in migration theory, the social, political, economic, and environmental forces that drive people from their previous location to search for new ones.

rain shadow - areas on leeward sides of mountain ranges characterized by much lower precipitation and humidity than the windward (rainy) side.

region - an area with one or more common characteristics or features, which give it a measure of homogeneity and make it different from surrounding areas.

regionalization - the partitioning of areas on Earth using a variety of criteria for the purpose of organizing elements in a complex space.

relative humidity - the amount of moisture actually in the air compared to the amount the air can hold at a given time at the same temperature (e.g., 85 percent).

relative location - the location of a place or region in relation to other places or regions (e.g., northwest or downstream).

remote sensing - information gathering about Earth's surface from a distance (usually referring to the use of aerial photography or satellite images).

renewable resource - a resource that can be regenerated if used carefully (e.g., fish, timber.)

resource - an aspect of the physical environment that people value and use to meet a need for fuel, food, industrial product, or something else of value.

resource base - the available resources in a given area at a given time.

salinization - the process by which high salinity soils are formed in arid areas where evaporation rates are high.

satellite image - an image produced by a variety of sensors, such as radar, microwave detectors, and scanners, which measure and record electromagnetic radiation. The collected data are turned into digital form for transmission to ground receiving stations. The data can be reconverted into imagery in a form resembling a photograph.

scale - on maps the relationship or ratio between a linear measurement on a map and the corresponding distance on Earth's surface. For example, the scale 1:1,000,000 means one unit (mile or kilometer) on the map and represents 1,000,000 similar units on Earth's surface. Also refers to the size of places or regions being studied.

secondary economic activity - the conversion of raw materials into finished industrial products (manufacturing).

sequent occupance - the settlement of an area by successive groups, each creating a distinctive cultural landscape.

settlement pattern - the spatial distribution and arrangement of human habitations, including rural and urban centers.

shifting cultivation - a system of agriculture in which a field or plot is cleared, cropped, and harvested and after a few years, with initial fertility exhausted, abandoned in favor of a new field. Also known as slash-and-burn, milpa, or swidden.

silting - the buildup of sediments at points along the course of a river where the flow velocity decreases (e.g., upstream of a dam).

site - the specific place where something is located, including its physical setting (e.g., on a floodplain).

situation - the general location of something in relation to other places or features of a larger region (e.g., in the center of a group of cities).

smog - a mixture of chemical pollutants and particulate matter in the lower atmosphere, usually found in highest concentrations in urban-industrial areas.

soil - unconsolidated material found at the surface of Earth, which is divided into layers (or horizons) characterized by the accumulation or loss of organic and inorganic compounds. Soil types and depths vary greatly over Earth's surface, and are very much influenced by climate, organisms, rock type, local relief, time, and human activity.

soil creep - the slow and gradual down-slope movement of masses of soil due to gravity, in combination with freeze/thaw and wet/dry cycles.

solar radiation - energy received from the sun, upon which all life on Earth depends.

South Pole - the geographical point farthest south on Earth. The southern end of Earth's axis. On globes and most maps, that place in the southern hemisphere where meridians converge.

spatial - pertains to space on Earth's surface.

subsistence agriculture - a form of agriculture with an emphasis on self-support in which crops or livestock are cultivated for personal consumption rather than for sale.

sustainable development - the capacity of a country to balance economic, social, and institutional needs as population and societal needs change over time.

sustainable environment - wise human use of resources designed to reduce stress on the physical environment.

system - a collection of entities that are linked and interrelated, such as the hydrologic cycle, cities, and transportation modes.

systemic - of or pertaining to a system as a whole.

tariff - an official schedule of taxes imposed by a government on imports or exports.

technological hazards - a disastrous event attributed to a failure of technology or a technological product (e.g., radioactive materials released from a nuclear power plant explosion or soil contamination from a chemical dump).

technology - application of knowledge to meet the goals, goods, and services needed and desired by people.

tectonic plates - sections of Earth's rigid crust that move as distinct units on a plastic-like mantle on which they rest. As many as twenty different plates have been identified, but only seven are considered to be major (e.g., Eurasian Plate and the South American Plate).

tectonic process - a physical process within Earth (e.g., volcanic activity, folding, faulting) that creates physical features, such as mountains, on the surface.

terrace - the step-like flat surfaces created on steep hill slopes for the purpose of farming land that is subject to erosion under normal cultivation practices.

tertiary economic activity - the provision of services (e.g., banking, retailing, education).

thematic map - a map representing a specific spatial distribution, theme, or topic (e.g., population density, cattle production, or climates of the world).

threshold - in physical and environmental processes, the point in the operation of a system when a jump or relatively great change occurs in response to a minor input; in an economic context, the minimum population needed for a service (e.g., auto dealer) to locate in a central place.

time-distance - the amount of time necessary to travel between two places.

time zone - a division of Earth, usually of longitude 15,° within which the time at the central meridian of the division represents the whole division.

topographic map - a detailed map on a large scale (e.g., 1:25,000 or 1:50,000) illustrating selected physical and human features of a place (see also **contour map**).

topography - the shape of Earth's surface.

tornado - a small, but intense funnel-shaped, low pressure cell with very low barometric pressure, strong and violent updrafts, high velocity converging winds, and resulting destruction.

transregional alliances - political and economic alliances between states that transcend traditional cultural regions (e.g., Organization of African Unity).

travel effort - the difficulty involved in moving from one place to another as measured in time, monetary cost, or physical distance.

Tropic of Cancer - latitude 23.5° N; the farthest north the sun is directly overhead during the year, usually June 22.

Tropic of Capricorn - latitude 23.5° S; the farthest south the sun is directly over head during the year, usually December 22.

urban heat island - a phenomenon of urban settlements where relatively warmer atmospheric temperatures prevail in the most heavily built-up areas and decrease outward toward the fringes.

urbanization - a process in which there is an increase in the percentage of people living/working in urban places as compared to rural places.

volcanism - a process resulting in the upward movement and expulsion of molten (melted) material from within Earth onto the surface where it cools and hardens. The Hawaiian Islands were created by this process.

watershed - the drainage area of a river and its tributaries.

weathering - the breaking down, disintegration, or dissolving of Earth's surface and subsurface rocks and minerals by physical, chemical, and organic processes.

zoning - a system of sectioning areas within cities, towns, and villages for specific land-use purposes through local ordinances (e.g., residential, light manufacturing, commercial uses).

Index

Q

questions, answering
  grade 4 48–49
  grade 8 50, 52
  grade 12 54, 55–56
questions, asking 42
  grade 4 46, 47
  grade 8 49, 50
  grade 12 53, 54

R

reference works 63
regions
  creation 152–153, 192–194
  culture and 203–204
  Earth's complexity 70–72
  formal 71–72
  functional 71
  perception 71, 117, 154–155,
    195–196
  physical and human
    characteristics 69–70,
    113–114, 150–151, 190–191
  places and 34, 69–74, 113–117,
    150–155, 191–196
resource management 221
resources 85
  changes in 98–100, 136–137,
    176–178, 216–218
  conflict 100
  demand 100
reviewers of drafts 251–252

S

settlements 87–88, 128–129,
  167–168, 208–209
skills 30, 41–44
  acquisition, assessment 45
  grade 4 46–49
  grade 8 49–52
  grade 12 53–56
  rationale 42–44
society, environment and 35,
  92–100, 132–137, 171–178,
  212–218
  see also **culture**
space, place and 31–32
spatial organization 18, 57,
  61–68, 110–112, 144–148,
  184–189
  past 179
squid-fishing fleet, night 13
standard 1 61–64
  K–4 106–107
  5–8 144–145
  9–12 184–185
standard 2 64–66
  K–4 108–109
  5–8 146–147
  9–12 186–187

standard 3 66–68
  K–4 110–112
  5–8 148–149
  9–12 188–189
standard 4 69–70
  K–4 113–114
  5–8 150–151
  9–12 190–191
standard 5 70–72
  K–4 115–116
  5–8 152–153
  9–12 192–194
standard 6 73–74
  K–4 117
  5–8 154–155
  9–12 195–196
standard 7 75–77
  K–4 118–119
  5–8 156–157
  9–12 197–198
standard 8 77–78
  K–4 120–121
  5–8 158–159
  9–12 199–200
standard 9 79–82
  K–4 122–123
  5–8 160–161
  9–12 201–202
standard 10 82–84
  K–4 124–125
  5–8 162–163
  9–12 203–205
standard 11 85–86
  K–4 126–127
  5–8 164–166
  9–12 206–207
standard 12 87–88
  K–4 128–129
  5–8 167–168
  9–12 208–209
standard 13 90–91
  K–4 130–131
  5–8 169–170
  9–12 210–211
standard 14 92–95
  K–4 132–133
  5–8 171–172
  9–12 212–213
standard 15 96–97
  K–4 134–135
  5–8 173–175
  9–12 214–215

standard 16 98–100
  K–4 136–137
  5–8 176–178
  9–12 216–218
standard 17 101–103
  K–4 138–139
  5–8 179–180
  9–12 219–220
standard 18 103–104
  K–4 140–141
  5–8 181–182
  9–12 221–222
standards 26–29, 34–35
  example 38–39
  grades K–4 105–141
  grades 5–8 143–182
  grades 9–12 183–222
  principles 60–104
  purpose 9, 60–104
  reading 38–39
  using 37
state boundaries 11
state sovereignty 90
Susquehanna River 15

T

technology 84, 204–205, 212
  resources and 99–100, 178
thinking geographically
  237–241
time in the classroom 254–255
turnpike, Pennsylvania 17

U, V

understanding 45
United States, topography 14–15
uses of geography
  see **applying geography**
Voyager 1 22, 23

W

weather 76–77
witnesses, public hearings
  249–251
world at night 12–13
world in spatial terms 34,
  61–68, 106–112, 144–148,
  184–189

To Order: GEOGRAPHY FOR LIFE:
NATIONAL GEOGRAPHY STANDARDS 1994
(product #01775-12160, 272 pages, paperbound)

For fewer than 10 copies: US $9, Canada CAN $16, all other countries
US $20. For 10 or more copies: US $8, CAN $15, all other countries US
$19. Postage and handling included.

Send your check and a written request with product number and your
name, institution, and address to: NATIONAL GEOGRAPHIC SOCIETY,
P.O. Box 1640, Washington, D.C. 20013-1640, USA.

Credit card holders may call 1-800-368-2728 (8 am–5:30 pm, EST).